Crimes Glass Vanity

A Takeover from Within

A MURDER MYSTERY

CHARLES HUNTER

NEWMAN SPRINGS PUBLISHING
320 Broad Street
Red Bank, NJ 07701

First originally published by Newman Springs Publishing 2021

ISBN 978-1-63881-066-7 (Paperback)
ISBN 978-1-63881-885-4 (Hardcover)
ISBN 978-1-63881-067-4 (Digital)

Printed in the United States of America

To all my siblings: the ones that have traveled
before us to their *homecoming* and to the ones still
here traveling along this path with me.

To the woman who dared me to prove to her that I
was a writer (*my fantastically wonderful movie marathon
partner!*) when she *really* didn't think I could write
but was *surprised* by the first chapter I wrote.

To all those people that had and showed faith in
me when I didn't have faith in myself.

And finally, to my *youngest partner in crime,* my stabilizing
force, who wondered how I *knew* about these things I
put down on paper but still read every word *anyway!*

You all are the "we" of "me"…

CONTENTS

CHAPTER 1

Rude Awakening

He was abruptly awakened by a solid impact on his back. It took him a few moments to orient himself and focus his eyes before he knew he was staring at the ceiling. Turning his head, he saw the royal-blue sheets to his right *(Were those…silk?)*, lifted his head, and saw the navy blue pajamas he was wearing *(Silk again?)*. Two and two dawned on him; more exactly two friction-free surfaces were the obvious causes of helping to deposit him faceup on the floor. The man braced his forearms on his sides, sitting up to take a look around the room. A sleek black marble hooded fireplace—a good distance from the foot of the bed, big enough to be a separate sitting area all by itself—softly reflected the rest of the room on its surface. Off to the left, at the back of the fireplace were two floor-to-ceiling windows overlooking a body of water he couldn't recognize but somehow thought he should. Left of those windows were glass sliding doors that looked out onto a medium-sized balcony with potted plants and deck furniture. Going out into the water were several flat buildings. *"Navy Pier"* shone in tall, lit letters at the front entrance. Further down the line of buildings was a huge Ferris wheel, lit pods where the seats should have been. Looking back into the room, at the opposite side of the fireplace front, he saw there were two more floor-to-ceiling windows that ended at what appeared to be the opening to a large bathroom. The surface of the vanity top, hung from the wall, was visible through the door. The man slowly got to his feet, his head clearing more as he stood straight up, and headed for the bathroom.

The flashback crashed into his mind from nowhere, and he literally jerked backward from the imagined physical contact, closing his eyes tight. When he opened them, he remembered a bar, loud music with colored strobe lights flashing to the beat, people bumping into and sliding against him. Someone…someone had been talking to him…about…*about what?* He felt that it was important, very important, but he couldn't put his finger on it. All he was coming up with was a headache.

The bathroom opening seemed still several feet away as he unsteadily moved toward it, passed through, and finally supported himself against the vanity with his left hand. He took another step forward with his right foot, and the second flashback hit him with the same force as the first. He staggered to the left, catching himself before he could fall, hands covering his eyes as he waited for the pain to stop. He could hear his heart beating in his ears. He was breathing rapidly through his mouth as he viewed the next set of images. He was talking to a woman, and the way she was dressed, she was either a highly paid hooker or just some skank who liked to be looked at. She had smiled, kissed him on the cheek, and handed him a wad of money. Was he a…*pimp?* Suddenly he realized he didn't know *who* he was! He had no clue about his life except for these flashback scenes that were popping into his brain. What had *happened* to him that wiped his memory out?

The man steadied himself as he turned on the sink's cold water, rubbing it on his face with both hands. He raised his head and looked into the mirror. A black, thin, oval face stared back at him, one he didn't recognize. The hair was curly, dark brown, slightly taller on the top than on the sides. His skin was very smooth, unblemished, and soft to the touch, somewhat feminine. He had three thin creases across his brow, almost from eye to eye, those being a slightly darker caramel color than his skin. His nose had the typical Black feature: wide nostrils. But overall, it wasn't as thick, somewhat longer as well. He wondered how many times he had been mistaken for a *woman*… *(Where the hell did that come from?)* He stood over six feet, probably closer to six feet, three inches or six feet, four inches, with a slight build but very toned. *Why the hell couldn't he remember who he was? This was stupid!* He knew he was over thirty *(How...?)*, but that was pretty much it. *All these are things you just don't* forget *all of a sudden!* There was no evidence of an accident or that he had been mugged as he checked over himself. *So what was the deal?*

This time he was somewhat prepared for the flashback, only slightly wincing at the continuing storyline.

Other women had come up to him, each as exotic as the last, all handing him large rolls of money. *So the pimp angle might not be too far off base*, he thought. He noticed several different levels in the building, crowded with people sitting, standing, or dancing in place to the beat of the loud bass-driven music. There was a sudden tap on his shoulder, a hand off to his right pointing at something— no...*someone* on one of the higher levels who needed his immediate attention. It was another Black man with possibly the same build and height as he, dancing with one of the women that had given him money. When she caught his eye, she quickly looked back at her dance partner's face, forcing him to look as well. The man's face was different than what he had seen in the bathroom mirror but somehow he felt it was similar, even familiar. He knew he had seen him before but couldn't pinpoint where. The sensation of moving through the crowd toward the other man began to fade along with the vision as he found himself back in the bathroom leaning on the vanity, the same unknown face staring back at him from the mirror.

He had started to sweat, and his heart was beating faster as he forced himself to calm down, trying to think this thing through. To his right was a glass-enclosed shower the size of his whole bathroom *(That was...in his...old apartment?)*. Another realized fact he knew was right, just not *how or why* he knew it was right! Maybe a hot shower would help jog his memory, give him a little more informa-tion to go with. The silk pajamas slid from his body without effort. Opening the door to the shower and stepping in, he closed it behind him. He turned the handles, adjusting the temperature of the water before turning the diverter to the showerhead. The multiple stinging drops of water beat down on his face, head, and shoulders, pushing whatever tiredness was left in him down the drain. He slowly turned, letting the water attack the rest of his body as he began to feel better, losing himself in the quickly growing cloud of steam. This time, his view in the vision was of a tall man making his way toward him through the crowd, gently nudging people out of his way. His face was pleasant with a slight smile as if they might be old friends. As the man came closer, he recognized the face: *It was the same face that stared back at him in the bathroom mirror!* As the man stood just in front of him, leaning in to speak, the man suddenly turned in the shower, slipping a bit as he grabbed the handles, turning the water off. His mind spun as he wondered how he could have both points of view from *two different perspectives*. This just jumped onto a whole new level of crazy!

He grabbed the shower door, swinging it open, and stepped out. Almost immediately he felt something touch him, a round metal on his stomach, and he looked down. The barrel of the pump-action shotgun glistened with the condensation from the shower. Further up, he saw the stock was held by leather-gloved hands. Quickly looking up, he saw the man's face holding the gun. For a moment he thought he was looking in a mirror because the face he saw staring back looked exactly like his own! There was no pain as the pellets disintegrated the skin on his stomach, perforating his organs as they passed through his body. Tissues, bone, and blood sprayed across the back of the shower, pellets digging deep into the tiles seconds before his body hit hard, sliding slowly down the wall into a sitting position, leaning slightly off to his right. Barely managing to lift his head, the last thing he saw before his world turned black was the sad, frowning face of his double looking down at him…

CHAPTER 2

Monday Morning

Chicago was showing its usual indecision toward the weather by having gone through all four seasons before noon.

Early-morning commuters were met by strong, cold winds that no matter how many layers of clothing they wore still chilled them to the bone. So when the bus operators arrived at their first stops of the day, *they* became the entire *CTA* management and operations staff, receiving every curse word ever spoken, along with the appropriate hand gestures, adding to the final emphasis. Some operators listened for a few moments before thoughts of days off, vacations, and warmer climates filled their minds. Others unfastened seat belts, stood, and gave back (in some cases) even worse than what they had received. And in the end, everybody present had to agree that *Mondays really sucked!*

Passengers traveling on the elevated rapid transit trains sped into heavy freezing rain that slowly covered the rails, platforms, surrounding buildings, and streets with a thin but solid coat of ice. One rapid transit train that was running too fast for conditions slipped past the end of a platform station stop by two car lengths before coming to a stop. *Dr. Daniel Reilly*, police senior pathologist, was standing with his back to the doors, impatient that they weren't opening. He switched his thoughts to several high-profile criminals that had recently come onto his tables. There was something odd about them all: minor scarring along the hairline and behind the ears, face-lifts for sure, but all of them? Odd indeed… Not sensing the movement of the train anymore, he wondered why the doors still weren't opening, so he felt along the top of the door for the emergency door release, found it, and pulled it down. Unfortunately, these were the older folding doors that opened to their full width instead of the newer sliding doors that popped open only a few inches then were manually pushed the rest of the way. With the shouting and several pairs of hands reaching toward him, his mind immediately jumped to the *"I'm about to be mugged and killed!"* conclusion. Unfortunately, as he quickly stepped back, it was only into the cold open air…

Officers Davis and Taylor, in their patrol car passing under the elevated tracks, had one more hour on their shift before they headed back to the station house to clock out and head home to nice, warm beds. The snow had been expected, and they had been ready for it, but this freezing rain was getting on their last nerve. Davis was driving much slower now, still sliding a bit when he hit the brakes, and Taylor was applying them also ever so slightly with a twitch of his body in the passenger seat. Taylor saw the shadow falling from the corner of his eye and thought someone must have dropped some luggage or a backpack from the platform above until he heard the distant shrill scream. The wet, muffled thud as the body hit the side of a building stopped the screaming abruptly. The body bounced into a smooth, slow, cartoonlike arc on its way to the street below, making both officers wince in sympathetic pain as it thudded to the ground, landing half in the street and half on the sidewalk. Davis hit the brakes too hard, and the squad car slid to an angled stop in the middle of the intersection. Taylor was out the door gliding on the ice more than running and fell a few feet in front of the prone figure, gently bumping into the man's side as he stopped against him. Much to the officer's surprise, the man was trying to move, lifting his body enough to turn his head in the direction of the officer. The nose had been pushed up to the right and was bleeding profusely. His left eye, completely closed, had a one-inch gash from the ridge into the hairline. The eyebrow was gone altogether, and the surrounding skin from chin to brow was scraped raw. His right leg was slightly bent outward midthigh and again at midcalf with the right arm hidden under his body. Despite all this obvious damage, the man was still trying to talk to Taylor! He leaned down closer to the man's mouth and listened. Davis had finally made his way over to them just as his partner was lowering the man's face gently back down to the sidewalk.

"Is he dead?"

"Nope, just passed out," said Taylor. "You know what he said?"

"He could talk?" said Davis. "What did he say?"

"He said, 'Mondays really suck!'"

*****

By *10:00 AM*, a light snow had begun to fall, and much to the delight of the grade-school children, it grew heavier with each passing minute. Most of them were already in their third class of the day, but thoughts of snowball fights, sledding, and just general playing outside shut out any lesson plan the teachers were attempting to start. Some of the teachers as well eyed the falling snow, going over alternate routes in their minds to get home after the children were bundled up and put onto school buses for the many trips to safe havens. After several frantic telephone calls from worried parents and a dire consensus from the senior teachers, the announcement came just before *10:30* AM. The snow didn't seem to be letting up, and the school buses had been called. The building engineers who had suited up to clear the walks so the kids could get out safely heard the students' cheers even down in the basement. Soon the halls were alive with the activity of books being thrown into lockers...coats, scarfs, and gloves hastily put on while plans for the rest of the week were discussed out loud. But by the time the first students had reached the side entry doors and stepped outside, all hopes of being out for the day, not to mention for the rest of the week, were shattered by the bright glow and warmth of the sun! The snow had stopped falling. The maintenance crew had cleared off the steps and walks, replacing the snow with quick-melt salt pellets for any ice that was left. The only sound was of the snowblowers going around the corner to the back of the school as the kids stood speechless on the top landing. Not a word was spoken as the principal made her way to the front of the crowd then, once there, waved her hands back toward the building, slowly shoving them all inside. As the last small student walked back into school, he turned to the principal, eyes welling up with tears.

"Principal Sanders?" he said.

"Yes?" she said softly.

"*Mondays really suck*, don't they?" Then he turned and ran back to his locker inside.

*****

When *11:30 AM* rolled around, the temperature was just on the north side of sixty degrees and climbing. Folks coming out of the buildings downtown for early lunches were in shirtsleeves or light sweaters praising the great, summerlike day. Food was ordered *"to go"* then rushed out the door to begin the search for a dry place to sit in the sun. Others took the opportunity to go for an extended walk, enjoying the bright, unexpected turn of the day along their way.

Bob Wilson decided to do both: eating a six-inch club sandwich as he walked over toward Grant Park. Working on Michigan Avenue downtown had its advantages, and being within walking distance to the park was one of them. By the time Bob reached the edge of the park, his sandwich was almost gone, and he had started a light sweat from his abbreviated power walk. Stepping off the sidewalk onto the grass, he brushed against some tall hedges and was surprised by several crows flying out from *under* them. Being a curious man and loving puzzles, he knew these were scavenger birds, so there had to be something dead close by on which they had been feeding. He sniffed the air toward the hedges and caught the unmistakable odor of spoiled meat, definite decay! Walking along the front of the hedges slightly bent, he saw a man's expensive-looking shoe first, then followed it forward along the leg and lower body. Judging by the pants and open overcoat, the guy had money or used to anyway—obviously the victim of a mugging, no doubt. Bob leaned lower, looking higher up on the torso and seeing the large bloodstained area that went almost across the entire chest. He saw small, darker clusters of what he could only guess were flesh and bone; a few spaces were just open dark holes, with ants crawling around and in the wound. Yep, this one was a goner, all right. Bob reached for his cell phone with his right hand as he pushed the hedge further away from the body so he could see if it was anyone important he might know. Maybe a couple of quick pictures before he called *911*, just to show the guys back at the office. *That would ruin a few lunches for sure*, he thought with a smile.

He saw the dead man's face just as his cell phone flipped open, falling from his hand to the ground. His whole body went numb as the information flashed through his brain: Murray *"The Monster"* Robinson, drug dealer to drug dealers. He made more money than most city budgets. He was known to personally kill his dealers that shorted him on their drug money collections. *Hell!* He even killed his *own* brother in his mother's basement, overdosing him slowly, for taking *$1,000* off the top of Murray's drug money! Bob turned to the right, dropping down to his knees, as his lunch forced its way out of him, his stomach convulsing from sheer fear.

Several passersby saw the man fall to his knees and quickly turned away, not wanting to get involved. Others, sitting on the grass several yards away, looked at him with total disgust, while one man continued eating his sandwich, slightly shaking his head from side to side. His only thought, as he balled up the sandwich wrapper to toss, was that for some people, *Mondays really sucked!*

CHAPTER 3

Adam Alan's Crime Scene

It was an unusual sight for some of the tenants at the lakefront luxury high-rise apartment building as they looked through the lobby front doors and saw the police cars parked in the entrance driveway. There had been rumors that someone in the building was involved in an altercation, probably domestic, that warranted this type of reaction. But overall, regardless of the reason, this was *not* the desired attention wanted in this area, let alone this building. Several calls to management, as well as individual lawyers, were placed within the first hour that the patrol cars appeared. One older woman even asked a uniformed officer if they would kindly park in the *"delivery entrance"* of the building because she was expecting guests shortly and didn't want them to think she lived in *"that type"* of neighborhood. He politely said he would ask, radioed his commander, and used all his willpower to stifle the smile and laugh as the explicit reply came out over his radio speaker. The officer thought to himself it had probably been quite a while since that older woman had moved *that* fast...

Stepping out of the elevator on the top floor, Stephanie and Alex saw the uniformed officer standing outside the second penthouse apartment belonging to *Adam Alan Anderson*. Once inside they noted how immaculate the apartment was; it looked more like a display showroom than a place someone actually lived. Unless he had fantastic taste and an eye for interior design, this had to have been put together by a professional designer. The living room furniture they passed on the way into the bedroom would easily have set them both back three months' pay, but living in this building said very loudly that money was not an issue.

The same pristine conditions were found in the kitchen: everything in its place, as if this room had seen very little use, if any. All the rooms looked untouched, nothing out of place anywhere until they went into the master bedroom suite. The bed looked like it had been slept in, top cover sheet partially on the floor. Energetic sex, or did someone get out of bed in a hurry? Or were they pulled out by force? No signs of things out of place on the dressers; tables and chairs in the sitting area looked unmoved. The massive black onyx hooded fireplace just added to the sense of how big the room truly was, reflecting their movements on its polished surface. A flash to the right of the fireplace caught their attention; they both turned and headed toward the open doorway. A *CSI* tech was taking pictures of the interior contents and body in the shower, the gun blast pattern visible on the back wall. Several more minutes of shots and the tech walked toward them, nodded, and left the bedroom.

"Mike! Don't you ever take a day off?" asked Stephanie seeing Mike stoop down to look closer at the body. He forcibly moved the man's right hand down to cover his genitals before he looked up at her, feeling the blush hot on his face.

"Just like you, Detective, *no!* Until *Reilly* gets better, I'll be pulling a lot of *OT*," he said.

"Yeah, that was a tough break for him falling out of that *'El Train.'* So I figured you'd catch this one too, seems to be a trend going on for killing crime lords. Another one up close and personal, I take it? Looks like this one was done right here though…"

"Yep. Who was he?" asked Alex.

"*Adam Alan Anderson. 'Triple A'* is what his friends and clients called him on the street. He ran mostly male cross-dressers, a few *real* women thrown in, to the rich and infamous. The majority of his *'girls'* were quite *'beautiful,' all* of them would *stand out* in a *crowded* room full of beauty contestants," said Stephanie.

"And you know this *how*…?" asked Mike perplexed.

"Some of his girls were in that roundup a few years back, you know, the dope-and-sex-ring thing with *Richardson*...," said Stephanie, stopping as she saw his cheeks redden more.

"That's a possible connection...but after all this time, could it be a motive? To prompt something like...*this?*" asked Mike.

Stepping further into the bathroom, they looked down on the man sitting on the shower floor. The spread pattern and fragments on the shower's back wall showed that he was standing up when he was shot. With the amount of damage to his abdomen, the barrel of the gun, if not directly against the skin, was a very short distance away. Being forced out of bed into a shower really didn't make sense now. If you wanted to remove trace elements, evidence, take the whole body and wash the entire place down. Or was the shot heard, forcing the killer to cut and run, thinking escape instead of cleanup? His eyes were open. Did he see who killed him? A client? A lover? *What kind of enemies could this guy have had?* thought Stephanie.

"Who called this one in, Mike?" asked Stephanie.

"Dispatch said they didn't leave a name and nothing showed up on caller ID. They got a confirmation on the address from the GPS. They pinged it back, the phone is still around here somewhere!" said Mike handing her the number.

She looked at it, walked over to a uniformed officer, and asked him to have the *CPD* cyber division run a more exact trace, maybe narrow down a location.

"Well, Mike, you've got all the signs showing this was the kill site, now work your magic and give me a *who*...," said Stephanie.

"Well, I can't give you a *who*, but if I'm right, by the way this buckshot looks, the same gun or type of gun *may* have been used in the other hit too," said Mike.

"Could be a power play from within his own shop maybe? Who was his number 2?" asked Alex.

"I think his sister worked with him. Not sure if they were close or not. Something else to look into...," said Stephanie.

"Well, these hits couldn't have been power plays coming from within, too coincidental. And both happening somewhat close together? Not likely...," said Alex.

"Maybe somebody's trying to do our job and help to clean up the city?" asked Stephanie.

"Or maybe something *worse*, Annie…," said Alex.

"What could be *worse*, Alex? They'd be doing *us* a favor. Give us a chance to relax for a minute or two."

"Helping us out by cleaning up the city? Okay…that's a thought. Or…could they be helping *themselves* to take *over* the city…?" said Alex looking down at the body.

CHAPTER 4

How's Your Day Going, Ole Man?

Charlie Conrad was making his way to his local street pharmacist. Today he was in no rush; for some unknown reason he wasn't hurting as bad as he usually did in the mornings, maybe because he had passed out last night *(got his hands on a half pint of* unopened *Hennessy)*, and his drug-racked body finally got the rest it needed. He had remembered back in the day a White boy that supplied this area. *Randy Rick* they called him, because he was always talking about jumping some woman and all the things he was gonna do to her ass, but Charlie knew he was probably all talk and no action. And if some chick had run up on him with an offer of free ass, he would have run for the hills quick, fast, and in a hurry! But no matter what he was talking about, he kept the people in the area well supplied. Then one day *Randy Rick* was just…*gone*, without a word no less, and this new Black boy, *young boy*, was taking over. *DJ* they called him, pretty friendly to the old-timers like him, but Charlie still felt that was just for show. Something about him just made him think that he had did something or knew something about why Ricky was…*gone.* He didn't trust DJ, figured he had that mean side to him that could hurt you bad, maybe even kill you, but he wasn't sure. He guessed that one day, like Randy Rick, DJ would just be…*gone*…too.

"Hey, CC. How's your day going, ole man?" the voice said.

22

Charlie stopped. CC was what they called him on the streets. He looked around and saw DJ leaning against the building. He had been so deep in his thoughts he walked right past him.

"*Fair to midland, youngster! Fair to midland!* Any mo' better they'd have ta' sedate my ole ass!" said CC.

"I *like* that answer, ole man! That's always a good one!" said DJ. "You out later than your usual. How you feeling, ole man?"

"Okay for now, long as my *discount* is still working from ya…?" said CC.

"No worries, CC. Just call it part of your Medicare plan," DJ said with a smile.

He turned to the left and nodded. A young boy, maybe ten or eleven years old, quickly came up to Charlie's side, putting his left hand close by Charlie's right-hand pants pocket. Charlie eased the folded money out into the little boy's open palm, and he was gone just as quick as he had come up, back around the corner into an alleyway. A few moments later, his hand waved around the corner of the building, and another little boy, just as young, just as quick, was on Charlie's left side dropping several small packets down into his pants pocket, then gone without a word.

"*Damn, DJ!* That was slicker then *cow shit* in the summertime! No matta' how many times I see it, I'm still impressed by it!"

"Just savin' my ass and givin' you a service, ole man. Anything goin' down out here I should know about? Somebody I might need to…*'talk to'*…maybe?" asked DJ.

There it was, thought Charlie. That feeling, that look. Even though DJ was smiling, his eyes were saying something a whole lot different. Almost like a need to go out and hurt somebody or even worse. He involuntarily took a small step back from DJ and put both hands in his pockets.

"Easy, *ole man*, easy. No need to go for that blade in your pocket. I got no worries 'bout you! You know you my eyes and ears out here. Things I *don't* see or hear, you just *might*…could save both our *asses* one day. I got yo' back, ole man. I *got* your back!" said DJ.

"Much obliged 'bout that, *Mr. DJ*, much obliged!" Charlie said not moving.

"You know, I got ambitions, CC. I don't plan to be out here on the streets supplying y'all forever. One day I'll have my own people runnin' the streets *for me*, not just around in this area but all over: uptown, suburbs, maybe even in other *states*. I want to grow and grow big, CC. *Be* the boss, not just a flunky makin' short coin runnin' hisself to death, but makin' *tall dollars*, the kind of dollars that make other folks do what *you* want them to do! Know what I mean, CC? Did you ever dream like that?" DJ asked.

For a second, Charlie thought back when he did dream, dream of being an engineer. Dreamed of helping to put up big houses, big buildings here in the city, suburbs, all over the world. He was gonna leave his name everywhere, and even after he was gone, *his name* would still be out there. But one day, the payment for a project he had worked on came through with a bonus of cocaine. The architect told him it was a onetime thing only, not to worry, wouldn't happen again. But that onetime thing was one time too many, and it did happen again and again *and again* until he lost his wife, his kids, his house, *everything!* Wound up on the streets doing shit he never even thought *existed* or anything he'd thought of *ever* doing…

"Naw, youngster, that's for you young'uns, ones that got places to go and ideas that fit in with those places. Ole-ass hypes like me just think about that next shot and hopefully dyin' in our sleep…," said Charlie. Then he turned and walked away, feeling that DJ really did have something to do with Randy Rick disappearing. And with an even more overwhelming feeling that DJ soon, *very soon*, would just be…*gone*…too.

DJ saw that faraway look in the ole man's eyes and knew memories had to be running through his mind and wondered what he had really been thinking and how he'd fit in, *or not fit in*, with *his* big ambitions…

CHAPTER 5

Murray "The Monster" Robinson

Murray watched as his Northside lieutenant snorted the line of coke. In all the movies he had seen growing up, the people were sucking up the white powder off mirrors, using rolled-up money, the really hard-core ones used a $100 bill, but he could never understand why. He had beveled-edge, tinted panes of high-gloss Plexiglas and heavy-duty four-inch-long Plexiglas straws for his people to use. He had tried it in his early days working for his uncle *Ronald Baker*, which was over twenty years ago, when he was *really* stupid as to how this *"game"* was played. His uncle had told him, much later, that he always wanted his people to use what they sold for two reasons. The first was control. He needed to have them *"beholden"* to him because he knew they'd be back not only to get their supply to sell but to get their *"so-called"* free samples for themselves, with extra added samples if they sold more than the week before. The second reason—if they did get picked up *"holdin'"* a portion of their stash, back then the judges would go a little easier on them because they were a junkie. But either way, in his uncle's eyes, they were still a pathetic bunch of asshole losers that were hooked on *shit!* Now Murray wanted them to use in front of him so he could gauge how much they were really hooked and if it was going to be a problem for his business.

Murray's thoughts jumped back to his mother, how she had always pushed him to excel, telling him and his siblings that her father had said that if the White man could make a watch out of a rock, then they damn well should be able to make two of them! His own father had tried to help them as much as he could, but as he often said, being a Black man on the Southside of Chicago not only worked against you; it literally wore you down. Some nights after he and his brothers and sisters had gone to bed, he could hear his mother and father arguing about everything under the sun: from money to living conditions to him not having any ambition to do any better, always throwing up in his face how successful her older brother Ronny was and that *he* didn't whine about his life.

Murray, at a very early age, began to hate his uncle *Ronald Baker*.

A few times when Murray's father hadn't made it home at his usual time, he'd stand at the front door waiting to see him come up the walkway, onto the front porch. And when he opened the front door, it was all he could do to keep from running to him so fast without knocking him down. One evening, Murray looked out the front door *(way past the time his dad usually got home)* and saw him sitting on the porch steps, head hung down. He quietly walked out, sat down next to him, and hugged him. He had never heard a sigh as deeply or as sad-sounding as what his dad let out that night, but somehow he managed to hug Murray back and give him a small kiss on the forehead, sitting that way in silence for quite a while longer.

His father, finally fed up with his wife's constant put-downs, went to work one Monday morning and never came home again. Murray, along with his brothers and sisters, thought the worst right off the bat and knew that soon that knock on the front door would come: the police telling them they had bad news because they had found their father's body in the *"most horrible"* way! Their world would be forever changed: no high school, no college, no future for any of them. Murray, being the oldest, tried to be brave for them all, always positive words and bright futures, but at night he would go down to a corner in the basement and silently cry. Even his mother began to question what had gone wrong. Did she really make him leave by talking that awfully to him? Had she really gone too far throwing her brother up to him every chance she got? And she knew she couldn't make it on her own with the house, bills, providing for the kids, and anything else that could, and would, pop up! Murray began to hate his mother almost as much as he hated her brother. Then there finally *was* that knock on the door, seven weeks after his father had not come home, and when he slowly opened it, there stood his uncle Ronald Baker.

Ronald and his sister talked softly *(and she cried often, hanging her head down)* at the dining room table, he reaching out to hold her hands in his several times, saying, "*There, there now,*" every once in a while. She stopped talking to him, came over to Murray, and told him to go put his brothers and sisters to bed, wiping her eyes, trying to smile for him. Getting them all together, guiding them upstairs, Murray turned to look back into the dining room and saw his uncle push a large roll of money across the table to his mother, her eyes widening in disbelief, not knowing what she should say or do. She quickly looked up at Murray and pushed the money back to her brother as Murray moved further up the stairs. Without looking back, he knew she would wait until he was out of sight then take the money back.

Murray and his siblings never saw their father again. But with the help of their Uncle Ronald, their lives didn't really change that much. His brothers and sisters even began to smile and laugh again... but not Murray. He had kept that hate burning, only letting it calm down when he went off to college.

CHAPTER 6

Murray Goes to College

College was a new and better world for Murray—freedom at last without the worry of his siblings. They were all older now, no more hoping for their dad to return. They all had a harder but realistic view of life. At first it was odd not hearing the usual noises of his brothers and sisters moving about, but that was soon replaced by the school noises: class schedules, work to be done, books to be read and the girls…*yeah, the girls!* He really wasn't prepared for some of them, not hesitating for a second to tell him what they wanted, most of them, and where they knew they could get it from. It was a wonder to him that he passed that first year with a B average. Much to his surprise, the Black girls he met were mostly cold to him and other Black guys. But after a while, he had understood why: lowlife brothers had gotten with them just to get laid then cut and ran as soon as the sister started to get serious. One woman he just said "Hi" to jumped back at him with, *"Nigga! If you ain't thinkin' 'bout a ring in my future, step the fuck on!"* Murray made it a point to not even nod at a sister unless she made some indication to him first.

Then he saw *Allison Thompson*, a White girl that looked too beautiful to be real but carried herself like a born *"sista."* She didn't talk like either one, Black or White, but somewhere between a perfect blend of the two, and she kept your attention regardless of what she was discussing. Murray kept his distance all the same, thinking of her in the back of his mind, knowing that their meeting would never happen.

One evening, down in the lounge on the main floor, Murray had noticed that a brand-new upright piano had been brought in. Feeling warm and in flight *(those joints with the guys were slightly wearing off but he still felt good)*, thoughts of how his dad played the piano when he was small flooded his mind. He stood to the side as a few brave souls plinked and plunked notes, laughing at the sweet sounds but awful combinations. Soon they tired, gravitating to the chairs and sofas, talking about other things; he sat down on the piano bench. Murray saw the notes and chords in his mind's eye as clearly as if they were written down on sheet music. The bass chord, soft and sweet, set the mood as the treble notes began to tell the story, his father's story. *Carl's Theme* was what he had called it, smooth jazz all the way. He lost track of time playing, eyes closing with the melody opening onto the scenes of happy times with his father, brothers, and sisters, days gone by. He sat for a moment when the music was done, still feeling the warmth of his family, when he heard applause. Looking up, Murray saw at least thirty, maybe forty, people had come into the lounge, crowded slightly around the piano, standing, clapping their hands softly. And there, right in front was Allison, a look of amazement in her eyes as she walked up to him and gave him a lingering hug. Taking his hand, she walked him out of the room into her life, *their life*, from that point on…

Murray's lieutenant finished his lines and gave him an update as to what was going on in his territory and quickly left, not wanting to spend any more time with Murray than he had too. He sat for a while thinking of everything yet nothing at the same time before he sensed someone coming up behind him. The footfalls were soft, steady, and familiar. His guard was never up here at home, but he was still in the habit of listening to his surroundings. Allison's right hand glided onto his right shoulder, gently sliding down to rub in short, easy strokes across his chest as she moved around his chair. Murray covered her hand with his left and turned to kiss her forearm.

"Penny for your thoughts, babe," Allison said, "as if I needed to ask."

"Or get paid that penny," said Murray.

He reached up with his right hand to circle her waist, pulling her down onto his lap. They held each other in their old, settled way, comfortable in each other's arms. Allison touched his face, leaned in, and kissed his lips softly, then looked into his eyes, truly a woman deeply in love with this man.

The years had been good to both of them. No one would realize, with her slender figure, that she had given him four children—all of them reaching or are in their twenties, all of them knowing what their father did for a living yet all loving him just the same. And Murray—people mistaking him for being in his mid or late thirties when on his next birthday, he'd turn fifty-two—loved his family with all his heart.

"We all know that 'The Monster' title is just that, a title. Nothing even remotely to do with you or describe who you really are. If your people knew who you really were, would you have built this business as big as it is? Would they have given you the respect that you now have? I don't think so, babe," said Allison.

"Yeah, baby, I know. You all loving me and caring for me means more to me than you'll ever know, but sometimes this duality gets to me, makes me tired, and wants to hang it all up. But to whom would I pass it on? Not any of the kids, not you, none of my lieutenants. I guess I'll be in this game until I get planted or I die on my own. Either way, baby, I still miss Davy," said Murray.

Allison touched Murray's forehead with her own, and it was almost like she could see into his mind images of those two unconnected days, only weeks apart, that put "The Monster" into his name...

CHAPTER 7

DJ's Big Ambition

DJ was one of those kids born to be no good, and growing up in the area beginning at *Forty-Seventh* and Indiana, it was a done deal. From an early age, he was always getting into trouble, one way or another. Sometimes it only took a look from somebody that he thought was judging him, and it was the start of a fight. He *knew* everyone was against him, so he had to make sure they didn't think he was just another little bitch that was going to roll over and take whatever they handed out!

At twelve years old, he was ditching school on a regular basis; all those books just seemed to make his head hurt every time he opened one and started to read, so he thought, *What's the point in going to school anyway? Who needs it?* During one of his many *"off days,"* he ran into an older kid named Mike Matthews. Mike was a child of the streets too, five years older than him, but he had already seen far too much for his age. He took DJ under his wing from the moment they met, showing him the ropes of running dope under the ever-watchful blue-light camera eyes of the police, no less! He also showed DJ how to keep his stash nearby, undercover, easy enough to get to for a quick sale but far enough away so the police couldn't get him for possession. When DJ's sales volume increased, Mike got him some younger kids to be his runners, paying them a few dollars each *(a lot more than what they got from home or a part-time job!)* so DJ could keep his customers in sight while the kids ran to one stash with the money and another kid delivered what he needed back to the buyer, all the time keeping mental track of product as well as cash. It got to the point that he only needed to handle the drugs when he got them from Mike and handle the money when he turned in for the night. After a while, the idea that running dope was a big mistake took on less and less concern as the money rolled in even faster.

At fourteen DJ's territory alone was almost thirty blocks in any direction, and Mike was branching out even further. He and Mike had taken over most of the other dope pushers that showed promise and scared off the others that Mike called *"weekend slingers,"* guys selling drugs on a *"part-time"* basis, not yet making enough money to quit their day jobs but enough to keep them interested. He had gotten so good with running his business that he always had a thousand dollars in his pocket and a Smith and Wesson *.380* automatic *(a gift from Mike)* tucked neatly in the back center of his pants. Mike had warned him not to wave it in anyone's face because that was the sure way for a young Black man with money to get shot quick, fast, and in a hurry! It was his protection—*period!*—when Mike wasn't around to have his back. In this neighborhood, when someone got beat down or shot, it rarely got looked into, let alone solved.

DJ's life had gotten even better at the age of fifteen, and when Mike told him it was time for him to meet their supplier, just in case something happened to Mike *(Seriously? Mike was forever!)*, he figured it had just gotten even better. At the back of DJ's mind, knowing who supplied Mike was one step closer to knowing who supplied them all. And that meant Mike and DJ were one step closer to cutting out the middleman ahead of them...

CHAPTER 8

DJ and Mike Meet Emmanuel Isaac

The sun was just beginning to set when Mike and DJ walked into the high-rise apartment building just off of Sixty-First and King Drive. The twenty-story building looked fairly clean and kept up for the neighborhood it was in, with several people sitting around outside on benches enjoying the slightly cool breeze. The variety of luxury cars in the parking lot ranged from Cadillac sedans to the latest Mustang Selby Cobra. But the one that really caught his eye was the silver Jaguar XJ with the charcoal-gray interior.

"Now that's a badass ride!" said DJ, nudging Mike.

"Yeah, that's why Isaac bought it! He knew it would *stand out*,'" said Mike.

DJ felt like this building was out of place here; it really should be somewhere else, the Northside or a suburb maybe. The residents seemed to be on a much higher level than he or Mike. Hell, most of them didn't even look up when they passed by. He wanted to shoot someone...*bad!* Mike's right hand tightened just above DJ's left wrist, and when he turned and looked at him, he knew Mike had read his mind. Just that look Mike was giving him said he was about three inches away from a really bad ass-whuppin'. Then Mike turned and looked to his left. About twenty feet away were two of the biggest men DJ had even seen in his life: both over six feet tall at least, easily weighing in at 260 to 270 pounds, all muscle! Their suits looked expensive and fit very well over their trim body armor he could just make out under their jackets, not to mention the slight bulges of the guns under each armpit.

DJ froze, for the first time in years, *out of fear!* Seeing him stop, one of the men quickly walked over to him.

"I take it this is your first time meeting Mr. Isaac," the man said in a velvet-smooth, professional voice. All DJ could do was look up at the man's face and nod his head yes.

"As Mike well knows, Mr. Isaac does *not* appreciate...*drama*... so ALL your personal *'affects'* will be left down here with...*us*," the man said softly into DJ's face, neither of them looking away from the other.

Before he could even think to move or understand what the man had said to him, DJ was slowly easing the *.380* from the center back of his pants and handing it to the man, handle first. It swiftly disappeared into a side coat pocket, a move done many times, both hands now going under both of DJ's armpits and easily forcing them away from his sides. The palms came up gliding along the bottom of his outstretched arms, fingers curled up, lightly touching the backs. Both hands worked in unison as they rolled over the front of his wrist, moving toward his shoulders onto his neck. For a second, DJ just knew this man was going to strangle him, end his life in a flash of brute strength, but the man's hands continued down, flat against his chest, around to his back, then down along the outsides of his legs. As the man slowly stood, his hands traveled up the insides of DJ's legs, cupping his crotch a moment too long, DJ thought. To his shock, he started to get a hard-on, quickly looking up into the man's dark eyes that smiled then winked the left one as his hand dropped from DJ's crotch.

"Mr. Isaac is waiting for you in the penthouse, elevator to your left...*sir*," the man said, still with a slight smile on his face.

As DJ turned and walked away, several thoughts ran through his mind, mainly how to kill that *fucker* as painfully as possible. Just as he reached Mike's side, the elevator doors opened, and he saw a third huge man standing at the elevator controls. DJ's thoughts intensified...

Emanuel Isaac had taken the top three floors of the high-rise building. On the lowest level of the three was primarily the recreation areas *(pool tables, card tables, fixed and portable video games, Blu-Ray movies, music CDs)* with sitting and food services at spot locations around the floor. Most of the people that were allowed this far usually stayed on this floor. Given the circumstances, the atmosphere on this level was always very relaxed, no need to constantly look over your shoulder. There were also five bedroom suites with private bathrooms *(an additional four half bathrooms down several hallways)* for his bodyguards, each housing a separate hidden, well-stocked arsenal. The next level up were six guest room suites, large lounge area with a bar/grill, and a thirty-four-seat home theater room complete with ticket booth and fully functional concession counters *(Isaac could not watch a movie without his hot dogs, popcorn, and cola!).* The top level was a massive living room open to a formal dining area seating sixteen, both sharing a 270-degree view looking toward the lake. The commercial-grade kitchen could easily handle food preparation for eighty-plus people or that midnight munchies run by Isaac and a special overnight guest. This was the level Mike and DJ were escorted to. Several casually dressed men were sitting around on various couches and club chairs, taking their turn talking to a man with his back to the window, looking at the elevator they were just walking out of.

The man held up his right hand, and the room fell silent.

"Gentlemen, this is Mike and his lieutenant, DJ. They are our top street dealers here on the Southside. Very soon they will be our top street dealers in the city. I asked them here today so you all could get to know them, as well as they get to know you. Young men, please have a seat."

Isaac's deep, smooth voice had a calming effect on DJ. Mike seemed to have relaxed a bit too. They sat on low cushions to the left of the elevator as the meeting continued.

At the end of the meeting, after a round of introductions and the other men had gone, Isaac had them move to one of the larger couches.

"You both have advanced faster than anyone else in my organization, and that lets me know you are serious about what you're doing. Mike, I'm giving you two of the suburbs to redo, make them run a lot smoother, what you decide is law there. And you, DJ, will take over Mike's territory here in the city," Isaac said.

DJ looked at Mike, giving him a half grin.

"So without Mike being around, does that make me the pickup for the...*product?*" said DJ.

Isaac turned and looked at Mike, slightly smiling. "I see your assessment of him was right, *very ambitious...*" Isaac turned to DJ. "Having that drive in you will take you far in this world, even if you *weren't* working for me, but you have to remember that you're not doing this...*job*...alone. Granddad always said, treat the people you meet on your way up well, because you *definitely* will meet those same people on your way down. Tread very carefully, young man, because that person you decide to cut out, possibly for personal gain, may one day come back to cut *you out*, *period*, for their payback," Isaac said.

DJ looked at Isaac and thought, *One day I'll be running your organization, old man...one day!*

Isaac continued to look at DJ then smiled and winked at him.

"I have gifts for you both downstairs to go along with your new promotions. Have a great day, gentlemen."

Then Isaac turned and walked toward the kitchen as DJ imagined putting several bullets into his back. Again he felt Mike's hand grab his left wrist, and this time he saw total anger in his eyes. He felt that same fear again but didn't have to ask him what was on his mind.

"So, Mike, have you ever thought about going direct? You know, cut Isaac out completely and deal with his drop?" asked DJ.

"You need to cut back on what you using, *little nigga!* That kinda *shit'll* get your ass *much dead!*" said Mike. "That's playing with the really *BIG* boys! Only one step above Emmanuel Isaac and you *don't* want to go *there!* That's *too* fuckin' high for both of us, *little nigga. And don't you get no fuckin' ideas either, DJ!* You're good at this, but you ain't *that goddamn good!*"

DJ watched as Mike turned and walked away, using all his will-power not to pull out the *.380* and light his ass up! *Shit!* The *.380* was downstairs in that son of a bitch's pocket! He had his answer now. Mike was just another punk-ass follower, happy as hell with the money he was getting that DJ knew, *just knew*, had to be chump change compared to what Isaac was getting. Shit! They were giving Isaac a cut of what they pulled every week on top of what he sold them the drugs for, and DJ knew of at least thirty other brothers that were paying out too!

After collecting their property and heading outside, they saw two new Ford Mustangs waiting for them at the front entrance. DJ couldn't believe his eyes, quickly jumping into the nearest one and taking off, but after a few minutes, the anger at what Isaac had said to him came back. This was a *fuckin' bribe!* A new shiny toy to take his mind off the important thing: *cutting out the middleman!* Either way, DJ had decided he wasn't gonna just sit and wait to move up *"behind"* Mike; he'd been in that shadow long enough. And just maybe, *just maybe*, later in the week, before they had their weekly meeting with Isaac, was gonna be his time for that move...

CHAPTER 9

Murray's "The Monster's" Crime Scene

Yellow and black tape strung about several trees and the mirrors of a few police cruisers defined a large area around the body of Murray *"The Monster"* Robinson. The medical examiner had bagged numerous samples, including insects found near the shredded wound. Hopefully, these little guys could help to narrow down the time of death. He called one of his attendants over to help him roll the body off its back onto its left side. Just like he thought, the wound went completely through, out the back. He had seen his share of gunshot trauma before, but this one took the prize. Powder burns on the front clothing along with this amount of damage had to be *00* buckshot, possibly a twelve-gauge shotgun. No pooling of blood or chunks of flesh/bone on the ground or in the bushes let him know that this was the secondary crime scene, a dump site. The actual shooting had been done elsewhere. Easing the body back down to the ground, he signaled to his attendants to bag the body for transport back to the morgue; there he'd find a bit more evidence, maybe even a clue to the *"where"* it happened.

Payback was a natural bitch in *The Monster's* line of business! If just some of the stories he had heard about this guy were true, then he deserved a lot more punishment than just being opened up in the middle like this. Murray had made a lot of enemies during his *"career,"* so figuring out who could have done this would be a long, not to even mention time-consuming process, and he was glad he didn't have to worry about doing all that footwork the detectives were in for.

"Hey, Ray, what we got?" said the female voice.

Dr. Raymond Walker didn't have to turn around to know it was his favorite detective, Lt. Stephanie Ann Caldwell. He had a secret crush on her from the first time they'd met, almost three years ago, when she was dressed as a runway model. He couldn't take his eyes off her as she stood at the end of the line of other models, all waiting to be booked for pushing drugs and sex at some of their shows. Two police women came up behind her and quietly escorted her away. *Must be their leader*, he thought, only to see her turn up in his lab twenty minutes later still dressed up, flashing her gold shield, and asking for a full *tox (toxicology)* report on the bag of brownish powder she had dropped on his table.

Standing up and turning around to face her, he was disappointed, as usual, to see her in the heavy bulletproof vest loaded with gear. The tight, small auburn curls of her hair still stood out and hung down to her shoulders, framing her caramel-colored face with those big brown eyes, instantly drawing him in as she looked his way...

"Stop thinking so hard, Ray, and talk to me," she said with a slight smile.

"From what I can see so far, it had to be a shotgun, double-barreled from the width of the front wound, put directly on his abdomen," he said, quickly looking down at the body to hide his glowing-red face. "Blew right through everything and out his back. I doubt he lasted more than a minute before he died. No signs of struggle or other trauma either."

Stephanie put her hand on one of the attendants' shoulder, motioning for him to stop zipping the body bag. She knelt down to get a closer look at the wound and concurred with Raymond's assessment: tie was still knotted sitting on a gold tie bar with diamonds, jacket *(Armani?)* was buttoned, and even the handkerchief was still folded in his breast pocket. She took out a ballpoint pen and forcefully moved his right hand away from his side. Odd, his hands were rough, somewhat scarred and calloused. These were the hands of someone who manually worked for a living, not someone that distributed drugs to an entire city.

"Ray, when you do the exam, get me a closer workup on his hands, palms especially. Something's not right about them...," she said starting to go through her mental catalog for similarities.

Stephanie stood up; the attendants finished zipping up the body bag, placed it on a gurney, and quickly wheeled it toward their van.

"Bet you dollars to doughnuts, Annie, he has a wet day-dream about you before he gets back to the shop," said Alex Smith, Stephanie's partner. They both turned and headed along the perimeter of the crime scene.

"No takers there, Al, that's a fool's bet for sure. *Dollars to dough-nuts*...really?" she said, looking at him in disbelief.

"So what's your idea about this whole deal? This is the second heavyweight asshole belly-up in three weeks, and these guys just don't get caught like that," he said looking down the path, a slow side-to-side scan.

"Yeah, you're right about that, Al. I looked at *The Monster's* hands just now, and they looked like he had been doing manual labor or *something* repetitive with them. When was the last time you think he picked up anything heavier than his dick or a rum and coke? This one's got a few questions from jump...," said Stephanie.

They continued walking the path, noting streets nearby, darker areas away from the main thoroughfares, possible quick exits leading away from the bushes into several different side roads and the direction of traffic on them. All the high rises were off to the west, streets inclining toward the lake to the east—too many places their guy, or guys, could have gone without being noticed. They continued their slow walk along the path, making mental notes to be discussed together later.

He pulled the dark-tan Italian leather gloves up, more out of habit than actual adjustment on his hands, letting them fall to his sides. The matching mohair overcoat, opened in the front, revealed a small glimpse of the dark-brown Armani single-breasted suit underneath. The knot of the gold tie rested on the 24-karat gold tie bar, half-karat diamonds on either end. His eyes locked on the crime scene across *Michigan Avenue*, taking in all the separate group activities, paying special attention to the two detectives walking north along the pathway parallel to the street.

The *S600 Mercedes* sedan, oxblood red, silently pulled to the curb in front of him. Almost instantly the front passenger was out the car, smoothly opening the rear door for the well-dressed man. He stood for a few moments longer before getting into the Mercedes. The front passenger closed the door with a muted thud and was back in the car just as quickly as he had gotten out. The car merged unnoticed into the southbound lanes, disappearing into the heavy afternoon traffic.

CHAPTER 10

Mason Lynn Richardson III

Mason sat in his chair, right leg crossed over the left, smoking one of his special-blend small cigars. They were a bit thicker than a cigarette but much thinner than an actual cigar. As he blew the smoke toward the ceiling, he thought of the similar cigars he had smoked growing up in Huntsville, North Carolina. Those had a hard wooden tip and made him feel more important than the other kids he hung out with; they only smoked cigarettes…and the *occasional joint*. He was much too good for that. If it wasn't for Tim and Daniel, he wouldn't even have associated with most of them. But in retrospect, he had figured out that was all three of their covers; *"beards"* was the word used back then. They were both his lovers, each afraid to mention it to the other, hoping that by not saying it out loud, their secret would be safe, making the thrill of going to Mason's bed even greater in their young minds than what it really was. Each new *"session"* with Tim or Daniel taught Mason not only what guys wanted but what they would do for or pay to get it, all the while giving him heightened feelings that a man, a *real* man, wasn't supposed to feel.

High school days had been great, but the college days were even better. The parties, the liquor, the drugs, and the really rich young men that put on the fronts for their upper-class parents during the day but were on their knees for him at night. The gifts and money poured in for Mason with little or no effort on his part, not only because he gave them what they wanted but from the fear that he might just tell someone their dirty little secrets.

Four years of college flew by, and he had a bachelor's degree in business finance, then a master's and another master's in business law. He took a break for a year and traveled around the world, experiencing delights that a gay American man didn't even know existed. With the money he had saved from his many *"lovers,"* he had invested wisely, growing it into a small fortune. He thought there was nothing that could stand in his way, and he wasn't even twenty-five years old yet!

But the wild, wonderful, devastating party in London brought him down to earth faster than a well-hung handsome man could take him to bed...

Alan Peterman was his name, and he was very rich, very beautiful, and *very twisted*. Mason felt the strong physical attraction from him across the room, and that should have been his first warning, but he was on his way to a solid drunk, and his ass had been twitching for a man the last few hours. As Alan walked toward him, Mason couldn't help but slowly look him up and down, getting hotter by the second with his stride. Alan stood next to him, staring into his eyes, no attempt to hide the lust that he was feeling.

"For some reason, I doubt the usual pickup lines will be necessary. What do you think?" he asked in a soft, smooth English voice.

"You're pretty much right own tha' a'count," Mason said. "Only thing ta figure out is yo' room or mine, darlin'."

"I didn't take you for a Southerner, but that will just make it all the more special indeed," Alan said. "Shall we go?" he said waving his hand toward the exit hall.

When the elevator doors closed, Alan pulled him close and lightly kissed his lips, then kissed down to his neck on the left. Mason could hardly contain himself and quickly reached out to rub between Alan's legs, pleasantly surprised to find him just as aroused as he was. The elevator doors opened, and they walked out holding hands, lost in the pure sexual attraction, or so Mason thought. At Alan's hotel door, they embraced again, the kiss deeper and more passionate this time, hardly breaking for Alan to take the key card out of his pocket. The door swung into the room as Mason turned to head in. Seated on the sofa was a bearded man, tie undone, suit jacket folded across the sofa arm. His head laid back as he steadily masturbated, he quickly turned toward the door. Off to the left were two very muscular naked men both holding short liquor glasses, now looking at him smiling. There was no pain, but Mason knew he had been hit from behind; his world had gone into slow motion as he sank to his knees. It felt like moving through syrup as he turned his head toward the two naked men slowly coming closer. One grabbed a handful of hair, pulling his head up taunt, the other man's balled-up fist growing larger in his vision from the right...*then blackness...*

He smelled fresh, clean odors before he finally remembered how to open his eyes. There was soft, white light off to his right. He followed it. The pain shot through his head, face, and neck as he tried to turn his head, quickly forcing his eyes closed again. His breath came in short, hard gasps as he waited for it to stop. He heard a door open, then soft footfalls walking toward him.

"Mr. Richardson? Mr. Richardson? I truly apologize for the intrusion, but your monitor at my station spiked. Can you speak, sir?" said the woman's voice.

He partially opened his left eye. A stout woman in a nurse uniform was standing over him looking down.

"Where...*where is this...?*" he managed to say.

"You are in the *hospital*, Mr. Richardson. You've suffered quite a bit of...*trauma...*"

"How...*how long...here?*"

"I'm afraid to say well into your second week, sir. It appears those...*associates*...of yours seemed to have had somewhat of a time with you. But not to worry to their whereabouts. The constables have them all locked away, trying to arrange for a solicitor to represent them. I'm sure there will be an officer 'round for your statement in due time, Mr. Richardson, when you're up for the inquiries," said the nurse, beaming her most professional smile.

"*What happened...? How bad...?*"

"I'm sorry, Mr. Richardson. I'll have *Dr. Walters* in to explain," she said, a slight pained look on her face. Once again the professional smile came on. "Is there anything else I might do for you till then, sir?"

"*Noooo...thanks...*" He closed his eye, and once he heard the door softly close, he felt the tears begin to flow...

CHAPTER 11

Michael Smith-Jones

Michael Smith-Jones, from a very early age, had known intermediate spots of violence, usually brought on by his father. But none of that happened because he was drunk or high; every once in a while he would just be…*brutal*, but never to him, his mother, or brother and sisters. His earliest memory of the violence was about eight years old when his parents were having a house party. A few friends over, who in turn brought their friends, and so on it went. The house was full, music playing, good food, people were having a really good time. As usual when you get a bunch of folks together, especially young Black folks, a disagreement will quickly turn into a major fight, regardless of what it started out as. Michael's father, Norman—six feet, two inches with a bodybuilder's physique—never raised his voice or seemed to be threatening in any way, always with an ear to listen and shoulder to cry on.

Two of the *"brought-along"* houseguests had started out quiet but soon were at a volume that caused everyone to stop and turn their way. Norman walked over to them and placed his hands on their shoulders, speaking softly as he looked from one to the other. For a few seconds they were quiet, staring in his direction, then turned and headed for the front door. Once outside, the party got back to a good time until the same voices, this time much louder, were heard even more heated. Michael watched as his father quickly walked to the front door; he ran to the window seeing his father take the steps down two at a time, getting between the two young men just as balled-up fists were beginning to swing. Grabbing both men by their wrist, he twisted them forward, forcing them off balance to the ground. The one on Norman's right tucked in his right shoulder, hitting the ground in a martial arts roll, landing on his feet, knees bent in a fighting stance that had broken Norman's grip midroll. The second man, attempting to do the same thing, was caught off guard as he was pulled toward the first man, one foot landing in his crotch and the other inside his left knee, sending them both into a heap on the ground. Before they could recover, Norman swung with his right fist balled up, hitting the second man just behind the right ear, sending him falling over the legs of the other man. Quickly spinning down on one knee, he caught the first man in the left side of his face with his balled-up left fist, making him twist awkwardly under the dead weight before falling back to the ground.

Michael was amazed. His father wasn't even breathing hard, and the moves that he made were awesome in his eyes! Norman stood, dusting his hands off before he reached down and grabbed them both by the collars, and dragging them to the edge of the lawn. He separated them both by several feet then rolled them onto the sidewalk close to the curb.

"Guttersnipes should be close to their natural homes…," he said then turned and walked back to the party. *AWESOME!*

The years that followed, with the help of his father, had Michael training in martial arts and light bodybuilding. Norman giving him personal training in boxing as well began to turn Michael into a very lethal young man, so by the time of his eighteenth birthday, he, along with his father, had gained a very tough street reputation. Even to this day, they still talked about the father-son duo that were always helping people who couldn't help themselves out of trouble. Several years had passed since his parents moved to Arizona. His mother's sister taking a turn for the worse with her asthma didn't keep him and his father from talking. Michael was getting tips and ideas about how to handle some of the more *"interesting"* situations in his present job…

CHAPTER 12

Melissa "Mel" Randolph

Growing up the typical family tomboy, Melissa really didn't stop to think about what path she was heading down. Having two older brothers, she was just as rough and tumbled with them as they were with her. She was constantly being told by her mother that little girls didn't behave like that, but it always went in one ear and out the other. So she ran right along with her brothers, learning to fight and curse and whistle just as well as them, her brothers thinking of her as their *literal* backup reinforcement.

The few times *(holidays, birthdays, special occasions)* when her mother deemed it necessary to put Melissa into the cute little girly dresses and patent leather shoes with the turned-down lace-trimmed socks usually turned out to be a disaster. Either her brothers would tease her to the point of anger, with her chasing them out the door into a scuffle, or they all would finally get a break from the grownups and head outside, resulting in Melissa coming back into the house covered from head to toe with dirt, grass, mud, or a combination of all the aforementioned plus anything else that would stick to her, the dress completely ruined. Her mother finally, with a heavy sigh, gave up on her daughter and accepted the tomboy.

Going through elementary school and moving on to high school slowly showed her changing from little girl to beautiful young woman. Still running with her brothers *(now her very best friends*

48

actually!), she got into their weight lifting and other exercise routines, toning a bit more than what the average female would want to look like but less than a major bodybuilder. Not even thinking about what was happening, her dates with other girls just seemed…*natural.* Even her brothers had assumed that she would date girls without a second thought, commenting sometimes about what girl was okay for her and the ones that were definitely one-night stands. When she had finished high school and moved on to college, it became quite clear, in her sophomore year, that it was time to drop out, get a job, and move forward. Physical fitness had been in her life almost from the start. Seeing the people in the gyms and giving some of them tips on how to work out made the decision to become a trainer a no-brainer, and her career took off. In less than two years, she had opened her own place; her brothers working with her on a part-time basis added the family and fun to a job she already loved. Now she had just resigned herself to settling down with the right woman, adopting a few kids, and living the standard *"plastic utopian"* suburban life…until she ran across *Michael Smith-Jones.*

Melissa was on her way home. Her date with Amy had ended leaving them both satisfied and relaxed. Amy would be a keeper for sure. Maybe she was the one she'd finally settle down with…

Melissa caught movement out the corner of her right eye in the alley she had just passed. She slowed, pulled over to the side, and parked. Did she see a woman in a fight with a *man?* A man much *bigger* than her? She remembered the rules of *"couple fights"* and knew getting involved would usually get them both fighting *you!* But somehow she was drawn to at least go back to that alley and sneak a peek; maybe she could call the police, if nothing else. Easing up to the opening of the alley, she snuck a peek around the edge of the building and saw the woman swing a pipe into the right side of the man. As he doubled over, she quickly spun around to her left bringing the pipe up then down at an angle across his back from shoulder to waist, dropping him to the ground. Obviously hurt, the man's arm slowly moved back to his body, maybe in an attempt to try and get up. The woman, standing over him, the pipe now in her left hand, reached into her coat and withdrew an automatic pistol, pointing it at his head. Before Melissa could stop herself, she took a step into the alley and yelled.

"Stop it, you bitch!"

The woman swung her body toward the sound, firing the gun as she turned. One bullet hit the man just below the shoulder blade and the other slightly above his waist. She hesitated for a moment before she took off after Melissa, who was already around the corner, running full out to her car. She thanked her lucky stars that she had left the driver's side door open as she literally jumped into the seat, hurting her fingers as she slammed the key into the ignition. It didn't register to her that the sound of glass breaking was the passenger side window shattering as the first bullet flew through, barely scraping her across her forehead, out the open driver side window. The second bullet sliced along her left cheek as she turned to her right, looking directly into the face of the woman pointing the gun. Like a deer caught in the headlights of an oncoming vehicle, all Melissa could do was stare, knowing that after the next second she'd be dead… The blood coming out the woman's upper arm seemed surreal, almost slow motion, as the gun moved away from her, firing over the hood of the car. The right side of the woman's neck exploded, sending flesh and blood flying, her head bending back toward her left shoulder only to be forced back upright as a sizable piece of her head above her right eye took flight.

Melissa, still looking out the window, was frozen to her seat, the car running but not in gear. The man walked up outside the car; the motion of his body indicated he had lightly kicked the woman, making sure she was no longer a threat. He bent down, looked into the car, and said something Melissa couldn't hear. He said it again, and then he walked away. She didn't know how long she sat there, still looking out the passenger side window, before hearing her driver's side door open. Hands pushed firmly on her shoulder and waist, moved her over to the passenger seat. Someone in front of her brushed the broken glass onto the floor of the car before she was settled and buckled in. As the car pulled away from the curb, her whole body felt as if it was made of gel, then she passed out.

CHAPTER 13

A Match Made in the Gym

Melissa reached up and felt the gauze on her forehead and a large bandage on her left cheek. The images of what she had seen flashed through her mind, making her quickly sit straight up in the bed. *Where the hell was she?* Going over her upper body then legs, she didn't feel any other bandages. She stopped moving and listened, hearing a muffled clinking somewhere outside the bedroom's open door. Easing over to the edge of the bed, then slowly standing up, Melissa walked softly to the door. The clinking grew louder as she peeked around the doorframe. To the left, further down the hall, she saw a tall, muscled Black man, bare-chested, working out his arms with weights attached to the wall. Jerking her head back into the bedroom, she looked around to see what she could use as a weapon. Lifting her head, she was suddenly aware that the clinking of the weights had stopped. Melissa took a few steps away from the door before she turned around. The man was standing just outside, wiping his face then his upper body with a towel, a large bruise on his right side.

"I guess you have…*questions*…?" he said, no malice in his voice.

"Yeah. Like why am I still *alive?*" she asked.

"Because you helped keep *me alive* last night. You can unball your fist now. I promise not to hurt you unless you try to hurt me, Melissa," he said.

She hadn't realized she had made fist, subconsciously ready for a fight.

"Now what? Twenty questions before you *shoot* me? Or should I get back in the bed to warm your ass up *first?*" she said, anger welling up inside.

"Questions, yeah. Bed, no. With the way you're built, I don't think I'm your type anyway," he said, looking her up and down. "What you saw last night was someone trying to move in on one of my…*bosses*. She had some info on him that didn't need to be put out there, so I went to make sure she didn't."

"Looked like she was *whupping your ass* pretty good, got to be a pro…*like you…?*"

He smiled, walked into the room.

"*Like me…!*" he said, dropping the towel to the floor. "Look, I know your name, address, company, and I have people working on your family and friends info too. So the question is, *Is that threat enough, or do I need to spell it out for you in more detail?*" the man said, looking deep into her eyes.

Melissa knew he had the upper hand and the threat to her friends and family was a very clear one, but just the way that he was looking at her brought her anger to a boil. Without thinking, she swung a sharp right to his head, surprised at his speed as he easily dodged the blow, but she caught him on the right side bruise with a hard left jab. As he moved to his left, she hit him with a right upper-cut, making him stumble several steps back. With the opening, she sprinted to the door, only to be hit just below the left shoulder blade, spinning her to the right and down as she fell through the doorway. Landing roughly on her behind, his speed put him almost on top of her as she tried lifting her leg for a kick, hitting the doorframe with her right knee instead. The wind was knocked out of her as he landed with his full weight. He then lifted up on his knees, slapping her open-handed on the left side of her face then backhanding her on the right side, bringing tears to her eyes. Both of his hands wrapped around her throat, pulling her up into a sitting position. Somehow, almost simultaneously, she hit him with fist under his armpits and hit him again as his hands loosened around her neck. Bringing her left knee up hard into his groin, he fell to her right, flat on his back. Quickly swinging her leg over him, landing on his stomach in a sitting position, she began landing blows into his face, right then left. Suddenly, she was airborne, arcing upside down over his head as she was slammed into the wall hard then thrown to his left. She landed hard on her right side, seeing spots swim in her vision when she lifted her head. Melissa sensed him coming over to her but couldn't clear the spots from her eyes. She felt him grab the front of her blouse, jerking her up roughly as the buttons began to pop off one by one. Up on her knees, held in place, the spots before her eyes cleared, and she cursed herself for not putting her bra back on when she left Amy's; her left breast was now fully exposed and the right one not far behind it. She tensed for the hit she knew was coming, then…*nothing!* What was he waiting for? Why didn't he just kill her? As her head cleared a bit more, she looked up at him as he stared down at her.

Both of them were breathing hard, not knowing why they had stopped their fight. The man helped her stand, looking in her eyes. Melissa watched his face as he slowly lowered his gaze down to her breast; the sudden heat starting within her was a surprise! When he again met her eyes, she knew she was about to do something she had *never* done before…

Sitting on the closed toilet seat, drying her hair, Melissa couldn't believe she had just been to bed with a *man* and *really* enjoyed it! *What the hell happened to her? What about Amy? Shit!* This wasn't happening! The man walked into the bathroom, naked, new bruises starting to show on his body and face. She felt herself getting warm again as he walked toward her and pointed to the toilet. She stood, lifted the top and seat together, and moved back to the wall, continuing to dry her hair.

"I've…*never*…done that with a…*man…before.* I…I didn't know I *could*…," she said, looking down, blushing.

The man finished and flushed the toilet. His back still toward her, he walked over to the face bowl to wash his hands. He turned to look at her fully and rested his behind against the vanity.

"When we started fighting, I knew, *just knew*, it would end with you *dead*. But I never fought a woman that fought me back...*the way you did!* And no, I didn't even think about having sex with you before that! I sure as hell can't think of *killing* you now! I don't know *what the hell* to do...," he said.

"How about...telling me...*your name*...for openers?" she asked, still blushing.

"Michael. *Michael Smith-Jones.*"

"Mike...Mike. What do you do besides...*kill* people, Mike?" Melissa asked, dropping the towel and walking toward him.

"*Bodyguard. Fixer. Only part-time killer*...when necessary," he said.

"*I saw you kill someone. You know where I live...*," she said, touching the bruise on his side.

He winced. "That's true. So you know what that means, *right...?*" He touched her left shoulder bruise.

She winced. Shook her head *no.*

"Only one thing...*partners...!*" he said as they embraced, slowly sinking to the floor...

CHAPTER 14

Mason's Cleanup Time

The sound of the body bag being zipped up brought Mason back to the reality of his apartment. His driver, Michael, and his *"helper,"* Melissa, had finished their cleanup and were ready to remove the body.

"Okay, boss. Anything else you need before we go?" Michael asked, looking at the two men just returning back into the room.

Melissa, not too far behind Michael, had her hand on the six-inch switchblade in her pocket. She had enjoyed what these two had done to the little girly fruit, but for some reason, she just wanted to gut both of these assholes...*bad!*

"Yeah, boss, *anything else* I could do?" said Melissa, eyeing the two men steadily.

Mason smiled, knowing that all he had to do was nod his head in their direction, and the two men would be leaving in body bags as well. "No, darlin'. Next time though...*yes*...su'ra'ly, next time."

He waved his hand, and they both reached down for the body bag, lifting it easily with one hand each, and then they were out the door, closing it behind them.

"He...*she*...was really great! Nice piece of ass and gave head like a real pro. With that first hit to her face, *man*, she didn't see that one coming! Being so small, she held on longer than I thought! Sweet, Mason, *real sweet!*" said Don. His friend Steve finished drying his hands off and dropped the small white towel on the floor.

"Yeah, you *fags* know how to show a guy a great time! *Really great time!*" said Steve.

"What about you, *sweet cheeks*, you available for some two-on-one action sometime, huh?" said Don rubbing his hands together and slowly licking his lips.

Steve, standing slightly behind him, had a big teeth-bearing grin.

Mason stared at them both, rested his small cigar in the ashtray on the end table next to his chair, and stood up.

"I act'sual'ly per'fer mah men quite hi'ah on the food chain, much mor'...*well man'nared* as well. But I doubt tha's anythang *y'all* would know 'bouts *any'ways*," said Mason.

Don turned and looked at Steve, the grin gone from his face. As he turned back toward Mason, he took a quick step forward, raising his right hand at the same time balling it into a fist, head high. Mason, faster than Don had anticipated, stepped to his right, left hand straight out with the fingers bent at the second knuckles. The quick jab into Don's throat collapsed his trachea, dropping him to his knees, his forward momentum taking him facedown onto the carpet and gasping in short, quick breaths. Steve, not believing what he had just seen, stood with his mouth hanging open, looking down on his friend. Mason's left foot glided along the carpet, stopping just a few inches in front of Steve as his torso twisted to the right, left hand in the classic karate pose hiding his fisted right hand. Steve looked up, seeing Mason's arm shooting rapidly toward his chest, and all he could do was stare. Mason's fist struck Steve off center of his chest to the left, slightly under his pectoral muscle, forcing it to literally separate as it continued to the breast bone, shattering that and sending the fragments into Steve's heart and surrounding tissues. Steve was knocked backward several feet, his hands bending up to grab his chest. He sagged to the right as his legs gave out, then he thudded roughly to the carpet, eyes still wide open, both hands curled upward in death.

Mason stood erect, tossing his head back to move the curl of hair that had fallen down into his face and smoothing it flat with his left hand. He turned and walked back to Don who was still gasping for breath, holding his throat with both hands, eyes full wide staring at him. Mason's left foot slowly rose into the air.

"A li'l bit of *trou'ble* catchin' yo' breath, *sugar?* Here, let me help *y'all...!*"

His foot came swiftly down, breaking Don's fingers as he threw his body weight into the movement to finish crushing his windpipe. A short, strangled gasp squeaked out from his mouth followed by a small rush of blood as Don slipped backward a few inches, head falling to his right, eyes slowly closing. Mason lifted his foot then walked back to his chair and sat down, picking up his thin cigar as he settled into the soft-padded leather. His fingers played over his cell phone lying on the end table next to him. He pressed Michael's name on his speed-dial list.

"I do *a'polo'gize* fo' *trou'blin'* ya, dear boy," he said after Michael answered, "but might y'all have a cou'ple extra...*con'tractas bags...?* I could use two right 'bout now? Yes, I'll be up...thank ya *kindly,* sweetheart."

CHAPTER 15

Stephanie Ann Caldwell

Stephanie Ann Caldwell had grown up in Dayton, Ohio—the baby girl with three older sisters and one younger brother. Her father, William, was medium height and thinner than most other Jamaicans of his generation. His keen features taken from his White father's side of the family and dark chocolate skin from his island mother seemed to soften him, but that didn't stop him from being a stern taskmaster with everything concerning his children. From the time they woke in the morning to the time they went back to bed at night, he dictated their lives completely. Her mother, Carrie Anna, was taller, with a full figure, caramel skin color with a round face and a gentleness about her that put people at ease. Almost from the first time people met her, she'd bring a smile to their faces after speaking with them for just a few minutes. She lived for her children, stepping in from time to time when she thought William was being *too* hard with them, usually sitting them down, explaining why he was that way simply in their terms, always ending with *"He is still your father"* regardless. After a bit of sitting to let their tears dry, a piece of pastry, or sliced fruit treat in hand, they were on their way outside to discuss with each other what they had just been told.

Stephanie, being next to the youngest, usually got the worst of his daily treatment, escaping into her schoolwork and adventure books once her chores were done for the day. The thought *"What would it be like away from him?"* popped into her mind quite often, intensifying with each repeated litany of his commands. It got to the point that when she would see him coming toward her, inwardly she'd cringe, and once he was done commanding her, she was off like a shot, gaining the nickname *Tornado* from her siblings.

One day while out grocery shopping with her mother at the open-air market, Stephanie saw Paul—a short local teen bad boy—snatch a few apples from the outdoor tables then try to hightail it out of there. Unfortunately, he started running without looking ahead of him, crashing into one of the policemen walking the beat. As he bounced back, he made his second mistake by swinging at the officer, not really seeing who he was, only knocking his hat off with the effort as the officer ducked to the side. Before Paul could recover, the policeman's nightstick was out, coming down on Paul's left shoulder blade with a muffled crack, forcing him quickly down to the ground. He landed hard on that same shoulder, yelping as he rolled onto his right side. Trying to gain his feet, turning his head to the left, he was caught broadside across his face at an angle, snapping his whole body around to land roughly on his back. Dazed, his body began to spasm slightly as the officer jerked him up by the front of his shirt. Still instinctively trying to fight, Paul raised his right arm and swung it limply against the officer's arm. The policeman's face turned into a picture of utter hatred as his nightstick rammed into Paul's stomach several times, forcing him up onto his toes. Finally spent, the officer released Paul's shirt, his limp body falling straight down to his knees, slowly tipping forward to land on the left side of his face with a wet, muffled thud. Roughly pulling his left arm behind his back, the bystanders could plainly see Paul's dislocated left shoulder extend further than it should have. Hearing Paul's low, sickening groan as his right arm was pulled back to meet the left, handcuffs being quickly locked around them both, the crowd knew this was just the start of his pain, because once they got him back to the station house, there'd be no civilian eyes to see. Standing, the officer looked around at each face, almost daring someone, *anyone*, to say something or make a move toward him. His upper lip turned into a snarl as he reached down, grabbing the collar of Paul's shirt, literally dragging him through the crowd, his knees still touching the ground.

Stephanie hadn't noticed she was standing behind her mother, peeking around her hip as she held tightly to her dress, until she had been pulled gently by the arm to continue their shopping. A few people they walked by were shaking their heads, looking down to the ground, while others had no expression on their faces at all, as if nothing had just happened, nothing at all.

CHAPTER 16

Heading Back to the Station

Stephanie and Alex were quiet driving back to the station, each lost in their own thoughts about the bizarre facts of these cases. Alex parked in front and shut the engine off as he unbuckled his seat belt. Stephanie, still buckled up, leaned back against the headrest.

"I just don't get it, Al. These guys have bad blood between each other all the time, but how serious could it have been to take somebody out and then leave the body belly-up in the open? Something just ain't right…," said Stephanie.

"Yeah, something else is definitely going on that we're just not getting…*for sure*," said Alex. *Triple A* getting done in his shower still freaks me out. Who the hell walked in his place, *with a shotgun no less*, and pinned him to the wall? And who called it in?" he said, looking down at his arms.

"Maybe the killer? Maybe one of his *'girls'* walked in and found him. Called before or after *'she'* got into the wind. Who the hell knows, Al, who the hell knows… You need coffee?" she said.

"I need coffee…," he said.

Alex took the keys. Then they both opened the car doors and headed to the building.

On this floor of the station, it had the appearance of a regular office space, desks facing each other in a two side-by-side layout with the offices along the outside walls. Interrogation rooms were one floor below, all of them reinforced with exterior Sheetrock on the ceilings and six inches of brick between the partition walls. The main standout of this office space was the number of uniformed officers and people walking around carrying guns. Several yards from their desk, Stephanie noticed one of the uniformed officers. He caught her eye because of his height and build: easily six feet, six inches tall, worked-out and well-toned muscled body. He passed by in front of her desk and turned left, moving along the office walls. There was a manila folder on her desk, one she didn't remember being there when she left for the crime scene, yet she had the strangest feeling that the tall officer who just walked by dropped it purposely. Looking over to the office wall, Stephanie was surprised to not see him. She turned to the elevator corridor, not there either.

"You look like you just saw a ghost, Annie," said Alex.

"Did you see that tall uniformed officer drop that folder on my desk?" she asked.

"If it wasn't a unique-looking '*she*'...no... Probably just an interoffice memo or report, Annie," Alex said.

Sitting down at her desk, Stephanie saw the manila folder was thicker than she thought. Opening it, she saw there were four medical reports, along with personal notes, from *Dr. Daniel Reilly*—the first pathologist on the crime-lord cases. The one thing that stood out to her was that three of them had gone under the knife: *plastic surgery*. With the latest two deaths, she wondered what he had found concerning them...

"So what's up with the file? Anything about the cases?" asked Alex.

"Yeah. One of them looks like a professional hit: *body, heart, and head shots.* Definitely left out in the open to make a point. The other three of our boys all had face work. What're the odds of that?" said Stephanie.

"Maybe one, even two, but all three? Naw, something's *all* wrong about that. What are we *really* looking at here?" he said.

"I don't know, but we just got some more questions we didn't even think to ask...," she said.

"Then maybe the first question should be to your *'doc in love'* about what he's found so far, huh?" Alex said smiling.

"You just *wanna* get cut, *don't you?*" she said sternly looking at him.

Flipping to the last page in the folder, the hairs suddenly stood up on the back of her neck. For a moment all she could do was stare at it, then she picked it up and turned it to face Alex. He read the handwritten note done with a thick, black marker and large letters. He sat back in his chair, letting out a low whistle. It read:

Ask Dr. Walker what he's found odd about these cases.

No signature. They both stood and headed down to the morgue.

CHAPTER 17

Something Odd in the Morgue

Looking at the morgue photos, Mike was cross-indexing Dr. Reilly's notes with the latest dead crime lord. He, too, had gone under the knife recently. His face job was still showing a slight bit of puffiness, unnoticed by a layman, but all in all, a really masterful job of surgery. Whoever did this was an expert in their field, and that kind of work did not come cheap. Looking closer, he saw there was something odd about the skin: the surface texture maybe…? Was it…*padded?* He couldn't put his finger on it, but something about it was out of place…

Mike stood up and walked back over to the body of Murray, getting a magnifying glass to look at the scarring behind the left ear. He wondered if Reilly had talked to the detectives about this, and if so, how much detail did he go into? A knock on the pathology doors broke his concentration. It was Stephanie and her partner, Alex. He buzzed them in.

"Sorry for dropping in without calling, but someone left me a note to ask you about what you've found so far on the cases," said Stephanie.

"*Really?* Just now I was thinking if Dr. Reilly had said anything to you before his accident. Going over his notes, I know he had found a coincidence, don't really know if that's how to describe it, but it concerns all of them," Mike said.

Stephanie and Alex looked at each other, then back at Mike.

"They were all killed by shootings?" Alex said.

"That plus the fact that three of them had plastic surgery, face-lifts *obviously*, reconstructive, *definitely* points to it in each case. And from the looks of things, in *those* cases so far, it was *recently* done," said Mike.

The silence seemed to grow more solid as the detectives stared at Mike, each not knowing what to say next.

"So…so the *Monster's* hands, manual labor, construction worker, maybe…?" asked Stephanie.

"Carpenter, most likely. I found a few wood splinters in his fingers, and those calluses on his hands could have been caused by repeated use of a hammer. There's nothing in the Monster's back-ground that states he was into carpentry, but from the condition of his hands, that had to have formed over a long period of time," said Mike.

"Something else for us to check into, Al. More questions just leading to *more questions!*"

"Oh well, Annie, that's why we get the little bucks…," said Alex.

"I'll keep going over Reilly's notes and go back to the other bodies besides the *Monster's*. Maybe I'll pick up on something Reilly or I missed. It's something about the facial skin that's still *buggin'*. Can't quite put my finger on it, but something's…*something's* just not right," said Mike.

"What are you seeing that we're not, Mike?" asked Stephanie.

"Well, right here…," Mike said, pointing behind Murray's left ear. They walked around for a closer look where he was focused at.

"Normally, with a face-lift, an incision is made here behind the ear going a short way down along the neck. The epidermis is '*lifted*,' microsurgery is performed for blood supply, and even facial mus-cles may be repositioned to give a leaner, more youthful appearance. Then the excess skin is trimmed, incision closed. A custom-made '*mask*' if you really want to simplify it, but with this work and the other work that was done, from what I can see at first glance, that wasn't the case."

"So what did happen? If whoever did this didn't follow the normal procedures, was there any plastic surgery actually done? And if not, what's the reason for the scar?" asked Alex.

"Oh, don't get me wrong, there was surgery done, but not in the true sense of *'plastic surgery.'* Here in the hollow of the cheeks," Mike said pointing then lightly touching and compressing the area. "It feels spongy, padded, like something was between the epidermis and the dermis, not connected like it should be in post-reconstructive surgeries."

Looking up, the questioning stares from Stephanie and Alex made Mike stop, not figuring out what they might have been confused by...

"English, Mike, *English please...!*" said Stephanie.

"Sorry...," he said, blushing a bit. "Something between the skin and the muscles after the face-lift that shouldn't be there."

"Can you find out? Do you think it's possible, or is this one of those '...*and then there was a miracle, ta da!*' type of thing?" asked Alex.

"Good questions. Skin sections will be the next step for *all* of them. After that, then I'll let you know what I find out about the latest two," said Mike.

The detectives turned, heading for the doors out of pathology. Mike went for scalpels and sample slides. None of them noticed the small, red, and green lights of the mic and video-recording indicators hanging above the autopsy table turn off.

CHAPTER 18

Murray's New Title

Murray had gone to college with a career of Social Services in his mind, to give people like his siblings and him someone to talk to after losing a close relative/parent for whatever the reasons. The four years had been hard, but he wasn't going to quit. He was on a mission.

The summer break after his fourth year, before going into graduate studies in the fall, had him in trouble finding a summer job. He wanted something to just tide him over, help keep him off the streets, until classes started again at the end of August. His mother had told his uncle about Murray's frustration, and he said he'd see what he could do, even though it had been a while since they had last talked.

It was a pleasant June Sunday, a bit cool for the time, but this was Chicago; *any type of weather was possible during anytime of the year*. Murray was enjoying being home with his family and was surprised to feel differently about his uncle. Obviously, the years away from him had softened his heart. During dinner, both of them even managed to laugh at each other's jokes, leaving his mother and siblings wondering who these two people were eating at the table with them. After clearing the dining room table and settling in the living room for movies, Ron nodded toward Murray, suggesting they go outside with a slight movement of his head to the left, then turned, and walked to the front door. When Murray got there and looked out, he saw his uncle sitting on the top step of the porch, and the image of how his dad had sat there almost in the same spot flashed into his mind. He hesitated for a moment, hand on the doorknob. He turned it and walked out to sit next to his uncle.

"Your mom told me you been looking for a job, just something for the summer, she said," he began, not looking at Murray.

"Yeah, things have been kinda frustrating. All these other people out looking too and not many employers want to hire you for just a few months," said Murray.

"Yeah, the bottom line is always money. Usually not enough to go around or finally doing some job that dead-ends until they give you a gold watch after two hundred years of service, a pat on the back and shuffle your ass off to the old folks home to die at breakfast, lunch, dinner, or hopefully in your sleep. Not good, not good at all."

"So what's your solution, Uncle Ron? Work for you as a runner? Bag man? Or did you have enforcer in mind?"

They both looked at each other and laughed out loud, smiling broadly after a bit.

"Naw, nephew, *naw*...a *lot* bigger than that! My *successor...period!*" said his uncle.

Murray wasn't sure he had heard him correctly. He didn't want to go down that road, but somehow it began to sink in and intrigue him.

"So why me, Uncle? Why me? Don't you have people that have been with you for a while that could take over from you?"

"Yeah, I do. But they ain't family, Murray. And since you didn't tell me to *'go to hell,'* I guess that means you're thinking about it...," said Uncle Ron.

"Yeah...*yeah*. But I want to talk it over with Allison. You know, she's special to me, been with me all these years, been with her... I don't want to mess that up, Uncle."

"Behind every successful man is a *woman* that loves him, no questions asked. She'll be your partner, lover, wife, *whatever* you need her to be, but she'll be there with you, *for* you. She'll have yo' back when you don't even know it *needs* watchin'. That's love, nephew. I wouldn't want you to mess *that* up! Nope, not at *all!* Go, go talk to her. She's probably been *listenin'* all this time anyway, makin' *sure* you didn't decide to *whup my ass* out here alone with me!" Uncle Ron said smiling.

Murray stood and walked back to the front door. Through the screen he saw Allison standing off to the left side, half hidden in the indoor shadows.

"You know, once you get involved with him, it won't be easy getting out...*if you really want to get out*...," said Allison softly.

Murray looked at her and knew she was right. Could he just work with his uncle for the summer then leave with Allison, *really* leave it all behind?

Allison stepped forward, opened the door, and walked out onto the porch.

"How did you know I was listening, Uncle Ron?" she asked.

"Because any *White* woman—matter of fact, *any* woman at all been with a *nigga* this long *gotta* be stupid...*or in love!* And, darlin'...I knows *you ain't stupid!* You'll be in this with him all the way, so if you want out or him out, say it now...," said Ron, his back to them both.

Allison stood, violent images going through her mind. People laid out on the floor, on couches, sitting in chairs, all with a glazed look on their faces. Some with needles in their arms, legs, others holding joints, so stoned that they had burned down to their fingers. She took a step backward and bumped into Murray, who immediately put his arms around her, nuzzling his face into the crook of her neck. The images were gone; now she was safely in his arms. Yes, she thought, this had to be *true love!*

"Okay, Uncle Ron. Okay...," said Murray.

"We're...*both in*," said Allison.

That summer had gone by quickly. Murray was walked through his uncle's day, learning the supply and delivery systems, the money trail that wasn't a trail but hidden in plain sight. How not to stand out because of all the money and there was plenty of that coming in! As he got the grasp of how the business was run, he had kept Allison in the loop, his loop, telling her all that he had learned, keeping her off to the side as best he could, but soon she was with him the majority of the time. The rest of the year was there and gone just as quickly, and before he knew it, two years had passed by, a career in Social Services long since forgotten, as the dealers and runners got used to his face as well as used to him telling them what to do. Soon they all started thinking of him not as next in line for the top position, but already there with his Uncle Ron fading more and more into the background with each passing day.

It was during Allison's fourth month of her first pregnancy that his life, their lives, would change drastically.

Murray had called Allison and told her he was finished at *"work"* and was stopping by the *"office"* to check in with his uncle, more so a courtesy visit than any actual business. He always liked going to Ron's place because the duplex penthouse was so unique at the time. But for the past few months, Murray had been hearing the hushed, low talk that his uncle might have started using his own product a bit too much. Some of Ron's bodyguards had let it slip that they were worried about him, and it really didn't help that he had started carrying a gun as well.

Murray got an uneasy feeling as soon as he stepped into the living room on the top floor, wishing now he had taken his own bodyguard Steven's advice and let him come up too. Ron was facing the window, dressed in a white shirt and dark tan pants, barefoot. He was having a very animated conversation with...*the window reflection!* As Murray walked closer, he began to hear what he was saying:

"My mistake *goddammit!* Young punk-ass nigga took over! *From me! FROM ME! SHIT!*" he said. "*Summer job my ass!* That nigga had this shit planned! *Planned all along! And I fell for the shit! Damn! DAMN! DAMMIT TA' HELL!*"

Murray stopped a good distance away before he spoke.

"Uncle Ron..." was all he got out.

Ron turned faster than he thought he could, gun coming up level with Murray's head in the same swift motion, and squeezed off two rounds. Murray felt the hand on his left upper arm pushing with a force, moving him out the way and slightly down. It was Willie, Ron's head bodyguard. Murray hadn't even heard him come up behind him! The first bullet caught him at the corner of his left eye, spinning his head with the impact as the second bullet hit him just off center of his chest to the left, ripping into his heart and out his back, adding momentum to the turn. Willie had his gun in his left hand and somehow managed to get a round off, hitting Ron in the ball and socket of his right arm, shattering the joint, knocking him off his feet and back into the glass window. Willie continued to spin around, dead, as he slammed into Murray's back, forcing him to the ground. When they both hit the floor, Willie's gun fell just in front of Murray's right hand. He grabbed it and quickly pushed up, rolling Willie's body off. Without thinking, he stayed low, moved over to the couch, and listened.

"Muthafucka shot me! Yo' ass put him up to that shit! Didn't ya? Didn't ya? Punk-ass bitch! I'm gonna kill yo' ass!" said Ron.

Murray heard him moving about and quickly looked around the edge of the couch, then pulled back into cover behind it. He had seen Ron on his back, the back of his head against the glass windowpane. The large bloodstain on the white shirt had spread across his right shoulder, down onto upper arm and chest. Ron's gun was just out of reach of his right hand as he tried to rise up and grab it with his left hand but fell back to the floor, head hitting against the windowpane. Murray stood up and walked around the edge of the couch, looking at his uncle as he slowly moved toward him.

"That's right, muthafucka! Come on! Get yo' ass closer so's I can kill ya! COME ON!" said Ron. He kept trying to reach for his gun with his left hand, only to fall back each time, rest a moment, then try again.

Murray stood a few steps away, wondering how Ron had ended up this way. All the times he had told him about not being an asshole and using your own product, turning into a loser like the ones you sold to. *What had happened to him...?*

"You wit' dat White bitch! Think you somethin'! Don't cha? SOMETHIN' better'n me!" He reached for the gun, fell back. *"You ain't, nigga! AIN'T SHIT! Just 'nother nigga wit' a White bitch fuckin' yo' ass!"* He tried to move, got halfway up, fell back. *"STUPID MUTHAFUCKA! I'll get her ass here, HERE! And have my boys, MY BOYS! Pull a train on her ass!"* His left arm twitched a bit, just moved slightly. *"KILL Y'ALL BOTH!*

BOTH, NIGGA!" Ron said, this time sitting up, left arm in a complete spasm but still trying to go for his gun.

Murray aimed the gun at Ron's head and squeezed the trigger twice. The first bullet hit him in the middle of his forehead, snapping his head straight back. The second bullet flew into his left nostril and traveled through, exiting out the base of his head. The body lifted to its right, flying backward a bit, hitting the window, bouncing on the floor, and settling. Murray walked over to it, aimed the gun at its chest, and fired two more rounds, watching as it jerked up and down then lay still, bloodstain growing a darker red against the white-shirt background. A calmness suddenly came over him as he tilted his head to the left, looking at the damage he had caused to his uncle. Somehow he didn't feel sad nor scared, just an overwhelming sense of...*relief*. He turned, about to walk back to the elevator, and stopped in midstep. Five of Ron's security guards were standing just outside of the elevator foyer, guns drawn, all of them pointing down to the floor, stern looks on their faces.

"We...we heard what he said, Murray... *Boss*...that was some... *cold shit!*" said Ed, Ron's number 2 bodyguard.

"What...*uuh*...what you want us to...*do?*"

Murray looked at them all, bent his hand backward under his jacket, and placed the gun in his waistband at the center of his back.

"Take care of Willie. Put him away good, good like family...*our family*. I'll foot the bill...*regardless*," said Murray, the quiet even tone of his voice sounding unnaturally odd, even to him.

They stepped out of his way as he walked to the elevator and pressed the call button.

"*Uuh...what about...Ron, boss?*" asked Ed.

Murray turned back, taking in the entire room with its two dead bodies, actually seeing for the first time the mess that had been made.

"I'll give Danny a visit at the scrap metal yard, tell him what's *comin'*...and to do his usual thing. I'll...I'll have him send over his cleaners too... They'll get...*Uncle Ron*...get him out and drop him off...*over there*. Tell them take him out the back door, no witnesses. Keep...keep this just between us, Ed, just between the six of us...

okay? Y'all okay with that?" asked Murray, looking at each one of them in turn.

Ed looked at the rest of them as well, turned back to Murray, and nodded.

"Yeah, boss man, yeah. We're all okay with that."

The elevator doors opened. Murray turned around and walked in and pressed the button for the lobby. As the doors were closing, he heard someone saying in a low voice, *"What kinda cold shit was that, man?"* and another saying, *"Fuckin' monster, man, fuckin' cold-ass monster!"*

He thought for a moment about *being* a monster. *Murray the Monster.* The lack of feelings for what he had just done was undeniable. Could it really be true? Had he turned into a *monster*? Right now all he could think about doing was stopping by Danny's, getting him moving on the cleanup...*then getting home to Allison.*

CHAPTER 19

Murray Adds More Street Credit

It had been just over two weeks since Murray had killed his uncle; the circumstances repeated verbatim. But the word *Monster* still made its rounds; even though they didn't say it to his face, he still heard it whispered behind his back. He had given the penthouse to his top lieutenant *Emmanuel Isaac*, simply because he was unable to even look at the building, let alone walk into it ever again.

When Isaac moved in, he took total control of the building, clearing out the entire floor below his duplex for his personal crew and bodyguards, actually putting several of them, dressed in business suits, down in the lobby, making it one of the safest buildings on the Southside. But Murray still owned it outright *(surprised his uncle had him listed as his only beneficiary),* so he cut the rents by *25 percent* for the paying tenants. He hired a live-in building manager that reported directly to him for repairs and upgrades to the entire property, five full-time handymen to work inside and out, and then finally he had Allison assure all the tenants that as long as they wanted to stay, they could. The majority of them were unaware that *Ronald Baker* had even died.

Things had gone surprisingly smooth for Murray as the new boss. Steven had stepped up as his head bodyguard, implementing new security protocol for every move he made as well as throughout the whole organization. Product was moved and delivered in confusing patterns to his lieutenants but perfectly logical once it was explained to Murray. The business was growing; his eyes and ears kept him in the loop about everything…*everything* except his brother Davy's growing drug habit.

The call came in on a Thursday night, about 6:40 PM. Seeing that it was from his mother gave him a very bad feeling from the start because she rarely called him, mostly talking to Allison about her coming grandchild, leaving any messages for him with her.

"Hi, honey, I really hate to call you about this, but I'm worried about Davy," she had said. "I haven't seen him for a few days and was wondering if he was doing something with you, you know, something that you didn't want to tell me about…"

He heard the controlled panic in her voice and knew that she was holding back a flood of tears. "A few days, Ma? Why didn't you call me sooner? You know I'm never too busy for family, for you…"

He knew Davy was seeing a guy on the Northside, up in the Rogers Park area. He had made it a point to know whom his brothers and sisters were hanging out with. Just in case he needed to *"help"* them.

"Okay, Ma, I'll get on it now. Somebody will know something. I'm sure of that. Don't worry, Ma. Luv ya!" said Murray.

While he was talking he saw Allison out the corner of his eye standing in the doorway to his study, a worried but guilty look on her face. Hanging up the phone, he turned to look at her.

"What is it, baby? You look like you know…*something*…that you didn't tell me…"

She slowly walked into the room, head slightly down, rubbing her extended abdomen but still looking him in the face.

"It's about Davy, isn't it?" she asked.

Murray nodded yes.

"His…his boyfriend…had wanted to try something new, a different kind of *'sex high, thrill.'* It…it involved using…*cocaine*," she said.

Murray stared at her long enough to make her feel uncomfortable. Without a word, she turned and walked away from his desk, her head hanging down as he heard the first low sob, then she was through the doorway.

Murray sat for a bit staring into nothing, his mind momentarily trying to get a handle on sex, drugs, his brother, and why they were mentioned in the same sentence. He pressed the house intercom and called for Steven to come to his study.

"I figured if anyone had eyes on my brother, it would be you or your people," Murray said as Steven walked in, closing the door behind him.

"Yeah, boss man. I put someone on all your immediate folks. Didn't want that to be an added worry for you," said Steven.

"So what's up with him? Did you know about this *drugs and sex* shit Allison was talking about?"

"Yeah, boss, but not the sex. One of the lieutenants told me he had come to him a month ago asking for drugs, so I told him step on it plenty, I'd cover the cost. I'd wanted to control it so he wouldn't sneak behind our back and get it from someone we didn't know that well."

"So where is he?"

"That's just it, boss, my people say he hasn't *been* out of the house for at least five to six days..." Steven's voice trailed off, eyes growing wide.

They both stared at each other for a moment. Then as Steven turned and walked toward the door, Murray was pushing away from his desk to follow.

In the car neither of them spoke, already knowing what they would find when they got to Murray's mother's house. Murray had called to check if anyone was home and didn't get an answer. Steven's people watching the house were called and said everyone was gone, but Davy had to still be in the house; they hadn't seen him leave in days. Murray was relieved that his mother was gone but even more apprehensive now at what they would find...

As they drove into the driveway, they saw Marcus Walters, the lieutenant selling to Davy, standing on the front porch. Once out of the car, Murray became aware of a dimness, darkness even, which seemed to hang over the entire area of the house. A cold chill crept up his back and stayed at the base of his neck.

Marcus backed off a bit from them as they stepped onto the porch; the presence of being this close to Murray always unnerved him.

"Marcus, what are you doing here?" asked Murray.

"Uh…sorry, boss man…didn't want to bother you with small stuff…uh…wanted to keep this between your brother and me…"

"I thought you were letting Steven know what your cost were, he was *paying* you. Again, *why are you here?*" Marcus took another step backward and swallowed hard.

"He started coming to me daily, boss! Wanted even more! I kept it stepped down, low, like Steven said, but it still added up with all his visits! Sorry, boss! Sorry!" said Marcus.

Murray and Steven both looked at him, unblinking, freezing him to the spot. Marcus knew, without a doubt, he was a dead man.

"How much, Marcus?" Murray finally asked.

"Five large, boss…!" Marcus barely got the words out, feeling like the air around him had suddenly gotten thicker.

After a moment, Murray and Steven turned toward the house, Steven unlocking the door.

"You stay here, Marcus. I'll *personally* pay you on my way out…," said Murray, not turning around.

As the door closed behind them, Marcus's mind told him to run, get the hell out of town, and don't ever look back, but he couldn't move. Frozen to the spot, all thoughts of bodily harm images floating in front of his eyes…he wet his pants.

The house was quiet, as if it was sitting there waiting for them to say or do something, holding back its secret until the last possible second. As they walked further into the foyer, a few steps past the basement door, they both caught the faint odor: *something spoiled, decayed…dead!* Opening the door, heading down the steps, the odor magnified, leaving little doubt as to what they would find. Looking to the far end of the basement, Davy was sitting on the floor, back against the wooden built-in bar. His legs were stretched out in front of him, arms down to his side. His head was at a slight angle to the right, chin resting on his chest, like an old man taking a catnap. Walking over, standing in front of him, Murray dismissed the strong urine and feces smells as he squatted down, looking closer into his brother's gray, ashen face. At least twenty small empty dope packets were on his right along with two disposable needles, a metal shot glass in a stand with a cigarette lighter close by. Murray reached out, touched the side of Davy's face, and remembered how they had grown up together. He was saddened beyond words that he had died like this, died alone.

"Please, Steven, call Joshua at the funeral home, have him pick my brother up. Let him know what...*condition...he's in...no surprises*. If...*if you can*...get a cleaning crew in, I...I don't care how many people, have them...have them concentrate on the basement, but do...do the whole house too. I don't want Momma...Momma and them to smell *this! Okay?*" said Murray.

"Yeah, boss. Yeah. I'll handle it myself... What...what about Marcus?"

"*I'll* talk to him. Pay him his money. Then we're *done* with him. He *walks* Steven, no troubles. Just let him *walk*, okay?"

"Yeah, boss, yeah," said Steven, knowing that *he* couldn't, *wouldn't* let it go that easy.

Murray's mother and other siblings were never told where Davy was found. His boyfriend, Christian told them about the drug usage, so it was assumed that's what killed him. He hung around the family for a while, trying to help keep the spirit of Davy alive; but a few months later, he was found overdosed in his own apartment, a picture of him and Davy still held in his hand.

Murray personally paid Marcus his money, giving him an extra *$10,000* for his troubles and cut him loose from the organization, never seeing or talking to him again. At first Marcus, was relieved to have gotten out alive. He packed his belongings and moved to a far western suburb. But after using some of his leftover product and talking to his friends, he began feeling he was being unduly punished. His anger got the best of him as the lies spread about why he was *really* cut loose. He was saying Murray had overdosed his own brother because he had used the drugs he was supposed to be sell-ing, owing *Murray $5,000*. Unfortunately, the rumor just added to Murray's street credits, making him an even more *"dangerous"* figure than what he was after killing his uncle.

Marcus, later that same year, was admitted to a nursing home, never to walk nor talk again. It appeared to be the results of a severe mugging. Apparently, he had been attacked quite brutally...*within*... his private, gated community condo.

CHAPTER 20

Stephanie's Thoughts

Stephanie woke and sat up in bed. She turned and saw Patrick was still asleep next to her, softly snoring. Sitting for a moment, letting the sleep slip away, she folded the covers back and swung her legs to the right, out of bed, onto the floor. Leaning forward, she slowly stood, not wanting to wake him by shaking the bed too much. With two steps she reached the chair next to the nightstand where she had thrown her robe. Normally, she didn't wear it around the house, preferring just a T-shirt or nothing, but with the sudden drop in temperature and Patrick spending the night *(it felt odd being naked around him out of bed, for some unknown reason!)*, she had a need to put it on.

Walking out into the hall, Stephanie headed to the kitchen, the *crème brûlée* ice cream in the freezer quietly calling her name. With the pint of ice cream and a teaspoon in hand, she went into the living room to curl up on the couch and watch the snow falling outside her windows. Being still and quiet usually helped her to think about the current case she was working on. Suddenly a chill ran through her, not from the ice cream but that different feeling you get that raises the hair at the back of your neck. The old folks down South would say someone just walked across your grave, and it never made any sense to her as a child because, she thought, how could you be alive *and* have a grave? Now, in her thirties, she understood it. All the strange, unexplained shit she had seen over the years not only opened her mind but let her know, with hard evidence, it existed.

She lowered the container, spoon resting inside, listening for something out of the ordinary. She scanned the room from right to left, not seeing anything different or out of place, and began to wonder what had set off her internal sensors. Stephanie raised the container, continued eating the ice cream. The *tox (toxicology)* report and close-up crime scene photos of Murray *"The Monster"* Robinson flashed, one by one, into her mind.

This guy was someone who knew how to handle himself, *period*, and nobody knew for sure how many people he was responsible for killing. If anyone needed to die just because of who they were, it would be *The Monster*. She hadn't thought that he would end up planted under some bushes, found by the first person that came close or got a whiff of him on the wind; it just didn't make sense. With his midsection blown out, powder burns on his coat and clothes—hell, that told her it was up close and *very* personal. Whom had he trusted enough to get that near him and with a big-ass gun, no less? Could he have been drugged, set up some way by his minions? Or did he catch that buckshot because he didn't *have* a choice? *Shit!* That made even less sense to her than his body turning up in public. If it really was a pro hit, he'd be halfway overseas in several dozen dog food cases. And why were his hands so rough, like a laborer's hands, someone that actually *worked* with their hands for a living?

Something smelled, thought Stephanie, and it wasn't just *The Monster*...

CHAPTER 21

People Are Suckers

No matter which way you sliced it, they were all suckers, thought Warren Bentley. He had seen his dad spend money like it was going to be banned the next day. Gambling on things that the average person knew was stupid, if not completely improbable. How many times had the bill money been spent because of a hot tip his dad had gotten on a horse? Or arguing with his running buddies about a baseball/ basketball/football/soccer—you name it, sports game and nine times out of ten losing all he had. Warren remembered listening to his mom trying her best to keep her voice down while telling his dad how much of an idiot he was and that his so-called-friends were even bigger idiots, before she stopped after hearing her own screaming voice bouncing off the walls! But no matter what she said, he kept doing the same stupid things over and over again, saying afterward how bad he felt about her paying the bills because *he* was *broke* from gambling!

Shit! People are suckers and always would be! he thought.

Warren made the left turn onto westbound *Chicago Avenue* off *Halsted Street*, going about two blocks down to a turnoff on his right. If you didn't know where the street led, you'd think it was a just another dead-end alley, but further down, past some piled-up trash it led to the back of the old abandoned granary that had been used in a number of movies, over the years, filmed here in *Chicago*. After one of those movies had finished filming, Warren was curious to see it; the size alone was intimidating for sure, and it looked like it could hold a good number of people too. But what the real surprise was what he found in the basement and subbasement by accident. The basement took up the entire footprint of the building, broken up by the large concrete support columns. Whatever the massive room was originally designed for didn't reveal itself, but water and drain pipes, ventilation ducts, areas obviously set up for mechanical spaces stood out, showing that this huge room was meant to be used. And the subbasement was similar, about two-thirds the size, with the same details.

On the outside, Warren had designed a covered entrance to a 250-car underground parking garage that also held four customized over-the-road buses for those clients that wanted to bring multiple guests. The small two-man guard shack, with an additional three armed guards further back, actually extended eighty-six feet back into the building for bathrooms, a break room, armory, and secondary video surveillance monitors and communication room. He even went so far as to having the overhead doors chemically treated to look rusted, adding to the "unoccupied building" appearance. The last thing he wanted or needed was to have anyone notice activity at a *"so-called"* abandoned building.

Warren had created different gambling areas on the first basement level: *blackjack, poker, roulette, slot machines, even off-track betting with overhead monitors.* Plush patterned rugs were throughout that level to help soften the noise generated, with paintings on the walls and columns as mild distractions for those not that much into the games of chance. Eight bars, each attended by five bartenders, comfortably seated thirty people on cushioned high stools. Several flat-screen TV monitors, hung from the ceilings just above the top shelves, were tuned to sports, news, and other broadcast shows. There were four food stations manned by servers that carved several prime cuts of meat: chicken, turkey, pork, ham, beef, ribs with side dishes that people of all walks of life enjoyed. Tucked close by were tables for sit-down dining with waiting staff in attendance or benches against the columns for self-served singles who just wanted to soak up the atmosphere before jumping back into the games. All the drinks and food were free on this level.

The subbasement was for the *"very" high rollers*. Warren had gone all out decorating this level. Even though the games were the same, the materials used for the furnishings were a step above. Rich walnut wood panels with contrasting wainscoting ran along the outside perimeter walls. All the furniture was dark leather, with lighter wood legs and accents. The four bars on this level were done in a darker walnut stain, hand-rubbed to a mirrored gloss finish. The two food stations with the sit-down dining areas had waiting staff that took food and drink orders and brought them back to the tables. Standing prime rib was number 1 on the list prepared by the top chefs that money could buy. Warren had seen one of his clients drop *$400,000* but stayed for the prime rib, spending another *$2,100* on dinner *alone!* Originally, he had paid for the drinks and food down on this level as well, but for some strange reason, the people always insisted on paying for everything. Another addition he had installed after opening was an eighty-seat indoor theater, complete with a full-blown concession area: *hot dogs, polishes, nachos with or without meat, candy, ice cream, popcorn, and soft drinks*—all requested by a client and staff survey.

Tonight Warren was down in the subbasement, full house; even the theater was almost full having an *Indiana Jones* movie marathon. The second movie had started, and he was standing at the theater entrance thinking back to when he had first seen it. He felt a soft tap on his shoulder.

"'Ren. That guy, Stewart, is back again. He said he needs to talk with you…*now*…! Says his *'boss'* wants an answer…," said Jerry.

They had grown up together, more like brothers than *actual* brothers. If anyone had his back, it would be Jerry.

"I'm really tired of this *asshole!* The answer was *no* last week, and it's still *no* this week. I don't give a *shit* what his boss wants. *No! I don't want in!*" said Warren.

"Yeah, and who the hell is this *boss* of his anyway? He never mentions any name, only *'his boss.'* I don't like it, 'Ren."

"Okay, Jerry, okay. Let's go see this *asshole* and make sure he don't come back knockin' anymore...*period!*" said Warren.

The elevator opened onto the garage lobby. The glass wall at the end looked out into the underground parking area. Stewart was sitting on one of the cushions in front of the glass wall, alone. Warren was immediately on alert because he didn't see any of his guards at the registration desk or entry doors. Just as it dawned on Jerry, before he could even reach for his weapon, a man stepped into the open door of the elevator holding a .38 automatic with silencer at arm's length. The first bullet hit Warren in the center of his forehead, forcing his head and upper body backward as the second bullet, lower to the left, hit him in the heart, knocking him off his feet to the back of the elevator, landing heavily on the floor. Jerry looked up as the third bullet hit him in his left shoulder, clean through and through, burying itself in the rear wall. He staggered back, stopping hard against the wall, the gunman stepping further in, gun now pointed at his heart and his other hand down to his side, holding the doors open.

Stewart stood, walked over, and stepped into the elevator.

"My *boss* didn't take kindly to the *no* I delivered last week and suggested I give him time to change his mind. Maybe even wait for him to give me a call... *I didn't receive a call!* So my *boss* said that's that and for me to go to plan *number 2.* As you can see, plan *number 2* was a bit drastic but cleared one hurdle, *most definitely,*" said Stewart looking down at Warren then back to Jerry.

"Now that Warren is no longer able to...*operate...or make decisions* about his business, you, as his number 2, are now in charge. And your decision shouldn't be based on the fact that my associate has several bullets left in his weapon..."

During the entire time Jerry noticed that the gunman's hand had not wavered from pointing at his heart, no expression at all on his face.

"I'm...*I'm in...!*" said Jerry, fighting back against the pain in his shoulder.

"Very good, Jerry, *very good!* I'm quite sure my *boss* will appreciate your cooperation. Thank you," said Stewart.

The gunman stepped further into the elevator, opened Jerry's jacket, and took out the gun from his shoulder holster as Stewart held the doors open. With one hand he released the clip on the carpeted elevator floor and backed out, Stewart moving out behind him. The gunman stopped and pushed the stop button on the control panel; no alarm sounded. A few feet outside of the doors, he stooped and placed Jerry's gun on the lobby floor, all the while keeping aim on his heart.

"By the way, I've called my people, they will be here within the hour to take care of this...*mess*... I suggest you have your guest stay for at least another two hours or so, before letting them leave. And please, when they do leave, have them use the other elevators... We'll have this one restored tomorrow. Good night, Jerry. I'll be in touch," said Stewart.

Jerry watched as they both turned and walked away. He stooped and painfully picked up the clip from the floor. He went out to get his gun, the pain beginning to make him slightly dizzy. Off to his right, he saw the three guards sitting on the floor, their backs against the wall. All of them had been shot in the hearts and heads.

Michael's cell phone rang on the nightstand next to the bed: *it was Stewart.* He listened, noting the address, mentally figuring out what he'd have to take with him for the job. As he ended the call, he turned toward Mel. She was already up on one elbow, her head resting in her open palm, her breast clearly visible in the moonlight from the window. She reached over, gently rubbing his stomach.

"I take it that was Stewart..."

"What makes you think that?" he asked.

"Just the look on your face, babe. He always gets on your last nerve," she said, sliding her hand down between his legs.

He let her massage him, and for a moment he forgot about what they had to do for Stewart. He rolled to her, lightly kissing her on the lips, and moved back.

"We'll finish what *you* started later, Mel. Right now we got to go clean up after that fuckin' psycho he's got working for him."

"*Shit.* How many...?"

"At least four," he said, "plus one to get patched up."

Melissa rolled to get out of bed.

"I'll call Danny and tell him to get his people and the doc on the move," she said.

CHAPTER 22

The Cleaner: Daniel Wallace Kavanagh

Daniel Wallace Kavanagh grew up in a stereotypical Irish home. Almost the entire family's every step was done with reference to the Bible and final seal of approval by his grandaunt Rose, his dad's older sister. It had been rumored that she and her husband were both high-ranking members of the *IRA* forced to leave the country after a mission had killed too many innocent bystanders, along with her husband and half their crew. In her atonement, she had become super religious. And because of that, Daniel always thought of her as an undercover nun with a direct line to *GOD* Almighty! Many a day when he and his running buddies would be about to cause havoc in the streets, an image of grandaunt Rose always popped into his mind with that stern, disapproving look, stopping him in his tracks. When his friends asked what was wrong and he told them, they all made a beeline for their respective homes, dropping to their knees. And once locked securely in bedrooms, they prayed until they felt absolved of the unrealized sin or the face of grandaunt Rose faded from their minds.

Daniel's buddy Will, on the other hand, only thought of her as a loser that got her ass handed to her for not being good enough at being bad! For the better part of their teen years, he was in and out of jail for one thing or another, pushing Daniel out of the way at the last minute, knowing that they both were about to go up for some jail time. But he never told anyone that Daniel was involved, taking the hits and always keeping his mouth shut.

It was the last time Will was paroled, now in his late twenties. Daniel picked him up at the front gate when he noticed Will was... different.

"They been treatin' ya wrong, Willie? You a' bit *quiet*...," said Daniel.

"No, Danny, no. Me Uncle Lou visited me almost as much as you done, let me in on *somethin'*...," said Will.

"Tha' bad...got ya quiet or dunna know wha' to due 'bout it...?"

"Aye...thinkin' a bit hard, but knowin' where mah next step a'be."

"Not a'one put ya back he're, hope to GOD not!"

"No, no... One, I think...I'm gonna want ya makin' wid' me though. Dunna know ah soul ta trust wid' this *but ya!*" Daniel stared straight, focusing on the road and hills ahead.

The way Will was talking and *"feeling"* let him know this was something far beyond anything Will had done before.

They had finally pulled up in front of his Uncle Lou's business: a funeral home of the family since the '60s, first run by Lou's uncle and dad until they both were lured away by the stories of the *IRA* battles and attacks. Lou's father had returned only because his brother had fought it out with the authorities while he and a few others got away. But now he was on the run, his face plastered all over the papers and airwaves, telling Lou how stupid he was to believe the fame and glory of fighting for his country instead of sitting down with the Brits, doing it right and legal. The beginning of decades to be known as *"The Troubles"* in Northern Ireland started.

Lou dropped the cigarette on the sidewalk, stepped it out, and then signaled for Daniel to drive around the back. A few feet from the front, he made a right, stopping on a driveway apron, at the end a wide metal roll-up door.

"Aye, Danny. I figa'd as much he'da pull ya in. Still time, lad, to drop 'um and head a' home wid' ya...," said Lou.

Daniel looked at him then turned and looked at Will.

"Ya *stood* up fa' me. Took the *time* fa' me! I dunna know how ta' giv' tha' back ta' ya... I'm *in*, Willie! I'm in *wid' ya! No matta' wha'!*" said Daniel.

"Right, lad! Right ya be! Com' on, this he're be tha' *or'ther business...*," said Lou.

They got out the car and followed him to a side door; he opened it and walked into darkness. When Daniel's eyes adjusted, he saw the four crematory vaults all not in use. Lou and Will moved along the left wall, heading behind the first vault. Reaching up, Lou pressed two bricks just above his head at the same time, swinging them out. He reached inside. Daniel heard a metal click, then a section of the back cinder block wall popped back a few inches. A low light glow came on around the section of the wall. Pushing the two bricks back in place, Lou turned, easily moving the section into a wide and long corridor. Wall sconces on the near and far walls extended to their right at least *120* feet, wooded boxes stacked up as far as the eye could see along the nearest wall. Once they were all in, he swung the wall section back until it clicked. Turning around, he went over to the wall behind him, another *thirty* feet, and he stooped down, pushed a cinder block in sliding it to the right, then slid it back into place. Another metal click, and the section of wall moved back as well.

"Back in da' dae, I'd hide mah booze in he're, so when da' *'garda'* (local police) come 'round, I'd let it out 'bout the secret door. They'd see da' hooch, takin' a' bit wid' 'em far' the payoff, nun da' wiza' thinkin' the're be two *se'cret rooms...!*" Lou said as he pushed open the second wall section.

Inside were eight more crematory vaults, all much bigger than the ones in the *"official"* crematorium. Daniel and Will both had no words to say, looking from the vaults to Lou, waiting for the explanation.

"Da' *tories* (politicians), da' crooks, one an' da' same *bas'tards* ya ask'in' me, pay ya well to keep the're secrets, or burnt 'em in this case! These babies! These hold two each! Ash 'em quicka' ya kin' blink! Sift 'em far' da' bone, metal, grind da' bone, smelt da' metal. Tak' da' bone and ash, mix it wid' Jonny's fir'talizer, no one's da' wizer! No one!" said Lou.

"Why ya tellin' us? Why ya brin'in' us inna *dis'* world wid' ya, Unc'?" said Will.

"Ah'm' no' long far dis' world, Willie, black lung, doncha' kno'. Ah dunna wanta' leave it be! Donna wan' me family ta go wid' out. Ya be parta' mah family, Willie. Ya be the one Ah troost!" Lou said.

Daniel saw the tears rolling down Willie's cheeks, face set in stone. He walked over to his uncle and hugged him as if he never wanted to let him go. When he looked up, he kissed him on the forehead and smiled, looking down into his uncle's face.

"Ahm' wid' ya, Unc…but…wha' 'bout Danny?"

They both turned to look at Daniel, then Lou walked over to him and looked him in the eyes.

"Ya be parta' mah family now too, Danny. *Mah fam'ly too!*" Daniel looked Lou in the eyes for a moment, then put his arms around him and felt the tears start rolling down his cheeks.

Danny was leaning back in his plush reclining chair, a small glass of scotch whiskey neat in his left hand. He had left Will back in Ireland almost twenty-five years ago, helping him to move the operation to a secret factory basement in the middle of Dublin before he left. When he arrived in New York, he soon found out there was nothing like what he and Will had done overseas. With a little help from some old friends *(and a lot of their muscle over here!)*, he had started operations going in five major cities within eight years, settling down in Chicago because of the *Cubs'* "never say die" spirit! His cell phone vibrated; it was Melissa. He listened, told her okay, then finished his drink. Time to go to work…

CHAPTER 23

Adam Alan Anderson

Alan was born into a middle-income family of all girls. The exact middle child, with two older and two younger sisters, he was, by tradition, overlooked. But not by his older sister, Ruthie, who gladly volunteered to look after him because now she would have a living, breathing baby doll to love and care for. He vaguely remembered earlier times before his memories picked up around the age of two or three. He had been told that his sister was ecstatic to learn that her larger doll clothes fit him perfectly, even down to the shoes. So many a day Alan went around the house in her dresses. His mother and father commented on how adorable he looked, sometimes slipping and calling him the cutest little *"girl"* they had ever seen. When he and Ruthie were alone, she always called him by the secret girl name she had given him, leaving Alan to believe that really *was* his name until he started to public school at the age of five.

As he and his sisters grew up, they all remained close, but he was always closest to Ruthie, frequently having *"girl talk"* with her into the early hours of the morning. None of his sisters noticed that they really didn't treat him like their brother but more like another sister. Frequent neighbors and other outside family members over the years always asked how their *"girls"* were doing, only adding *"and Alan"* afterward. Even though Alan didn't admit this to himself, nor did he correct them when they referred to him as *"her,"* he felt comfortable being one of the girls.

Alan had begun trying on his sister Ruthie's clothes when he was about seven, continuing well into his preteens when one day, as he was wearing a pair of her shorts and sleeveless top, she walked in on him. His blood ran cold because he knew that she was about to blow up at him.

"*Shit!* Another one of my sisters taking my clothes! *Amazing!*" she said walking past him, throwing her purse and book bag on the bed. She undressed down to her bra and panties before she turned to him, shaking her finger in his direction.

"And you better wash them, *girl*, before you give them back!"

They both froze, her arm and finger still stretched out pointing at him.

"Okay, Ruthie! *Okay! Sorry!* I'll wash them myself! *Really! Please don't be mad at me!*" he said.

Then it dawned on him as well, his eyes opening wide.

"You really feel okay wearing…*girl clothes?*" she asked biting her lower lip.

"I feel…*comfortable*…maybe even…*natural…dressed as a girl.* I feel good about it…" Alan said looking her straight in the eye this time. "You really think of me as…*a girl…?*" he asked.

"I…*I guess I do…!* Okay. Okay…*little sis!* I'll keep your secret. We'll *all* keep your secret… I don't think our…*other sisters*…will mind either." She walked over to him and gave him the warmest hug he had ever felt.

As the years passed by and Alan grew, he and Ruthie went out more and more on shopping excursions, his female wardrobe growing larger with each trip. When she finally decided to move out of their parents' home, her thoughts were of a place that would be big enough for the two of them, eventually giving Alan his own room where he could openly store and have access to all his female clothing and accessories. And at least twice a month, they invited their other sisters over for "*girls' night out.*" They truly were the best of friends.

Once Alan turned eighteen, they started double-dating as sisters, excited just to be out as girls, even more so when most of the guys thought they were twins! If a guy became interested in Alan, that guy was made very much aware of not only *who* Alan was but *what* he was, no surprises in store for him later! But they did not stop to think what could happen if they both drank a bit too much and went home alone. That night happened a few days before Alan headed off to college. Returning from a double date, Alan had noticed that Ruthie was drinking more than usual and was being very sarcastic to his date. Saying goodbye to the guys at the restaurant and driving home in silence, Ruthie walked into the apartment, went straight to her room, and slammed the door. Alan hesitated a moment before he walked to her door and opened it cautiously. She was standing by her closet, just stepping out of her dress.

"Honey? What's wrong?" asked Alan.

She quickly turned and looked at him with murder, then tears in her eyes. "I felt left out!" she slurred slightly.

"Left out of what?" he asked.

"Dinner! They liked you better!" she said.

"They thought we were twins... How could they '*like*' me better?"

"Because they know I love you more than them!" said Ruthie.

Alan began to get angry. "I love you too, but I don't say shit 'bout the guys you date!" said Alan walking toward her.

"What about them? What about them, bitch?" said Ruthie, running forward toward him.

"I'm better! I'm better than any of them, you bitch!" said Alan.

They both met in the middle of the room, bodies pressed together, breathing heavily. Slowly the tension in their faces softened; their arms wrapped around each other's waists. Ruthie lightly kissed Alan on the lips, pulled back, and looked into his eyes. This time their lips met more intimately than they should, but they were unable to stop. Completely lost in the heat of the moment, it would tear them apart for years but strengthen their bond forever.

CHAPTER 24

Adam Alan's New Business

Many years later, after Alan had graduated from college, he was mired in the in-between zone of just out of college and not having a job yet. So like most people his age, he was hanging out at a local coffeehouse up north, with several morning interviews behind him and having a Grande mocha latte. The first thing Alan noticed about the older lady as she walked toward the counter was how elegant she appeared. The double-breasted navy-blue suit with medium-gray pinstripes seemed so out of place for this coffeehouse, not to mention the navy-blue, red-soled, high-heeled, ankle-strap shoes she was wearing. Don't see too many women in five-inch stilettos nowadays, let alone older ones able to walk in them so...*gracefully*. His gaze followed her body upward past the full hips, small waist, ample breast showing a good amount of cleavage, until he stopped at her perfectly made-up face: *which was staring directly at him with a warm, sly smile!* Alan quickly turned away, dropping his head and looking down at his latte, completely embarrassed. Out of his peripheral vision to the left, he saw her turn toward the counter, the thick black back seams of her stockings making his heart skip a beat. Without looking up, he just knew she would be walking over to his table; he waited for the telltale click of her heels on the concrete floor...

"I thought you would appreciate a closer look...*if I'm not being too presumptuous?*" the smooth, silky voice said.

He hadn't heard her walking over and was totally surprised that she was standing at his table, involuntarily looking down at her shoes.

"Real rubber soles and tips, honey, not leather. In my business, I've learned to walk softly...*and carry a big stick*..." she said trailing off as if she had already said too much. "May I sit with you?"

"Yes! Yes, ma'am, please!" he said half standing, gesturing to the chair opposite him with his right hand. When she was seated, he couldn't help looking at her face down to her cleavage.

"I guess I was right about you wanting *a closer look...!*" she said.

Alan's head snapped up, looking into her face then down again at his latte.

"Sorry, ma'am! I really don't know what's wrong with me right now," he said in a low voice. "Please excuse me."

"Don't worry about it, sugar. I think you see someone that you're attracted to and would like to *dress like* is all," she said in that smooth, silky voice.

Alan looked up, this time really caught off guard but somehow put at ease.

"You have beautiful skin, dear, and your features are very much girl-like. With the way you have your hair in that short, curly natural, most people would assume that you *are* a female, which I think you kinda like. *Right?*" she said smiling. "And you *probably* will look even *more feminine* with makeup and women's clothes on..." Was she reading his mind? How could she know that he really liked her outfit, not to mention the back seams! And how did she know he dressed up in women's clothing? *Who was this woman?*

"My name is *Sheila*, and I run an adult entertainment business farther north of here. You're like a lot of young people that come in here fresh out of college, *in between interviews*, taking a breather from the harsh view of reality, *etc*. But you, my dear, you stand out because you are...*pretty!*" Sheila said.

"*Wow! Do I stand out that much? Am I that obvious?*" Alan said, wondering if she just had above-average *gay-dar*.

"To me...*yes!* I have a job for you, honey, one that I think you would fit perfectly in. Care to come home with me, *sugar?*"

It was a thirty-five-minute drive further north to the gray area that was part *Chicago*, part *Evanston*, a toss-up as she explained it. Sheila parked in the back of a six-flat, three-story building, the first one of five that she owned on that block, all sitting on oversized city lots. The patio, well maintained, had several seating vignettes placed about, opposite the parking spaces. He walked up two steps onto a raised platform before entering through a glass-door ultramodern rear foyer. He was following behind her down the wide corridor, intently watching the back seams and heels as she slightly swayed from side to side. He saw another indoor sitting/lounge area, with a full bar against the long wall off to his right. There was medium-colored stained-wall paneling with large floor-to-ceiling paintings placed in groups or single, apparently cut from one long-running scene. Sheila stopped in front of one of the single paintings and pressed the side of the wall next to it. The panel slid back against a group of two, lining up perfectly to extend the scene, with the matte stainless steel elevator door behind it coming into view. It, too, had opened, revealing the same colored paneling up to the stainless steel handrail, beige smooth walls above that. The soft glow of valance lighting gave the car a warm, inviting feel. Once inside, the door closed. Sheila walked over to Alan and kissed him deeply on the mouth, lightly gliding her tongue across his top lip as she pulled back, moving away.

"I always...*taste*...my new employees before I get them up to my personal space, just to see how they may react to...*things to come*...," she said.

Alan walked over to her, giving her the same deep form of kiss, rubbing her back with his left hand as he traveled along her behind to the top of her leg with his right.

"*Oooohhh!* You're going to be *a fast learner!* You may even teach me a thing or two...," she said as she pulled away.

"I doubt that seriously, Sheila, I really do," Alan said.

The elevator door opened onto a view of a well-furnished living room: dark-beige sofa facing them in front of a long floor-to-ceiling window, end tables on either side. On the right, a small three-seat sectional, a whitewood coffee table placed for use by both, all sitting on a brown shag rug. Sheila walked in holding his hand, guided him to the sectional, and gently pushed him down to sit. Moving his legs apart, she stood in between them and began to unbutton her jacket then let it drop to the rug. The thin, white lace front-hook bra barely containing her large breast, areola, and nipples in stark contrast.

"Yes, dear, they are real. I *paid* enough for them to be…!"

Alan was rendered motionless, completely enjoying the sight. She reached to the left side of her skirt, unbuttoned the single button, and began to turn to her right as she unzipped it.

"Most men I…*service*…love to see my bare bottom along with the seams and heels, it excites them to no end…" Sheila said, letting the skirt fall down her legs and bending over halfway to emphasize her behind and the matching white lace garter belt.

"But what *all* my men really enjoy…is the view from the front…!" she said as she slowly turned back to face him.

The fully erect male member caught him off guard, making him sit back a bit, before it dawned on him: *With "her," he'd have the best of both worlds!*

CHAPTER 25

DJ's Big Mistake

The day of the meeting, DJ had gotten there a full hour before. He parked down the block and walked back to the building. He saw that Isaac's silver *Jaguar XJ* was sitting out in front of his building instead of its special place in the parking lot, which was odd… Why didn't he park it in the lot for his people to watch it? Even though everyone knew whose car it was, there was still that chance that some hype or dumb-ass car thief would cruise by and mistake it for an opportunity waiting. He felt something was wrong, instinctively moving back closer to the corner of the building across the street, until he saw someone sit up in the front seat then disappear again. He quickly looked over to the passenger seat. Maybe Isaac was with his bitch before the meet, a quick piece to relax, but he saw the passenger seat was empty. Still staying on the opposite side of the street, DJ slowly walked toward the Jaguar, staying close to the parked cars for a better look inside. Isaac popped up again; this time he could clearly see his head rolling loosely to the side, like he was drunk or high. Did Isaac use his own drugs? Was he sick or hurt? He slumped back over out of sight again, and with the closer view of the car, DJ could see that the driver's window was all the way down. Looking up and down the street and scanning the windows of the buildings, he quickly walked to the corner then crossed the street keeping the car in sight. Once again Isaac seemed to struggle to sit up, falling all the way over to the car door, his head hanging out the window for a few seconds before arcing forward and coming to rest on the steering wheel. DJ froze, thinking that the horn was going to go off with the impact, but it stayed quiet.

He finally reached the back of the car, and looking in, he saw that Isaac really was alone. His head was still on the steering wheel moving slightly as if it was way too heavy to lift. With four quick steps, DJ was at the car window. He reached in with his left hand, pushing Isaac back into the seat while pulling the *.380* with the twelve-ounce plastic bottle taped around the top of the slide. Isaac's head bounced on the seat headrest and moved forward coming in line with the bottom of the plastic bottle as DJ squeezed the trigger. There was a muffled pop as the bullet tore through the bottle into Isaac's left temple. He wasn't ready for the amount of skin, blood, and bone that flew against the passenger side door as well as out the window. Isaac's head snapped to the right, the dead weight breaking free of his grip, then settled into the passenger seat. DJ jerked to the left, turning his head as the vomit exploded from his mouth, dropping the gun inside the car. Holding onto the fender of the car, DJ slowly straightened up, not wanting to look inside the car, but he knew he had to get his gun.

"*Wow, DJ!* Your ambition was a lot more then I had *thought!* Thank you for helping me out though," said the deep, smooth voice.

DJ quickly looked to his right and saw the muzzle of the silenced .32 automatic no more than six inches away from his left eye. But the real shock was the man that he recognized holding the gun in his face! Before his brain could process the image, he felt the hot blast of the gun firing into his face, slamming into him like a sledgehammer as he was literally thrown back off his feet. He couldn't feel the left side of his face anymore, but he felt the second bullet bore into his chest, quickly followed by a third and fourth into his stomach as he turned to his right in midair on his way to the ground.

The man watched as DJ's body bounced once on the ground, twitched slightly as it slid a few more inches, and then stopped. He looked into the car just to make sure that that body was dead as well. He unscrewed the warm silencer with his handkerchief, putting them both in his left hand coat pocket, then put the *.32* automatic into his right hand coat pocket. He took one last look at DJ's body lying in the street then turned, walking back to another silver *Jaguar XJ* parked further down the block at the corner…

CHAPTER 26

Stewart's First Contact

Stewart Albert Jamessen had always been a follower, but a follower with his own agenda in mind. All the lectures from his parents growing up were contrary to what he believed; they really didn't have his insight or ability to see the big picture. His loyalty to his ideas as well as his concept of *their* plans was far better formulated. He was able to make subtle statements, planting a seed in them that, later on, they would adopt as their own. He could see the pitfalls of any plan/idea that was presented to him and knew beforehand when to get out after he had gotten what *he* wanted. Stewart always managed to escape any and all repercussions. But this time he would miss a very important pitfall…

The majority of Stewart's adult life was spent in the employment of various crime bosses who had heard of his meticulous organization abilities. Several of his past affiliations lasted for years after his departure because they continued to follow the procedures he had outlined. The main reasons for him to move on were *bigger challenges and obviously more money*. But the real cause for his change of locations was to prove that he *was* smarter than those so-called crime lords. A few of his second-in-commands asked why he had never started his own organization and carved out his own territory somewhere; he definitely had the people that would follow him anywhere. His simple answer was always: *complacency*. He felt if he stayed in one place too long, he would begin to get *too* comfortable with the way things were running, miss the little things behind the scenes that eventually turned into bigger things, and once that happened it was only a matter of time until they caused you to get caught.

At the end of his last employment, Stewart had decided to drop off the radar for a while, looking to relax his mind. His investments put him into a seven-figure bank account, so anywhere in the world was available to go for downtime.

His thoughts were broken when his cell phone rang. Less than a handful of people had his number, and of those, they had no need to call. Unless a name showed up *(all aliases of the actual person)* with the number, he always let it go to voice mail; if it was important, they would leave a message. The message, spoken by a deep male voice, said an account with *$1,000,000* had been opened for his use. If he was interested in controlling an entire city, he was to call the cell phone number left for further information. Stewart had made a lot of money over the years, but no one had ever started a conversation by *offering a million dollars* up front. After a moment's hesitation, he decided to make the call.

"Promptness is a quality I quite admire, Mr. Jamessen. Thank you for returning my call," said the deep voice.

"It isn't every day someone starts a conversation with me by offering a possible citywide takeover, let alone a *million-dollar* payment upfront, *Mr....?*" said Stewart.

"*Aurell. Marc Aurell*, Mr. Jamessen. I prefer using *'controlling'* instead of *'takeover,'* something that another *Southside Italian* was credited with. Even though historians have written that *'control'* did *not* include a *Northside Irishman's* territory. I believe that Irishman knew his days were...*numbered*...though. Let us not forget our history, Mr. Jamessen."

"*'He who forgets the past is doomed to repeat it,'* Mr. Aurell? What has history taught you that will make a difference today?" asked Stewart.

"An outright attack from the front can be seen and may be countered. While an attack from within is totally unexpected and usually more...*devastating*."

"That sounds plausible, but how do we get inside those areas we wish to...*attack?*"

"Very simply, Mr. Jamessen—*information.* Know the answers to the questions well before you ask those you are confronting. Everyone has weaknesses that they may or may not be aware of, not truly understanding how deeply those weaknesses are embedded or how much they could be *injured* by them. Being able to use that as an advantage is key to holding someone hostage and, if necessary, *destroying everything* they consider dear," said Mr. Aurell.

"And if they are able to circumvent those weaknesses, take them out of harm's way, or even eliminate the threat to them altogether? What then, Mr. Aurell?" asked Stewart.

"Then, Mr. Jamessen, you would direct your associate *Edmond David* to resolve the situation with his usual *extreme prejudice.*"

The hairs on the back of Stewart's neck stood up. He had worked with Edmond many times before, and each time, it never ceased to amaze him how coldly efficient at killing he was. A sociopath he could rely on but, for that same reason, from whom he maintained his distance.

"You really have done your homework, Mr. Aurell. Once I have been brought into your complete information loop, I'll contact Edmond. Until then, I'd rather tread slowly."

"Of course, Mr. Jamessen, quite understandable. Mr. David is under our...*surveillance*...as well. Busy man... Further information, Mr. Jamessen, will be presented at a later time if you will make yourself available...?"

"Yes. I'm at your disposal, Mr. Aurell. When and where shall I meet you?" asked Stewart.

"My driver will be there shortly, Mr. Jamessen."

"I haven't given you my address..."

A knock on the hotel room door made him turn; he walked over and opened it. A tall young man in a tailored suit, obviously well muscled. Very slight bulges under both arms caught his attention before he looked up to his face.

"Mr. Jamessen? I have a car waiting for you downstairs. Would you mind getting your jacket please?" said the young man.

"You *have* done your homework, Mr. Aurell," said Stewart as he turned back into the room, heading for his jacket.

"Yes, Mr. Jamessen, I'm not one for...*surprises*." The call ended.

CHAPTER 27

Marc Aurell, I Presume?

Stewart sat back in the rear of the *Maybach* listening to the classical music played on satellite radio. The ride, extremely smooth, definitely expected of a *$2 million plus*, finely crafted automobile, something he would never choose to own. With some of the *"duties"* performed in the service of his many past employers, this mode of transportation would make him a bit *too* visible. He preferred to go about his business, *his clients' business*, in a much lower key.

The idea of taking over a city had piqued his curiosity, but whether it could actually be planned, let alone carried out, was what he was truly interested in seeing. It was one thing to take over a company, a criminal organization, those had been done many times before—where as an *entire city…unheard of!* The thought was quite impressive, though just as equally insane. Even at the height of *Al Capone's* power, he managed to only unify the *Southside* gangs, control the major crime. With policemen and judges on his payroll, he was able to go a long way only to have *Bugs Moran* still maintain control of the *Northside*. Would it have been any different if the Southsiders had high-quality breweries to give the Northsiders' direct competition in the liquor trades? Or did the ethnic hatred of the Irish and the Italians go too deep, with total lack of respect for each other as well as wanting only *one ruler* for *Chicago*? Power, money, and egos—*never* a good combination for a business. Even *worse* for a criminal organization.

Once prohibition hit, that made the feud even more problematic. They took their violence into the streets, creating an even higher public profile than needed, *or wanted*, by the start-up members of the *true* organized crime syndicate. The *Capone/Moran* feud ended with both men going to prison: Capone dying after he left prison from heart failure brought on by third-stage syphilis and Moran passing away from lung cancer while still incarcerated. Both nonviolent ends for two *very* violent men.

Stewart's thoughts were broken when the *Maybach* began to slow, making a slight shift to the right-hand exit drive. At the second stoplight, they made a left turn into a parking lot and drove to the front entrance of a modern glass-and-steel-walled high-rise building. Another young man, he too well muscled and armed, was standing at the curb. He opened the rear door.

"Mr. Jamessen, please follow me," he said, closed the door, and walked ahead of Stewart.

The office was located on the top floor, a slightly bronze-tinted glass wall going across the width of the elevator lobby. The two four-foot-wide glass doors, both trimmed with highly polished chrome plates at the tops and bottoms, stood out in the middle of the open space. A burnished chrome plate at the edge of the right-hand door, head-height, had black raised block letters that read, *"BARTLETT, DOUGLAS, AND ASSOCIATES,"* two inches high, and *"ATTORNEYS-AT-LAW"* half that size centered below. The young man walked through, holding the door for him, turned to the right, and walked to a clear-glass-walled conference room. The glass-and-chrome conference table inside seated twelve. The young man, again, held the door open for him.

"Mr. Aurell will be with you shortly, Mr. Jamessen. Please have a seat. May I get you anything while you wait?" he asked.

"No, thank you. I'm fine," said Stewart.

The young man turned and left, the door slowly closing behind him. Stewart took the seat opposite the door, his back to the windows. The glass wall of the corridor and the windows behind him turned white opaque, overhead valance lights coming on reflecting softly off the white ceiling. The end wood panel to his left swung in, and a tall man in a tailored suit stepped out of the small inner office. He obviously worked out but was not a fanatic to the routine. At first glance, his face made Stewart think of an action hero or enhanced super being. The slight smile to help ease the tension made him wonder if this was going to be a waste of his time.

"Privacy glass, Mr. Jamessen, as well as an audio-encrypting sound source making any recording impossible," the man said. He pulled the wood panel, and it closed behind him in line with the other wood panels. Moving to the head of the conference table, he rolled the chair back and sat down.

"Obviously, the thought of what *Al Capone* had done, in his day, has run through your mind. Along with *Bugs Moran* being the ever-constant thorn in his side...," he said looking Stewart in the eyes.

"That *is* the obvious place to *start* when contemplating taking over a...*sizable turf*...so to speak," said Stewart.

"Your skepticism is duly noted, and if not far off the mark, the word *insane* came up at some point, I take it...?"

"Of course," said Stewart.

"Then we are at the beginning of the same book's first chapter. The problem with those two businessmen, clothed *gangsters* really, was quite simple: *ego*. They both wanted to be *number 1*, no second-in-command, complete control over all the areas, *North* and *South*. Because of their violent *history*, their violent *nature*, the concept of working together would never have entered into *any* actual realm of their thought. The outright warfare of the two rival factions could only escalate through the frequent killings and destruction of property, each thinking they had dealt a grave blow to the other, succeeding only in producing larger headlines carried by all the local newspapers."

"It can't be as simple as ego and ethnic prejudice, a very small portion of an enormous undertaking," said Stewart, slightly irritated at the history explanations.

"Unfortunately…yes. *That is why they failed*. Removing those two conditions allows a clear view of where to begin: *from within existing organizations.*"

The idea caught Stewart off guard; his way of thinking takeovers usually, at some point, would involve violence.

"And how are you planning on getting inside these existing organizations? Strangers attempting to infiltrate at the ground floor are automatically suspect. Trying to put your own people in not only would be a waste of time but a waste of that person's *life* as well," said Stewart.

"Yes, quite so. *But not if that person was already in that organization to begin with…!*" Stewart sat back and thought through a few scenarios, seeing the beginnings of where this was headed.

"You're speaking of the ones at the bottom, the so-called *'foot soldiers,'* disgruntled for whatever reasons. The one's that could be… *bought*…?"

"Exactly! Once their price is met, along with other…*motivations*…to solidify them to our control, we find the weak areas, exploit them, before moving in with…*an offer*," the man said, a slight smile on his face.

"And by having several of these…*informants*…working for you, unknown to each other, the information would be readily verifiable," said Stewart.

"Working for…*us*…Mr. Jamessen. My information concerning you was very accurate about your intelligence," he said, the smile on his face widening.

"What if your…*our offer*…isn't accepted by the so-called leaders of these organizations?" asked Stewart.

"Then that is when you will let your man, Eduardo, with his unique abilities, *persuade* the others to follow us," said the man.

"Yes, *Eduardo*, of course," said Stewart looking deeper into the man's eyes.

"I'm sure you have him located and he's able to travel at a moment's notice?" the man said with a nod of his head.

"Thank you, Mr. Raymond. Your services will no longer be required," said the voice filling the room from the overhead speakers.

The man's eyes widened, his hands going flat on the conference tabletop. "I...*I apologize, Mr. Aurell! I...*"

"No apology needed, Mr. Raymond. Thank you for your time," said the disembodied voice.

The end wooden panel swung open, and the young man that led Stewart into the room was standing in the opening.

"Mr. Jamessen, come with me. This way please," he said, turning with his left arm extending into the smaller office behind him.

Stewart stood and walked toward the opening as the outer door to the conference room opened. Two additional young men walked in facing Mr. Raymond. As the wooden panel closed completely, he heard the soft sounds of silenced guns being fired, followed by something heavy hitting the floor.

CHAPTER 28

Marc Aurell's Proposal

"My anonymity is not a condition brought on by a heightened sense of awareness for my surroundings but a tool that enables my observations of those individuals pertinent to my future intentions, at most times, within arm's length of the subject, *their* awareness of myself *negated*," said the voice of Marc Aurell over the small office speaker system.

Stewart sat back on the sofa and crossed his legs. This was the voice he had heard over the telephone, with the enhanced sound of the larger speakers; it was an *exact* copy of the late Mr. Raymond's voice.

"Quite understandable, Mr. Aurell, but still bordering on an *implied* sense of paranoia...especially with the sudden...*termination*...of Mr. Raymond."

"On the contrary, Mr. Jamessen, a precaution taken due to a lack of focus, on his part, toward the information supplied to him. Not knowing the names of your...*important personnel*...would have *grave* consequences moving forward."

Stewart was amazed at the matter-of-fact tone, making the comparison to Edmond, on a much higher level, without a doubt.

"As mentioned by you, previously, taking control of smaller areas is relatively routine, seeing that the law enforcement agencies have done most of the work for us by incarcerating the *'gang leaders,'* leaving the infighting among the neophytes, the primary cause of the frequent street violence, innocents becoming collateral damage almost daily. These individuals you cannot dialog with, their way of problem-solving is with primal impulses: *eliminate the opposition with extreme prejudice.* That solution will be used against them, with our *'cleaner'* and *'his organization'* taking care of any *'telltale residue,'*" said Marc.

"That would possibly work for the street gangs, a *'larger intimidator'* moving in, showing them that the only way to continue is to submit...or definitely *disappear.* But what about the *main crime lords?* The ones whose organizations are more sophisticated, under intensive scrutiny? I'm quite sure they won't *'roll over and die'*...," said Stewart.

"That is exactly what I *can* offer them, Mr. Jamessen. What better way to remove intense scrutiny of a *subject* than to remove the *subject* being scrutinized? A *'deceased'* crime lord is no longer of interest to *anyone.* How they may have died is not an issue that will be of concern nor investigated. Infighting, a competitor finally achieving the desired goal, only another criminal becoming a statistic. Focus is now placed upon their second-in-command, allowing the *'deceased'* crime lord to continue their control over their people, major decisions still made by the original leader. Therefore the business will continue, the income will continue, increasing the capital needed to acquire the services of key personnel in city/state government managerial positions, bringing along with them, under their command, official armored security instructed as well as compensated to cast a blind eye," said Marc.

"And this offer...*to die*...? Obviously, someone has to die, but if it isn't the crime lord, they *continue* to remain intact, then who becomes the *statistic?* Possibly...the body...*of someone*...burned beyond recognition? Partially dissolved by sulfuric or carborane acid? In either case, dental records or some other identifying feature will have to be used," said Stewart.

"Those would be generic at best, causing an automatic investigation leading, eventually, to the realization of mistaken *'assumed'* identity. The average person in a position of coroner, forensic examiner, for any extended period of time, will not institute a minute inspection of the remains if the face is intact and an irrefutable cause of death is present," said Marc.

"*If the face is still intact...?*" asked Stewart.

"Yes, Mr. Jamessen. Science has progressed far beyond our standardized way of thinking, bringing into any dialog elements never considered. Cloning was only presented in science-fiction stories until a mere sheep was created from cells removed from another. Artificially produced appendages of flesh, bone, and blood have been successfully used to replace missing limbs in humans. The next threshold was the human face, how an individual is recognized, basically, by sight alone. That challenge has been met and realized. Once a *'duplicate'* is achieved, the original disposes of them, recorded without their knowledge, as insurance, my way of controlling them, at a future date...*if necessary*," said Marc.

Stewart was now very curious. What did he mean by *"the human face challenge had been met"*? Could a face transplant have been perfected? *Even possible?* This was something that he had to see through, but until all the information was given, he couldn't begin to make changes that would benefit him.

"So, Mr. Aurell, are you recording *me now?* And what if I say *no?*"

"No, Mr. Jamessen, I am not recording you. Nor would I expect you to say *no*. Your mind works quite similar to mine, a truly unfortunate waste if it should end...*prematurely*."

Stewart thought, not believing for a moment that he would walk out of this room alive if he refused to work for this man.

"Then we are agreed. I am at your service, Mr. Aurell. Please tell me more..."

"I shall, but first, sustenance and libations," said Marc.

The end wooden panel opened, and a young man walked in carrying a tray with several cold-cut meat selections. A second young man, right behind him, carried another tray loaded with cheeses, condiments, and a bottle of twelve-year-old Hennessy cognac, Stewart's favorite *(he had done his research!)*. They were both placed on the coffee table in front of Stewart. The second young man went to a small refrigerator on the opposite wall and removed a small full ice bucket.

"Enjoy, sir. The door to the bathroom is located behind you on the left," he said, turned, and walked out.

Stewart began to make himself a sandwich.

"Shall we continue, Mr. Jamessen?"

"Yes, Mr. Aurell. Please continue…," said Stewart.

A third young man, sitting outside at the conference table, took another bite of his first baked ham and cheddar cheese sandwich on seedless rye bread. He picked up the chilled bottle of Dr. Pepper next to the silenced Glock. He listened over the Bluetooth headset, on mute, as the conversation continued in the small office, the periodic low beep letting him know the recording was in progress.

CHAPTER 29

Charlie Tells What He Saw

Charlie Conrad was sweating even more than the junkie that he was, a junkie that hadn't fixed in almost two days because he was scared! He was so scared that he was afraid to go to any of his secondary suppliers for a hit because of the awful image still in his mind of what happened to his *main supplier!*

The plastic chair with the thin steel legs was working into his behind, not letting him find a comfortable position, shifting from one side to the other then back again. Why in the *hell* had he come down here to tell his story, and who in the *hell* would believe *him?*

Shit! What was that crawling on his left arm under the sleeve? Nope! *Nope!* Just his nerves! He needed to shoot up! No. *No!* That's the last thing he should do! They'd see him and take him down! He'd be *dead* before he could even *cop* a fix!

Charlie leaned forward, his head in his hands, a thousand voices screaming in his head to run! Get the hell up and out of here before somebody let them know he was here!

"Mr. Conrad? I'm Detective Smith. The desk sergeant said you had some information about Emmanuel Isaac...?"

Charlie shot straight up out of the seat, his head swiftly looking from side to side, total fear in his eyes. Alex took a few steps back, holding out both hands in front of him.

"Whoa, *whoa!* Nobody's here to hurt you. Settle down. Settle down..."

115

Charlie could feel his heart in his throat. For a minute he forgot how to breathe; the urge to bolt was *almost* too much to ignore!

"*It's too open out here! Too many people lookin' at me! I gotta go! I gotta go!*" he said.

Then just as suddenly, he plopped back down into the seat, eyes wide staring up into Alex's face. And the tears began. Charlie's left eye began to twitch uncontrollably, mouth slowly opening in a silent scream as his head lowered to his chest. Alex watched as his shoulders shook, sobs barely heard. He felt helpless. What had this man seen that reduced him to this crying, frightened wreck? Let it run its course for a minute then get him something to eat and drink, then start all over...

By the time Charlie had gotten to the third cheese burger and second cola, he was in a much better state of mind. Alex had noticed that Charlie's left eye had stopped twitching and his hands were shaking a *lot* less. He took another bite of the cheese burger, a sip of cola, and settled back in his chair.

"I didn't know if I should even be *down here*, didn't know if you guys would even want ta' listen to a junkie like me. I've been... *usin'*...forever and saw a lot of crazy shit, *lots of crazy shit!* Seen nigga's like Isaac come and go plenty of times. Other dealers, their own people would cap they ass or set 'em up for the fall, gettin' them out the way so they could move up. But *man!* I *never* saw *shit* like *this* go down, wish I hadn't, *wish I hadn't!*" said Charlie.

"So you saw who shot Isaac? Can you describe what they looked like?" asked Alex.

"*Yeeaah*, man, and that's the *really* crazy part! You *won't* believe it! Just *won't believe what I saw!*" said Charlie.

"I'm a cop on the *Southside* of *Chicago*... What *haven't* I seen? Try me...," said Alex.

"Okay. Okay. I was going to Isaac's building. He'd have me over regular, you know, tell him the shit goin' down on the street that his people, I guess, wouldn't tell him. Sometimes he'd fix me food. Most times we'd just talk. But always he'd give me a couple hits on my way out the door with a few dollars too. That night, *that night*, I was *comin'* out the alley, usual, *the usual*, and out the corner of my eye, I see that youngster DJ, so I cut back in the alley. He's just hangin' on the other side of the street, across from Isaac's buildin', moving like he's tryin' ta' sneak up or *somethin'*. He even ducked down behind a car!"

Alex made a mental check; that must have been the young man they found in the street shot in the face. Charlie stopped and took a long swallow of the cola. The twitch started in his eye again.

"Go on, Mr. Conrad."

"He made it 'cross the street, came up behind Isaac's car, and went over to the driver's side. Isaac popped up in the window like a *jack-in-the-box*, then gone! I guess he fell over in the seat again. Scared the *shit* out of him the way he jumped back! *Really* jumped back! Anyways, Isaac came up a couple more times, and that youngster pulled *somethin'* out his jacket. That's when I heard the pop, real soft, and the boy turned quick to the side and threw up in the street, *threw up!*"

"Is that when Isaac got out of the car and waited to shoot DJ in the face?" asked Alex.

"Naw. *Naw! That's the crazy part!* When DJ, DJ turned back 'round from throwin' up, the man was already *standin'* by the car's *back door!* I didn't even see him get out the car! He was just there, *standin' up!* He said somethin' to the boy, smiled, and shot him in the face! Before he could even hit the ground, he shot 'em couple more times, then he just walked away, *just walked away!*"

"*Another man?* Isaac had somebody in the car *with him* when he got shot? You sure?"

"*Naw, man, naw! Nobody* else was *in that car! NOBODY!* I'm a junkie, not *fuckin' blind!*"

"Then why'd you say you didn't see him get *'out the car'?* Can you identify this other man? Can you describe him?" asked Alex.

"I didn't see him get out the car *because he didn't get out the car! He couldn't have got out the car! And yeah! I can describe the nigga' with my fuckin' eyes closed in my sleep!*" said Charlie.

Alex reached over, picked up the telephone handset, and dialed a number.

"Bill, see if we got a sketch artist in-house and send them to *interrogation number 8.*"

"Won't *need no* sketch artist, man! You already *got* pictures of him, for sure!" said Charlie. "*Plenty pictures!*"

"What? Who the *hell* was the guy that shot DJ?"

"*Isaac, man! Emmanuel Isaac hisself!*"

CHAPTER 30

DJ Figured Wrong

The police SUVs blocked the flow of traffic eastbound and westbound on Sixty-Third Street in front of Emmanuel Isaac's building. A white covering with a plastic liner had been placed over DJ's body still lying in the street. The driver's door of the silver *Jaguar XJ* was open, a *CSI* tech taking pictures of the interior as other techs walked the area placing markers at evidence to be documented and collected.

The word about DJ had traveled fast along the streets to Mike. His people gave him updates every few minutes as he rushed there to see for himself, still hoping that he was only hurt and not dead. But as he got closer, the information coming to him wore away that little hope altogether.

Mike had gone through the back entrance of the truck and railway marshalling area directly across the street from the building, knowing that he wouldn't be able to get closer on the street. He stood back from the fence, staying close to the shadows as he could, surveying the scene. It was true: the white covering in the street obviously had a body underneath, DJ. How could he have been so stupid? Going up against Isaac's by himself! He always knew he wanted more, wanted to be a boss, *big boss*, but just didn't have the patience to wait for it to happen. Damn you, DJ! He saw a man walking over to the silver *Jaguar XJ*, touched the tech on the arm, backing him up as he bent, and reached into the car. He stayed in that position for a few moments then backed out himself, slow, as if he was bringing something out. When the man stepped aside, he motioned to the tech, who stepped forward and started taking pictures again. In the camera flashes, Mike could plainly see it was Isaac's; he had been shot in the left side of his head, dead for sure.

Well, DJ, he thought, *you cut out the middleman all right. Yeah, you did, brother!*

Mike hung his head, knowing there was nothing he could do for his friend or get revenge on that *son of a bitch* Isaac. He turned and began to walk away when it hit him like a ton of bricks! Isaac was shot in the *side* of his head. DJ was either on the side of the car or came up behind him as Isaac turned his head; he couldn't have seen it coming! That was an instant kill shot, so how the *hell* did he shoot DJ? *Who shot DJ?* Something was *very* wrong; it just didn't add up! His Bluetooth earpiece rang; he reached up to answer.

"Yeah…!"

"This's Billie. One of my runners said she saw a car headin' *away* from there 'bout the time the shit went down."

"She know what kind? Get a plate? *Nigga drivin'?*"

"No plate, Mike, but she knew the car *and* the *nigga drivin!*"

"Who, Billie? Who the *fuck* was it?

"Isaac, man! Isaac!"

Mike's head shot up as he saw the techs put Isaac's body into a black plastic bag on the ground, zipped it up, and carried it to a waiting coroner's van.

The Deal with the Devil

Alan was sitting in the office area of the apartment. He turned to the side, looking out the window. He was thinking of Sheila; she had passed away almost six years ago. He remembered working for her that very same day she took him home to her place; he had serviced three men, along with two of their wives, all the while dressed in women's lingerie.

Over the years they had gotten closer together, not only as lovers but true friends, she showing him all the ends and outs of the business, knowing that one day she would pass *everything* on to him. He, eventually, told her about Ruthie and what they had done with each other years before, not having spoken to her since. Sheila had listened, tears in her eyes, then she told him about her father, a minister down South. He had preached, one Sunday, about truth. The *only* truth was the truth of the heart. True love for all, regardless of color, status, or position in the community was truth you felt in your heart. But that obviously didn't extend to his son, who *very stupidly* brought his boyfriend to the church and had sex with him in the balcony...*sex that was a little too loud...* Both of them, caught by his father, were beaten to within an inch of their lives with his belt, vowed *never* to go back to their hometown ever again in life. They went their separate ways.

It was over thirty years later when his sister tracked him down and said that his father's last words to her were he was sorry he kicked out his son for doing what he had preached. Regardless of what he had done, he would always be loved, *always be his child!* Just like Ruthie, regardless, would always be *Alan's sister*.

Sheila, behind Alan's back, invited Ruthie to their apartment for a *"business meeting"* with a *"mutual friend,"* knowing that he would come upstairs to change clothes. When he stepped off the elevator, he took a step back in, wanting to leave but unable to move. Ruthie, sitting still in one of the club chairs, looked as if she had stopped breathing, then the tears began to flow. Without hesitation, Alan walked over and knelt at her side, hugging her tightly, as he too began to cry. That was the moment Sheila fell in love with them both, all becoming lovers as their relationship deepened. Working together, they grew the client base. Alan was in charge of the scheduling, while Sheila and Ruthie continued to service the clients and interact with the other *"girls"* for collective teaching of what they were all learning. Before they knew it, their ranks had grown to forty-five, including five actual women and four more six-flat apartment buildings.

The day Sheila passed away, she had serviced five men as well as had a threesome with Alan and Ruthie before going home to her bungalow in Darien. At first they thought she was just resting up from such a busy time, not hearing from her the next day; but when the second day rolled around with no contact from her, they both headed straight for her place. As they walked in, they felt the house was cool; she always had it set for 68 degrees. Nothing looked out of place; soft, easy listening music was playing upstairs. Neither one of them wanted to go and see what was there, but they knew they had to. Holding hands, they slowly started up the stairs.

Sheila's bedroom was at the far end of the hall facing the back-yard. The door was open, music obviously coming from inside. When they slowly pushed the door open, they saw she was lying on her left side facing away from the door, wearing a white lace gown, a metal box along with various papers spread out on the bed in front of her. Ruthie stopped, tears flowing down her cheeks as Alan stepped closer. Reaching out, he touched her shoulder: *it was cold*. He turned to Ruthie and shook his head. She backed out of the bedroom door, and he could hear her running down the hall. Alan stepped forward and looked down onto her face; *she was smiling…*

Sheila was *ninety-two* years old. After the services, which all the girls had attended, Sheila's lawyer, the same one they used for the business, met with them privately. He had told them she left everything to him and Ruthie: *money, all the properties, even the cars that she had stopped driving years before.* Her last wishes were to take care of the *"girls"* and create some type of *"retirement plan"* for them, the preliminary drafts she had already laid out. All the girls, that very same day, were immediately set up with *$1,000,000* in savings, added to each year and fully vested after four.

Alan's thoughts suddenly shifted, and he remembered the look on that stranger's face after he had shot him, and the poor guy didn't even know *why* he had died. That was a look that he knew he would take to his grave. The more he thought about this situation, the more he wanted out of the deal with Stewart *and* his mysterious, unseen boss. But what would happen to him? His sisters? He really had no clue, but between him and Ruthie, they would have to figure it out…

"I'd say a penny for your thoughts, but I already know what they are…," said Ruthie from behind him.

"What was I thinking, honey? What is this *'deal with the devil'* going to do for us in the long run? And if I decide to tell Stewart to go pound sand up his ass, what's going to happen to you and the rest of our sisters? Not to mention what he's going to do to our friends…?" said Alan not turning around.

"At the time, you really didn't have a choice, *boo.* Look at what happened to Warren and his people. But now that the police are looking into those other killings, maybe we can go to them or even start dropping some hints to them anonymously."

"No. I'm not sure how much of a deterrent that's going to be to them. Who knows, they may even have someone on the inside at the police department tracking all the information that comes in and giving them updates," said Alan. "No, honey, we're going to have to face this on our own, and even if it means paying the girls off, shutting down the business, and disappearing…*so be it!*"

"Either way, *boo*, we all need to be careful. You and me doubly so," said Ruthie.

Just then the desk telephone rang, making them both jump slightly. They both stared at it for a moment. Alan answered on speaker. It was Stewart.

"I was just calling to check in with you, Alan. Ask how are things going with the business and...*Ms. Ruthie*?"

"The business is just fine, Stewart. As far as my sister is *concerned*, you'll have to take that up with her."

"Really? Most *'men'* would be rather protective of their sisters, especially inquiries from a newly acquired...*associate*," said Stewart.

Alan didn't miss the *men* reference or the plural added to the word *sister*, but he was not going to jump to the bait.

"Ruthie has dealt with a lot of...*newly acquired associates*... Most of them survived. What can I do for you, Stewart? Or is this call intended to just keep me aware of your existence?"

"No, nothing of real importance, other than sending you a few new clients. And I may even stop in myself if...*Ms. Ruthie*...will be *available*," said Stewart. "I'll call beforehand." The call ended.

"Well, girl, I guess we should have known that he would eventually get around to asking for *'free services'* from us, but I didn't expect him having a thing for *you! Wow!*"

"That makes *two* of us! Let's play along for a while. We might learn something else about him, something we can hold over *him*," said Ruthie.

CHAPTER 32

Wrong Toes to Step On

The image of the man Alan shot stayed in the back of his mind, moving into full focus at the oddest times. It didn't matter if he was happy or having one of those days; the noise, the blood, but most of all *the look* on that man's face were sharp and clear. Stewart had told him that if he hadn't gone through with the plan, his own family could...*would*...be at risk. Family was everything. His sisters meant the world to him, and whatever he had to do, he would keep them safe. But this was beginning to be a heavier burden to carry than he thought. The guilt was eating him from the inside out, killing him as well. How much longer could he hold out, and with Stewart *"dating"* his sister Ruthie, that was just adding insult to the injury!

Even though Stewart had been taking Ruthie out for only a few weeks, Alan had noticed the change in her. He knew the dinners, movies, and bunches of flowers were only to soften her up before he'd ask her to his bed, which they both thought was inevitable anyway. The way he looked at her with the contained lust of a predator, not for food or even sport, only...*control*. But once it happened, she seemed to draw away from him, spending a lot of time away from the buildings, a few times turning around to go the other way when she saw him coming toward her. Today sitting at the rear bar on the ground floor, he would talk to her, regardless of how she was feeling. He needed to know what was going on with his sister.

She came in, head slightly down, looking but seeing nothing as she walked. Ruthie was past him a few feet before he spoke.

"A penny for your thoughts, dear," he said.

She turned, startled by his voice and stood still, eyes wide open. Alan stood and moved forward and put his arms around her, drawing her near. Ruthie's head fell onto his shoulder as she began to silently cry.

In the top-floor personal apartment, Ruthie had stopped crying, sitting in one of the plush club chairs, Alan sitting on the floor next to her.

"The sex we have isn't anything I haven't done before, it's just the way he *controls* the...*details...before we start...*," she said.

Alan reached up and held her hand.

"He wants me to wear a dark-red, long-sleeved, front-and-back low-cut dress, thin enough so he can see the imprint of my nipples and the garter belt underneath. Back-seamed stockings and six-inch heels, not five inches or seven inches, but *six-inch stiletto heels*. I turn around slowly so he can see them. Then he tells me, *not asks me*, but *tells* me to walk over to him sitting on the bed and kneel down on my knees between his legs, unzip his pants..." He felt her squeeze his hand a bit harder.

"When I...*when I finish*...as I'm cleaning him off, he lets his head fall back...and tells me...tells me in a very relaxed soft voice... *I'm a really great whore! The best he's ever had!*" Her tears began again, slowly running down her cheeks. "Then he tells me to get up and get my *filthy whore ass* out of his house!"

Alan moved over to her, kneeling, holding her tight as she continued to cry, this time sobbing uncontrollably.

After a while Alan had gotten a sleeping pill into Ruthie along with some warm tea and tucked her into bed. Still pissed off about how she had been humiliated by Stewart, he began to think about ways to take him out, maybe even asking Mason if he or even his bodyguards had any ideas. All Alan knew was that Stewart needed to *die!* Reaching for the phone to call Mason, it rang. Caller ID showed it was Stewart.

"What can I do for you?" Alan asked.

"From the sound of your voice, it seems I have caught you at a bad time, dear boy. Anything I can help *you* with?" Stewart said.

"No, nothing. Nothing that I can't take care of myself, Stewart."

"Try not to *bite off* something more than you can *chew*, dear boy. Others may be better at that sort of thing *than you are...*" Stewart said.

"You son of a bitch!" Alan exploded. *"I'll get your ass! Be sure of that, you bastard!"*

"I'm sure you would *like to*, but I prefer the *fairer sex*, my boy..."

Alan slammed the phone down into its cradle. That was it! No call to Mason. He was going to go see him now.

Once downstairs Alan grabbed his coat from behind the bar, rushed over to the rear glass door, unlocked it, and swung it open. It felt as if someone had hit him over his heart, full force, with a heavy round ball, moving him backward a step, knocking the wind out of him. Before he could recover, a second hit, lower to the right, forced him to turn to the left as his legs gave out, sending him falling toward the ground. Turning his head to look out the door, Alan felt something scrape across his right temple. He felt as if the right side of his face had been set on fire. Then, without a doubt, he knew: *he had just been shot three times!* Hitting the floor hard on his right side, he rolled to his back and watched the darkness slowly consume him.

The man sitting in the middle row of the minivan had fired through the open driver's side window. He reached over and picked up a slice of the deep-dish pizza on the other passenger seat. Finished chewing, he took a drink of root beer soda and pressed *number 3* on his cell phone.

"Yes, Edmond?" the man heard over his earpiece headset.

"You were right, Stewart. He came running to the door as if the building were on fire. What did you say to him?"

"I simply complimented him on his sister's wonderful *oral* talents..." Stewart said.

"Yep, that will do it every time..." He ended the call.

Picking up the slice of pizza again, he had to admit that it was better than what he was getting in *New York*. As he chewed, he wondered how he could take a few pizza pies back with him...

CHAPTER 33

Keeper of the Money Trail

The long line of apartment buildings had been built back in the early 1950s to help accommodate the returning soldiers from *World War II*. The two-, three-, and four-bedroom apartments were just what the veterans were looking for, especially the larger apartments that had two and a half bathrooms, no waiting.

As the years went on, the neighborhood along and nearby *Jeffery Boulevard*, starting at *Sixty-Seventh* Street, began to change. The wealthy men that worked in the downtown *Chicago* area had wanted a place in town, only taking the trek to their suburban homes every other weekend. So when the veterans moved out of their apartments into single family homes, the businessmen moved in. One businessman in particular, *Milton Stevens*, had been shown one of the four-bedroom apartments on an upper floor. To his surprise, the other three apartments on that same floor were also empty, and the quiet was a much-welcomed difference from the noise of downtown, so he decided to purchase them all.

Before Milton knew it, his wife had ordered walls taken down, rooms rearranged, open spaces created, until their original four-bedroom apartment had been expanded to an eight-bedroom, eleven-bathroom, full-floor home. Years later, when Milton and his wife moved to a suburban home to live out their retirement, he passed the apartment on to his middle son, *Robert Stephen Stevens*, who promptly bought the whole floor below, turning that into his at-home offices, soundproof home theater, and multipurpose game room. The handful of people he had working for him knew only code names he gave to his many clients, their accounts around the world coded the same way, protecting the actual locations of the banks and the people using them. Because of what Robert was paying *"his people,"* along with *wonderful perks*, they *all* kept their mouths shut. Robert and *his* personal lawyer were the only ones that could tie all the varied pieces together. But just to be on the safe side, Robert had an account set up with a private messenger service to deliver all his files, along with the code keys, to the local *FBI* office if he missed his weekly check-in.

Robert was in the upstairs living room, sitting on the large, medium-brown leather-and-wood sectional sofa. The copper-tinted glass-and-chrome coffee table was placed within arm's reach on the plush tan rug. There was a lone wine glass full of his favorite *Don Perion* white wine. Directly across the room, opposite the sofa, was a custom-made cabinet unit suspended on the wall. There was a large seventy-inch flat-screen TV on a single pedestal mount sitting at the end closest to the open skylight-lit dining room behind him. He loved sitting in this room because he could see from one end of the apartment to the other, no walls in between, nothing hidden, unlike what he did for his clients: *hiding all their assets*.

"You have a wonderful home here, Robert, quite modern yet extremely warm and comfortable, not cold and uninviting as some I've been in," said Stewart. He was standing at the end of the living room looking through the large front window.

"Thank you, Stewart. That is a true compliment coming from someone…*like you*. Thank you," said Robert, turning his head to the left toward him.

"*'Like me?'*… I take a small amount of *offense* to that statement, even though I understand where it comes from. I may seem somewhat…*distanced*…from a particular situation at hand, but I do have *feelings* very similar to yours. I'm just very *attentive* to details concerning my employer," he said, still staring out the front window, his back to Robert.

"Normally, criminals are taken down due to the *money trail* being followed by law enforcement. They're not clever enough to hide their *paper trail* like you do. Even looking directly at the information, you have found a way to make it…*unconnected…quite amazing!*

"You, *the keeper of the money trail,* are the most important, as well as the *most dangerous,* of employees to these organizations. Your testimony could send them away for a very long time…or keep them in line and under total…*control…?* That's why my employer wanted me to ask you to join us, somewhat helping your clients to see it our way," said Stewart.

Robert sat for a moment then leaned forward, picked up his glass, and took a sip. The *Don Perion* always tasted delicious, regardless of how *distasteful* the situation at hand was. He sat back on the sofa, still holding the wine glass, making himself comfortable, and crossed his legs.

"A very *blatant* case of old-fashioned blackmail nonetheless. I suppose if I said *no* I'd be another statistic listed in the *Chicago* violence tally…," said Robert.

"No, far from it. You see, my employer, as do I, know you are much more valuable left *alive.* Besides, you probably have safeguards in place that would release all that information in the case of your death to the local authorities, and *that* would put a serious glitch in my employer's plans," said Stewart.

"But I still wouldn't be able to just…*walk away…either,* right?"

"Well, that may be true, though harshly put. Unfortunately, we do have some *unpleasant* ways of *convincing* you to come over to our side… Not that I would have any hand with those ways. Once my employer sets on an agenda, it's usually followed to a…*conclusion…*"

Robert took another sip from his glass; knowing this was a *"no-win"* situation, he came to the only decision he could.

"Well, I guess I have *a new client…*or should I say… *'employer'?*"

Stewart finally turned and faced Robert smiling, walking toward him to the foyer.

"It will be quite an experience working with you, Robert," said Stewart.

Robert placed his glass on the table, stood, and followed him.

The man on the roof of the building across the street disman-tled his rifle as he had done hundreds of times before, placing each piece into its custom-made section. During their entire conversation, he had kept a watch on Stewart's face, waiting for the signal letting him know to shoot Robert: a nod of his head, a look to his right, and two bullets would have been in Robert's forehead. He snapped the rifle case closed and stood. As he walked away, he called and ordered a pizza from the pizzeria next to his hotel.

CHAPTER 34

Mason Is Asked a Question

Mason could not believe that Alan had been shot. With their client base, there were bound to be people pissed off about something, but enough to *shoot* him! He thought about how over the years that they were in business together, they had not only become great business partners but wonderful lovers as well. He was amazed at Alan's transformation; when he dressed as a woman, he was quite *literally* able to pass as Ruthie's younger sister.

Working out of the buildings in *Evanston*, Mason's wealthier business associates had spread the word to their *"celebrity friends,"* most of whom were still closeted. They felt the need for a higher level of privacy during their gay *"dalliances,"* politely referred to, and were very skeptical of the inner-city locations. Almost immediately, Mason saw the necessity to have a location far away from the scrutinizing eyes of the big city, settling for the much-overlooked serenity of the *plastic utopian* suburbs. So he purchased several large townhouses, remodeling each with a different theme, keeping the one corner property for himself. Now the *VIP* gay clients had a *"hideaway in plain sight"* at their disposal, some keeping a regular reservation throughout the year. Much to Mason's surprise, even a few major crime lords became frequent clients.

Last month two men had shown up on his doorstep, very well dressed. The first one introduced himself as Stewart and the second one his associate, Edmond. Last names were almost never used in his business, even though some of his clients couldn't help themselves from speaking *far* too much. Stewart had said that Alan referred him, but without a call from Alan, Mason knew he was lying. When he was asked to work for this "*Stewart*," he had politely said *no*. Stewart told him to think about his offer and he would return. He never did.

A week had passed since Alan's funeral. Mason was sitting in his favorite armchair smoking and sipping a brandy, thinking of him. His cell phone rang.

"Hello, Mason here."

"Good day, Mr. Richardson. I trust I am not disturbing your day...?" said the male voice.

"Own tha' con'trary, suh'r, just a' qui'et moment ta' ma'self... How may ah' be of ser'vace?" asked Mason.

"Quite the Southern gentleman, a rarity in this day and age. Manners are much the thing of the past. I have a proposition for you, Mr. Richardson, one that will bring you substantially more clients," said the voice.

"Mor' biz'nuss fo' mah' biz'nuss is al'ways a' good thang. But Ah' have biz'nuss part'nas..."

"Minus one...if I am not mistaken, Mr. Richardson. You have my condolences," said the voice.

Mason sat up, putting out the cigarette.

"An' jus' who *are* ya, suh'r?" said Mason angrily.

"My name is *Marc Aurell*, Mr. Richardson. You have met my associate Mr. Jamessen, who I am sure presented you with an invitation to become a member of...*our*...organization?" said Marc Aurell.

"Yes, suh'r, an' if mem'ry servas me, Ah de'clined tha' offa'! Tha' has *not* changed!" said Mason.

"I am quite sure *Alan* felt the same way...*during his last moments...*," said Marc.

"*YA'SONAVABITCH!*" screamed Mason. "*Ah'll kill ya ass!*"

"That, Mr. Richardson, is highly improbable. But I may reach out and touch someone...else...close to you. Your client base will *increase,* as well as your income, due to my previous offer. You are a *'means to an end,'* Mr. Richardson, an important component within a larger vision. Please keep that in mind when your new *clients* begin to arrive…," said Marc. The called ended.

Mason was at a loss for words, throwing his cell phone across the room, smashing it against the far wall. He jumped to his feet, both fists balled tight. He started to walk forward, took a few steps, and stopped, looking around, too angry to even think straight. Suddenly the front door bell chimed, bringing him slowly back to a calmer frame of mind. Finally he walked to the door, opened it, and saw a man dressed in a suit.

"*Uhh*…my name is Brian. Mr. Aurell referred me to you…," he said.

As the man stood outside on the landing, Mason saw across the street, sitting in a bronze-colored *Jeep Grand Cherokee*, Edmond, and it looked like he was eating a slice of pizza…

CHAPTER 35

Should Have Listened, Dante

Dante was sitting in the basement of the mom-and-pop store that was under his "*protection*." He made sure that nobody did anything inside or outside of here because he knew this place had to keep running, *neutral territory*, so to speak. If it was one thing he had learned from Rich, his pop, it was don't take over a *place of business* and run it *out of business* by not letting it *do its business!* At first he didn't understand: If this was gonna be their place, they could do what they *wanted* to in it, no worries. But after Rich went down to his summer home in *Joliet (Joliet Correctional Facility)* and the store ran out of products to sell, plus the water, gas, *and* electricity were turned off, he knew what Rich had meant. With the money his people were bringing in, he quickly got the store back on track; he even had a *"geek"* come in once a month to do the books! Once the neighborhood saw that this was a safe place to shop, the store started to turn a profit with more people coming in; they then passed the word to others on the outside. Dante wanted to keep most of it, but the *"geek"* said put a portion back into the business, upgrade, get more of a variety of items to sell. Damned if the *"geek"* wasn't right! Now with the store making it on its own, *plus* turning a profit, he could look into these other gangs disrespecting him, moving into *his territory* trying to stake a claim! He was gonna move them out, *feet first, goddammit!* Show those *other punk asses* just what *he* was about!

But right now, he had to deal with this guy, *Stewart*, talking about working *"for him,"* cut down on all this rival gang *killing!* Who the *hell* did he think he *was? Son of a bitch! Coming into my house trying to tell me what to do!* That second time he showed up, he had wanted to cap his ass so bad, but something about the way that other dude with him was looking, the vibe coming off that guy, freaked him out. He didn't act crazy, didn't even look crazy, but he knew that guy was just…*wrong!* After they left, Dante had sent one of his guys out to follow them, wanted to get some information about them… That guy never came back. He sent two more out, and those two didn't come back either! It had been a few weeks since Dante had seen Stewart, but the thought of him coming through his doors raised the hairs on the back of his neck.

The lights flickered briefly, came back on fully for a moment, then went out completely. Another damn power surge, he figured, but then someone had to have overloaded the system down the line. Dante waited until his eyes adjusted a little to the darkness before he stood up and walked toward the desk. He heard footsteps above moving around, spreading out across the store, and thought nothing of it. He heard something heavy hit the floor, a muffled *"Hey…!"* then a second sound of something heavy hitting the floor. Then it suddenly dawned on him: *the store was closed, and only his guys were upstairs.* For a moment he froze, ran to the desk, and got behind it on the floor. He pulled the .*38* automatic from his waistband, pulled the slide back, chambering a round. The light footsteps above moved steadily across the store, seeming to make sure they would cover the entire floor, finding anyone else that was up there. Only a matter of time before they got to the stairs in the back leading to the basement.

Dante knew he had to make it to the basement door going out, up a few steps, and escape down the alley. He felt for the keys in his pocket, then around the desk to his left, keeping low as he made his way in the dark. He heard the footsteps above him getting closer to the back of the store as he fumbled with the padlock on the inside gate, finally getting it open. Another heavy thud to the floor above made him jump, almost dropping the keys. He managed to get the other two locks open, swung the door in, and bolted to the steps, taking them three at a time. At ground level, he turned to the right and started a sprint to the alleyway when the first steel-jacketed bullet hit him slightly above his left pectoral muscle. So intent on running away, he literally ran into the second bullet that went lower, going through his rib cage and left lung, slowing him considerably as the third slammed into his left bicep, shattering the humerus on its way out the triceps. Spinning awkwardly to his right and falling fast, the next two shots flew over him as he landed on the ground. Quickly using his right elbow to sit up, he was hit in the right side of his neck. It tore through his carotid artery, forcing him forward as the last bullet hit and shattered his right collarbone, leaving him in a sitting position, very much dead.

As Edmond walked over to Dante, he kept his eye on the basement entrance, not knowing if anyone else was coming out. With the flash suppressor/silencer on the *M-17*, he knew no one inside could have heard anything except the muffled sound of this amateur's body and gun hitting the ground. Standing behind Dante, he touched him with the end of the suppressor and watched as the body slowly tipped over to the left, falling solidly onto the ground, upper torso black from the massive blood loss. He saw one of his own people from inside cautiously move up the basement stairs and look around the opening.

"You all done inside?" Edmond asked the man.

"Yes, sir. Only five people were inside, all *canceled*," said the man flipping his night goggles up.

"I'll make the call to Danny and let him know that he has six to pick up. The money will be put in all your accounts once I'm done with Danny," he said.

"Pull him back down to the bottom of the basement steps. Let's not have any unwanted attention, if necessary. Danny will have his cleaners with him as well."

Edmond turned and walked back to his van, hearing Dante's body being dragged down the stairs and back inside. His cell phone vibrated as he was unlocking the door; he retrieved it from his jacket and read the message. His pizza was ready, delivered to the front desk of his motel. Great! He was starved.

CHAPTER 36

Dr. Patrick L. Procter

"Not to worry, Mrs. Roberts, with the new medical procedures and instruments available today, the chance of something going wrong with your plastic surgery has dropped considerably. And *any* doctor worth his salt will lessen that chance even further," said Dr. Patrick L. Procter as he gently felt along her neck.

He could see that the fear in her eyes wasn't as prominent as when she came into his office. Just barely into her fifties, back in her day, she must have been quite a looker and really didn't look one tenth as bad as she thought, especially with her toned body and larger-than-average breast *(implants, most definitely!)*. Guys would still give her a second, even *third* look. And knowing her, they would probably be in the sack with her by nightfall. This was all an act from her to get his sympathy, in her mind only, of course. *Amazing!*

He stopped to think about how he had gotten to this point in his life… After several years out of medical school, he had finally interviewed with a small group of other plastic surgeons who had banded together after bouncing from one hospital to another. With their combined lists of clients, they all worked and covered for each other to constantly growing salaries, while really enjoying the work that they were doing. Sure, they had their ups and downs with each other, interoffice affairs, disagreements, but they all loved what they did: helping people change themselves into someone who the client thought looked better.

Patrick's personal demon was the infrequent client with diagnosed tissue rejection or later abnormal keloids, thicker-than-average scaring. The preliminary testing or ethnic types *(some people with Mediterranean lineage scarred more than others)* coupled with small surgical procedures always exposed these traits, usually starting heated arguments that always ended with, *"You're just too young to know what really can be done!"* as they stormed out the door, leaving him with the question, *"Could they possibly be right?"* Patrick researched everything he thought was relevant to plastic surgery, maybe something wasn't covered or overlooked in his schooling. He needed to stay ahead of the game in order to give them what they *thought* they wanted.

It was during lab work on new liquid solutions for skin preparation that he accidentally came across something straight out of a *"sci-fi movie."* He had used a lower-level saline solution with denatured water to first soak the recipient skin cells, weakening their structure but not killing them. Then for the donor tissue, he did just the opposite: a higher saline solution with nutrient-rich water to help strengthen the cells. But just as he was applying the two specimens together, a static charge somehow jumped between the forceps, attaching the two segments together quickly, like magnets. At first Patrick thought the experiment had failed, throwing the forceps down in anger as he walked away. After a few minutes of berating himself, the gods, and all people on the planet in general, he went back to the lab table to start again. But instead of finding two dead skin samples, the donor sample on top seemed to be getting some color back, still attached to the recipient sample below, and it looked to have grown! The first slivers he cut, when viewed under the microscope, proved that the combined sample *had* grown, actually appearing healthier. Repeating the procedure a few times, all failures, increased his frustration level until he remembered the static charge that jumped across the forceps. He added the charge, then waited and watched, totally surprised that he could see the combined sample color slowly coming back as well as growing larger. He knew he was on to something big but held off from telling his colleges until he could apply this technique to a living patient.

Patrick got the chance he had been waiting for a few weeks later. As he was closing up the office, the night duty nurses had been filled in on the new patients, his cell phone rang.

"Hey, sorry to bother you at this hour, Pat, but I've got a really bad one that just rolled in the doors...," said Larry.

He and Patrick had done an internship at Northwestern Hospital after college, both of them vowing to start their own private practice when done. Two years later, Patrick left, Larry stayed, the higher calling of helping the people in the community his main and only reason. Almost fifteen years later, Larry was still helping the community.

"And you need a plastic surgeon...? *Really?*" said Patrick.

"Yeah, I know, but this call came from the daughter's own mouth. Seems her mom was going to be a patient of yours later this month, face-lift. But they got T-boned tonight. The daughter's got several pieces of car sticking through her *and* the passenger seat. Mom's face is cut to shreds from flying glass and debris. As far as I can tell, she's gonna need skin grafts, *big time.*"

"So how'd my name come up from the daughter? With that much damage to her, I'd think she'd be out," said Patrick.

"Yeah, me too. But in some cases like this one, the person is totally conscious and rational, the bad part is that once we pull all that shit out of her, she's gone, *done!*" said Larry.

"What do you mean *she's gone...?*"

"Just that—*too much internal damage, Pat.* The organs that are keeping her alive are still intact because of the car parts' pressure on them. Once those objects are gone, the organs collapse, we can't sew them up fast enough to stop the bleeding. All we can do is deaden the pain. We knew she was dead before she came into the doors..."

Patrick couldn't believe the sinking depression he was feeling; he didn't know what he could do. When he looked up, he was standing in front of his lab down in the basement, unaware that he had even been walking.

"On my way, Larry," he said walking into his lab.

The scene at the emergency entrance had the usual ambulances and police cruisers outside with the addition of several local news vans diagonally parked, their respective *"on-the-street anchors"* doing lead-ins to the breaking story. The car that had T-boned them, an older minivan, was running from a high-end shoe store robbery, being chased by the police. When they ran a red light, locking them and the sedan together, they skidded across the street into a lamp pole. With the impact, the sedan spun to the left along the lamp pole, sending the minivan to the right along the sedan's side into a parked car. Before the occupants in the minivan could jump out, the police cruiser pinned the doors closed.

Patrick was led into the emergency triage room where the daughter had been sent. He was not ready for what he saw: she was up on a lowered gurney, still in the passenger seat. Several long, flat pieces of metal and plastic protruded just below her right breast almost extending down to her right leg. At their angle, he knew they were very close to her spine, maybe just missing a lung and her heart. The ends were sticking out a few inches past the back of the seat. Larry had a blanket draped over her right shoulder covering the objects from her sight as he examined the wounds.

"Hi…," she said in a low voice. "I'm…*Lizzie.*"

For a moment, all he could do was look at the horrific scene before his professionalism kicked in.

"Hi, Lizzie…I'm Patrick."

"Kinda…bad…*huh*?" she said. "*Sorry…*"

"No. Don't be. Not…*not your fault*, sweetheart. You…asked for me…?" he said.

She nodded slightly. "Yes. My mom…is a…*diva…extreme…*! Her face…*her face…*" she said taking a slow breath. "Can…you help…*her face…*? *Grafts…skin…mine…to her…*" She slowly turned to try and face him.

Patrick stepped forward to get closer to her line of sight. For the first time, he noticed that her face was untouched, makeup-free. A natural beauty. Someone must have cleaned her face off, checking for injuries.

"I haven't seen your mom, but I'll check and let you know immediately, Lizzie."

"I don't…I don't want…*grafts*…from her…*body…used…*," she said. "I…I won't be…*needing mine…really!*"

Patrick thought he saw the barest hint of a smile just before her eyes closed. He stepped closer and touched her forehead, moving the brown hair back as he stared at her, his head slightly angled to the right.

"*Promise…?*" her eyes still closed.

"*Promise,* Lizzie…"

Lizzie's mom's triage room was next door as Patrick left Larry to make her comfortable. She was unconscious, face bandaged from hair line to neck, the small opening for her eyes showed the lids had been scraped as well. From what he could see, if the rest of her face had suffered these small scrapes and cuts, the skin grafts would have to cover large areas just to, hopefully, smooth out the skin texture. Upper shoulders and a portion of her chest showed the same damage. After some time to heal, he could make a better assessment. He saw her paperwork on the cart next to the bed and picked the pile up to read. Maybe he could get a jump on prepping for her face surgery: *blood type, allergies, and drug reactions.* Her name hit him like an electric shock to his body: *Norma Roberts.* She had been afraid before. What would she be like now with more extensive work needed? And would his untried procedure even work? In the next few months, Patrick would not have thought that these questions would be the *least* of his worries…

CHAPTER 37

Dr. Patrick's Special Patient

Norma Roberts's daughter, Lizzie, had passed away a few minutes after Larry and his team removed the last piece of the car debris; she felt no pain with the sedative *IV* drip they had given her. Patrick, standing outside in his scrubs, fought back tears, knowing there was nothing he could have done to save her but determined to keep his promise. It had taken him and two of Larry's staff to harvest portions of skin from her face and upper shoulders, placing them into the special solution-filled trays for storage. Another week had gone by when Patrick stood by Larry as he told Norma about her daughter's passing, then took over telling her of his promise to Lizzie. The tears rolled down her cheeks as he spoke, knowing all the while her daughter wasn't going to survive the accident and surprised that Lizzie would, *could* even be able to make such a statement. No matter what, she would help him to keep that promise as well.

It would be almost three months before they could start keeping those promises.

Norma's facial skin had been prepped. Patrick applied the first section of skin graft, positioned it, and sent the charge. To his amazement, it jumped slightly then it spread, growing brighter in color as he watched. The section had to be taking blood and nutrients from direct contact with the living skin itself! He applied the second graft close to the first, leaving a small space for expansion. This time, once shocked, the edge immediately attached itself to the edge of the first section placed, becoming a hairline mark and fading as he watched. Patrick looked up, his assisting nurse wide-eyed staring at him, breathing rapidly.

"I know, Jenny, I know! This…seems to be working!" he said in a whisper.

"What seems to be working? And *how*…is it working? What have you done? What…are we doing to her?" she said, matching his whisper.

"Giving her her face back…! Giving her her face back!" Patrick looked up and took a deep breath.

"Continue…," she asked.

"Continue, Jenny…"

They worked on in silence, Jenny scared as well as amazed.

Patrick adjusted the tautness of her skin along the hairline and behind the ears after the last sections had been applied to her face. The sections applied to her shoulders and upper chest went the same way, both of them noticing a younger appearance after just a few minutes. With very little bleeding, except along the adjusted areas, Patrick decided to apply bandages to go along with *"the standard operating procedures."* The attending nurse came in and wheeled her to her recovery room, instructions for the night listed on the chart.

Outside in the rear parking lot, Jenny's hands shook as she tried to light a cigarette. Patrick walked over to help by holding her hands steady, then lit one for himself.

"I saw it, Pat…*I saw it!* But I sure as *hell* don't know *what* I *saw! Did you tell anyone else about this? The other doctors in the office?*" she asked, still trembling a bit.

"No. *No!* And I'm not *going to* until I see what the results are. If it goes south, then I'll take the hit on my own, leave the rest of them out of this, even you, Jenny! You just handed me the skin sections, nothing more, NOTHING MORE! If it goes right, then we both talk, tell the others everything. But until then, this is between us. They know I did skin grafts from her daughter. They know I did the prep of the grafts, but they don't know about the '*procedure.*' That's between us Jenny. *That's between us…!*" he said.

She looked down at the ground, blowing out a long stream of smoke, then looked back up into his eyes.

"I'm scared, Pat."

"Me too, babe. Me too. But I got your back, for sure, on this one, Jenny."

A few days later, Patrick decided it was time to take the bandages off. He was anxious to see how the grafts were healing, to know if they were still even alive. Jenny had taken over from the attending night nurse, staying by Norma's side day and night, telling the others that it was the circumstances surrounding the operation that made her care so much instead of her *real* nervousness about the outcome.

"Okay, Norma, it's unveiling time. Let's see if our promise to Lizzie has been kept and, *maybe, exceeded...,*" said Patrick.

After taking the bandages from her head and face, what he saw made him drop them to the floor, taking a step backward, eyes and mouth both wide open. Jenny, startled by his actions, quickly stepped forward for a closer look, trying to see what *he* had seen. Norma, now suddenly afraid, sat up straighter in the bed.

"What...? *What is it? What's wrong?*" she asked.

All Patrick could do was stare with his mouth still slightly open.

"*Give me a mirror! Give me a mirror, goddammit!*" she said reaching out to Jenny.

Opening the nightstand top drawer, Jenny pulled out a mirror and handed it to Norma, still wondering what Patrick had seen. Looking in the mirror, Norma saw her eyes were the same, but the forehead, cheeks, nose, even her lips...*were Lizzie's!* Her face was broader, true, but the overall look was that of her *daughter's!* She smiled, and *Lizzie's* face smiled back, and *her* eyes began to cry.

"How? *How...how* did you do this, Patrick?" she asked through tears of joy. "*How...how* did you give me *such* a *wonderful* reminder of my *precious Lizzie?*" she asked.

"It...it had to be...*all* Lizzie's doing, Norma. I think...*I think...* she just guided my hands...," he said, totally unsure of what had happened.

Jenny looked from Patrick to Norma, hoping that one of them would tell her what the *hell* was going on...!

The Monster's Warehouse

The anonymous tip had come in through the station receptionist lines, Stephanie's name mentioned specifically for the contact. It had been almost three weeks since Murray's *"The Monster's"* body had turned up in the park, out in the open for just anyone to see. That was suspect to her and Al from the start of walking the crime scene, not to mention the roughness of the corpse's hands. When was the last time Murray did any hard manual work with his hands? Al had gone out to run down a few other leads, some of Murray's people that were their *CIs (confidential informants)*, while she went online checking older reports. Maybe something would pop out that they both were missing. Then the call came in. At first Stephanie thought it was just another crazy seeing things not on this plane of existence until she saw the mention of Murray's Benz and accurate license plate number. She reached for the phone to call Al, touched the handset, but decided if this didn't pan out, she would only have wasted her time, not his too. She headed to the locker room to change into some off-road *hunting clothes…*

It was close to sunset when Stephanie drove past the front of the warehouse along *Seventy-Third* Street. Several panel trucks were parked outside, east of the main entrance, two truck trailers sitting in the loading dock. Over the entry doors and truck docks were video camera domes, regular cameras mounted midway and at the building corners. At the west end of the building was a Suburban with blacked-out windows parked at an angle where the occupants had a clear view of the front and side… She kept driving past until she got to *Central Avenue* several blocks away and made a right turn and drove up to the tree line just before the railroad tracks. Making another right, off-road now, Stephanie drove into the cover of the trees and waited until full darkness.

Before getting out of the SUV, she added two more sixteen-round clips to her shoulder holster rig, bringing the total up to six. Something in the back of her mind was telling her even those might not be enough. A moment's hesitation then she was out the door. After a few dozen yards, the terrain began to slope down, dropping more as she got closer to the edge of the rear parking lot / truck turnaround, a stone retaining wall rising up on her left. Stephanie saw typical industrial windows on the building back wall; a few were open toward the end, somewhat in shadows but still in full view of what had to be a guard shack about a hundred yards away. Sticking to the retaining wall cover, she quickly made her way to one of the open windows and looked inside. The ceiling height was easily twenty-five to thirty feet. Metal wire shelving units between the vertical I-beams held medium cardboard boxes, row after row, throughout the warehouse. A series of numbers, two rows stamped in the lower left-hand corner of each, probably their way of an inventory reference. Stephanie heard a car coming her way and stepped further back into the shadows.

The *S600 Mercedes Benz* turned the corner, its oxblood pearlized paint job shining in the rear entrance overhead lights, and stopped at the entry doors. A man got out the front passenger side and stepped back to open the rear passenger car door. A well-dressed taller, heavy-set man emerged. Stephanie knew without a doubt, not believing her eyes, that it was Murray *"The Monster"!* He opened one of the building doors and was followed inside by two other men from the Mercedes.

What the hell *was going on?* she thought.

She saw him on the ground, a big chunk blown out of his middle… *He was dead!* This was too crazy! She heard footfalls behind her, but she moved too late to miss the kick aimed at her back, catching her on the left side instead, spinning her down to the pavement. She ended up sitting on her behind. During the spin, Stephanie had pulled out her steel collapsible nightstick. The second kick, aimed at her head, was met midcalf with the steel rod as she moved to her right slightly, getting up on one knee. The man twisted to her left, screaming in pain, and landing at an awkward angle on his injured leg. Stephanie was up, jumped closer, striking him hard on the left side of his head, stopping his screaming abruptly, his now-dead weight forcing him backward to the left. He hit the ground with a thud. She was off and running to the tree line at an angle to go behind the guard shack. Hearing the door open just as she passed the corner, Stephanie continued to the rear of the shack and pressed her body flat against the wall. She could hear several men run to the man on the ground, another standing near the front of the guard shack going back in. Seconds later a pulsing, deep hum sounded, the low frequency alarm felt in her bones. She eased off the back wall, heading deeper into the trees, circling back in the direction of her car. The truck turnaround area was flooded with light now; other men had come out of the main building all crowding over the man on the ground. Three of them picked him up, making their way back to the building while the others drew their guns, fanned out, and walked toward the tree line. Moving further into the trees, Stephanie drew her gun as well, not wanting to get into a firefight but glad she had brought along the extra clips. She moved forward, parallel to the lot, keeping her eyes on the men as they entered the trees.

Now the fun begins... she thought.

She heard someone crossing a few yards behind, moving to her far right, others to her left snapping fallen branches, stopping for a moment before slowly moving again. A snap of wood close behind her made her crouch down at a wide tree trunk, scanning the darkness as her eyes adjusted. Unfortunately, she saw him just as he saw her and opened fire immediately. The bullets flew past on her right, not even close, as she returned fire, two rounds to his chest, knocking him off his feet. Turning to her right, still crouched, a second man began to run in her direction. Stephanie fired away from him, hoping that he'd take cover, but instead he broke into a zigzag pattern, firing as he ran forward. Holding her gun steady, she waited for him to run back into her sight line. The first shot caught him in the right shoulder; as he spun, the second hit upper chest, and the third his left side, twirling him to the ground. Continuing her slow arc, she fired just above the heads of the still-advancing men, hoping to slow their progress. They all dropped as bark and branches were hit, falling down in their general directions as she quickly moved forward, keeping a low profile. Fifty or sixty yards away, she heard them start to move again, this time a lot slower than before, faint footfalls further away, probably more men coming out of the main building to help in the search. The shot rang out somewhere behind her, turning instinctively to her right and moving lower; she felt the bullet skim across her right upper thigh, leaving a hot burning trail; the second missing by just inches forced her down onto her left knee. Out the corner of her eye, she had seen the muzzle flash and got off two rounds in that direction, her gun locking on an empty clip. Another shot went wide, a few feet above her head; her left hand swung up with a new clip, the empty already on the ground as the new one locked into place, slide released, and three more rounds fired.

The quiet, not lasting long, was unnerving to Stephanie. It couldn't have been five to six seconds before she heard the thud of a body hitting the ground a few yards away, then movement again from the others tracking her. Stephanie forced herself to stand, started a quick sprint, with the pain in her leg seeming to attack every nerve in her body; she knew if she stopped, she would be dead. Bullets crossed in front of her as she continued her forward run, a few almost parallel to her body on either side. In the pale light, she came upon another low retaining wall, this one made from different-size stones instead of poured concrete; it made her aware that she had lost track of where she was, no idea which direction to go for finding her car. Easing down over the low wall, the pain in her leg was not as bad but still very electric. Checking the clip in her gun, she counted two rounds left; she put that one into her cargo pants pocket and put a third full clip in. The *9 mm Glock* in her right hand began to feel heavier than usual. She had put down three men, using up two of her clips, and the three extra clips she had left would have to count to the last round. If she got out of this situation...*this craziness...alive*, she would *really* have to rethink this whole independent woman lifestyle...

CHAPTER 39

Stephanie's Fight

The soft sound of pebbles falling somewhere behind made her turn and jump to the right. The force of the bullet's path close to the base of her neck rattled her for a second, but she still sighted along the quickly fading flash of the gunman's shots. Pumping two rounds above and one to the left, she rolled easy onto her shoulder, coming up in a squatting position further along the short wall. Falling out of the shadows, the man dropped to his knees, a surprised look on his face that faded as he bent forward and tumbled down the grassy slope. She caught her breath, looking into the darkness; then she felt fingers slide across her forehead, pulling her by the hair back and up out of her squatting position. Her head was forced to the left just in time to see the other massive hand closing toward her face. Instinctively, she raised her gun, meeting his fist in the air, and pulled the trigger. Stephanie saw the bullet fly out the back of his hand as small specks of blood hit her on the right cheek. The hand instantly was blown back, causing her attacker to lose his balance on the wall behind her, forcing both of them into a sideways roll for several feet. When they settled, Stephanie on top, she didn't even stop to think as she pulled the trigger, her gun just under the man's left armpit, and shot twice. The first bullet went through, shattering his collarbone as it came out the top of his shoulder, barely missing his head. The second bullet, along the same path, shifted left and hit him behind his left ear, making his eyes bulge, then they slowly closed to a thin slit.

Stephanie was up within seconds, the dead man on the ground forgotten for now, over the low wall and running as best as she could to the tree line she had seen on her way onto the property. Hopefully, she would get some cover and breathing room to figure out her next move. She must have stumbled onto something a lot bigger than just some drug stash warehouse of a major distributor that was evident with all this armed muscle around. She ran into the trees a few yards before kneeling down behind a large trunk, trying to soften the quick inhales of her breathing. She heard a branch snap close by…

For some strange reason a scene from an old monster movie flashed into her mind, where the woman who was running through the woods, chased by the monster/vampire/bad thing, stopped behind a tree, slowly looking around the tree, only to see the monster/vampire/bad thing inches from her face. Then a scream, sickening thud, blood flying. Fade to black…

The sharp sting in Stephanie's leg brought her back to reality as she quietly chambered a round. She slowly looked around the tree, back toward the way she had run to see if someone had crept up on her.

"*Got yo' ass, bitch!*" he said as he pressed the barrel of the *Desert Eagle* into her forehead.

"You killed my boys, *bitch!* Com' on! Show me some of that fancy shit you were doin' back there! Blow *me* the *fuck away, bitch!*"

"Shut up…" the deep voice said flatly, no emotion.

Stephanie was suddenly aware of the presence behind her *(When, how did he walk up on her?)*. The gun barrel slid quickly across and off her forehead, guided by another's hand, going off with the shell casing ejecting just over her head and the gun, forced out of her attacker's hand, falling to the ground. She had heard the gunshot explosion for a second, then her world was muffled and went silent. Still looking up, she saw the long stiletto blade quickly jab into the man's throat, several times to the handle, a slight fling to her right side to discard the excess blood. The man stepped from behind her, pulling the choking gunman away, and knocked his feet out from under him as his hand on the man's chest pushed him to the ground with a bone-breaking thud. He knelt down over the man, his back to

Stephanie, and leaned over him. The man's head and upper part of his body was blocked from her view; his legs jerking frantically was all she saw, and then…they were still.

"You need to work on your *guerilla skills* a bit, you make *far* too much noise traveling about in a wooden setting," he said in a slightly deep, *DJ* type of voice.

The man stood, walked over to her, and looked down. He extended his hand to help her up, and she knew *(somehow)* he was not going to kill her. She grabbed it and was gently pulled to her feet. The man bent slightly, looking at the dark stain on her right pant leg; he gently probed inside with his index finger. She winched, not wanting to cry out, but the pain was *electric!* He felt her quick tremble, stood, and looked back into her face.

"It feels like a good chunk of flesh was blown out by the bullet. Unfortunately, that *will* leave a scar," he said.

He walked forward with her away from the tree, turned left, and headed up into the denser tree line about *forty* feet away. He moved as if he had done this type of thing many times before, almost soundlessly, making her move, *almost glide*, with him at every step. The slope up leveled off, and she could see the dark-colored Hummer backed into a clump of covering trees. Within *thirty* feet, she barely heard the engine turn over, starting remotely. When he opened the passenger side door, no interior lights came on, and the dashboard lights were softly dimmed. He easily lifted her into a sitting position, placing her into the Hummer. As she turned to look for the shoulder seat belt, their faces were less than an inch apart, and she looked deeply into his eyes, almost feeling as if she was falling into a dark, warm pool. Stephanie snapped back into reality as she heard the seat belt softly click shut; the man backed away to close her door. *What the hell was that about?* Her thoughts raced in several directions at the same time, not really knowing which one to pursue. The driver's door opened; again the interior lights didn't go on. He buckled up, shifted into gear, and pulled out all in quick, smooth movements, letting her know beyond any doubt this man was a *pro*. But why had he been following her? *How long* had he been following her to turn up just when she needed him? And above all those questions, *who the hell was he?*

"I'm taking you someplace secure where I can see how bad your leg is, do what I can for it before I take you to a hospital…" He turned and looked at her. "Because I know you have questions to ask me, Detective."

"Yes, that is *soooo* true! A *lot* of questions, especially, *how* do you know me, and what the *hell* is going on?" she said.

Looking at his profile, she suddenly had a feeling she had seen him before!

"I'll answer what I can, but for right now…*I truly apologize…*"

She felt something softly stab into her left leg, not very deep nor painful. Stephanie felt an instant warmth flood into her, falling back into the soft cushion of the seat. She was aware of the muted glow coming from the windshield… *Heads-up night vision? Military? Why…? Stephanie fell soundly asleep.*

The Hummer, without any exterior lights on, continued along the back roads away from the city.

CHAPTER 40

Stephanie Wakes Up

Stephanie was running; the gun in her hand seemed to weigh a ton. It was really tough holding it up as she continued running. Turning to take a quick look behind her, all she could see was a moving, changing darkness, slowly gaining on her. Panic kicked in, and she knew that *wasn't* a good thing. Without a clear head, she would make mistakes, deadly mistakes! She turned again looking behind; it had gotten even closer! How the *hell* did that happen? She was moving faster than she thought she could *(wishing now that she actually had the speed of a tornado!)*, but it was still closing the gap! Stephanie suddenly felt as if she had run into a huge mass of dense liquid, slowing her forward speed by half. Still in running form, she strained to keep going, knowing with every step the darkness was going to engulf her any second. She felt something touch her right arm above the elbow, flow around it, and begin to increase the pressure; it felt like…*a hand!* She was being pulled to her right, nothing she could do about it. *Caught!* But something was…*different.* Stephanie was moving faster to the right, literally being pulled off her feet. The panic was gone; a warmth came over her. This wasn't the darkness that held her; this…*was something…good.*

Stephanie lifted her right hand before she opened her eyes: it was empty, no gun. She saw a blank ceiling above her and sat up… *in a bed!* Her heart still racing, she knew she wasn't at home nor a hospital, but by the looks of things in the room, she had to be in a high-end hotel. Lifting the light cover over her, she saw the bandage on her right leg and wondered where her pants and top could be. The thought of always wearing clean underwear in case you got into an accident, like Momma always said, flashed into her mind suddenly. The least of her worries, she thought considering, and who was that guy that helped *and* drugged her? Over to her right, she saw camouflaged clothes on a chair by the window: *they looked new.* Thick socks on top of a pair of boots underneath the chair. Directly in front of her was a low dresser drawers, a large flat-screen TV sitting in the middle on top with tall lamps on either side. On her left was a closet with louvered folding doors, the entry to the room at the end opposite the dresser drawers. Lifting the cover, she swung her legs to the right, lightly touching the carpeted floor. Slowly standing, testing the strength of her bandaged leg, she felt a sharp electric pain shot through her hip as she put weight on it, quickly forcing her to shift to the left leg. Again she shifted her weight; the pain wasn't as severe this time. A few more tries and she could make it over to the chair, get into the clothes, and find out just *where the hell she was.*

"Some days I start out the same way, taking my time walking until the pain goes away. Hopefully, yours will just be tender until it heals," said the deep, familiar voice behind her at the door. It was him.

"But I take it you don't wake up in your underwear in strange surroundings either. Not to mention being drugged, *huh?*" said Stephanie not turning around.

"Yeah, you got me there, Stephanie. But don't worry, I only touched what was necessary to clean your wound and get you out of those soiled clothes."

"That's supposed to make me feel *better? Safer?*" she said.

"No. Just filling in a few gaps."

Stephanie stepped forward toward the chair, stumbled a bit, and was surprised to feel his hands on her forearm and waist, supporting her easily. How did he move so quickly and quietly? How did he know *her name?* A chill went up her spine.

"The people I work for had been following your case with these *'crime lords'* from the beginning. After the body count continued going up, they decided to send me in for a closer look."

They were at the chair. He moved the clothes with his right hand, dropped them on the floor next to the chair, left hand still holding her left arm. She felt the warmth of his arm against her back; again, that good protected feeling flowed through her as he helped her to turn and sit down. Stephanie looked up into his eyes and saw a dark coldness there, something she had never seen in a human before, making her slightly pull back. But just as quickly, she knew, beyond a doubt, that it didn't include her, would *never* include her. She saw he recognized the look on her face, but in a split second, he smiled. At that moment, for whatever reason, she trusted him with her very life. The thoughts going through her mind made her wonder at herself: *What did this man just do to her? And she still didn't know his name.*

"And just who *are* these people you work for?" asked Stephanie

"They are a group of men and women who have *'vested interest'* in pretty much every major city around the world, especially *New York, Chicago, Los Angeles,* and *London*. They force the issues for finance, housing, munitions, and technological advances, just to name a few things they have their hands *'in,'*" he said.

"Well, they seemed to have screwed up with *ISIS* and other major crazies overseas, don't you think? And what about all the bullshit that's going on here in the States? If they force issues, force *those* issues off the *goddamn maps!*" Stephanie said.

"All in due time, dear lady, all in due time..."

"And by the way, since we're having such a *pleasant conversation,* who the *hell* are you?" she said as she bent over and picked the shirt up off the floor; it was already unbuttoned.

"You can call me Carl, if you like. *'Hey you!'* will also work."

"Okay, *Carl,* if that really is your name, what next?"

The shirt was warm as if it had just come out of a dryer. Slipping her arms into the sleeves, she found it felt heavier than the camo *(camouflage)* material she had worn before. She stood a little too fast, leaning to the side, and saw him move toward her. Holding up her left hand, he stopped, but she knew he was still ready to assist if needed.

"I would say, getting some food into you for starters, after you get dressed, of course," he said.

"Room service, or do you already have something set up that will knock me out later? *After eating, of course...*," she said, looking him in the eye as she pulled up her pants, fastening them.

"You really do have a *suspicious* mind, don't you? Well, I can't blame you for that, after drugging you earlier, understandable. No, I can honestly say, I won't be doing that to you again, *promise!*" said Carl.

"Uh-huh. *And the checks are in the mail, right?*"

He smiled, and she felt it was genuine. Why, she didn't know, but he seemed to be growing on her.

Out in the living room area of the suite, a movie was playing on the flat-screen TV; she recognized it as the remake of *Total Recall*. Looking out the window, she could see other buildings in the area, a scene very similar to *Denver* with all its trees. Obviously, somewhere in a suburb but no markers to tell her which one. Carl was over to the right standing behind the small bar; he reached down and put three wrapped glasses on the countertop. Then he brought up plastic bottles of Dr. Pepper, orange and apple juice. She walked over to the bar without hesitation and took the middle wrapped glass, the bottle of orange juice. They both appeared to still be sealed, so she opened them. The juice felt cold going down and seemed to give her a slight boost of energy.

"Now that that's settled, I'll order the food. Being a detective, I'm guessing sandwiches will be okay, or did you want an actual '*sit-down*' dinner?"

"Sandwiches will be fine... You've seen too many movies about cops to think we always just eat sandwiches. We sometimes do '*sit down*' for dinner at a table, not cramped in a car or comm *(communication)* van all the time...," said Stephanie.

"Never thought you didn't. I know from experience that sandwiches are simpler and easier to handle at times," said Carl.

After her third ham, turkey, and cheese sandwich *(she couldn't believe she was that hungry!)*, she settled back on the sofa, satisfied and tired. Her internal system working to digest the food, using up her last bit of energy. Stephanie leaned forward, slower than she thought it would take, and felt even more tired than just a moment ago. Looking, up she saw Carl glancing at her, his head angled in her direction. He didn't have a drink, didn't have a plate for a sandwich. He hadn't drank or eaten *anything!* Trying to stand, all she could do was plop back onto the sofa, knowing she had been drugged again.

"You…*promised! No more…drugging me…damn you…!*" She was trying to stay awake, losing the fight rapidly.

"I *didn't* do it. It was the juice *combined* with the food, they both worked as a time-release sedative…"

"You…put it…put it in the…*food*…?" she said, eyes closed.

"No, Stephanie, my helpers, here in the hotel, *put it in the food*…," Carl said.

Stephanie slowly laid her head on the couch back…and slept.

CHAPTER 41

Patrick's Concerns Grow

After mistakenly seeing the crime scene photos of Murray *"The Monster,"* Patrick found it impossible to be around Stephanie anymore, scared that he might drop something about the cases that she didn't know, then questioning him about where he had *gotten* that information from. How did he get himself into all this mess, *with organized crime, no less?* All he had wanted to do was expand his research, further his use of the radical procedure he had lucked up on. Instead he was in knee-deep with someone he had never even *met!*

All this from one single answered telephone call…

Weeks after Norma Roberts had left his recovery room, she would call him every other day, always asking him how she could help. If he needed *anything* that she could give him or sponsor an application to. Patrick didn't miss any opportunity to have her come in for an examination, marveling at the way the skin grafts were healing, leaving the faintest of hairlines where he had pulled the skin taunt. But one day, quick to answer his cellphone, thinking it was Norma, he would take the wrong turn down that dark road with Marc Aurell.

"How are you feeling today, Norma?" asked Patrick.

"Better than she could possibly express to you, Dr. Procter, I am quite sure," said the male voice.

Startled, Patrick was momentarily at a loss for words.

"I'm sorry... *Who*, may I ask, am I speaking *with?*"

"My name is *Marc Aurell*, Dr. Procter, and I wish to aid you with furthering your breakthrough procedure in cosmetic surgery. Excellent artistry you and your assistant Jenny performed on Mrs. Roberts," he said.

"How...*how do you know about that?* I haven't even told my associates about what was done to her...!" Patrick said, getting angry.

"I know of the things that will be useful to *my* agenda, Dr. Procter. Your procedure will enable my associates to go about their varied businesses without the focused attention they are now under, while following *my* directives," said Marc.

"And if I say *no*? This is still trial-and-error as far as I'm concerned. It's only been less than a month so far with this *first* patient. Who knows what the long-term effects will be?" said Patrick.

"Spoken like a true scientist, Dr. Procter. Your research with extended results, to be discoursed among your peers, written into journals so as to receive accolades from the scientific community at large. Quite commendable, but all that is of no interest to me, because my needs for *your* services are of a more *transient nature*," said Marc.

"So if you don't care about the long-term effects of these people you have in mind for me to work on, what's the point? Why go to the time and effort?"

"The *'means to an end,'* Dr. Procter. A small part of the larger scheme of things to come. Mainly control of the smaller organizations that will be built into the base, then spread across the city, *ultimately...* But enough of *my* wants, this is what I *will* do for you, Dr. Procter: *that 'wish list' of equipment to further your research*. Expansion of your present facilities, along with the additional trained staff required to oversee that expansion, as a beginning."

"That sounds like it'll take a large sum of money, not to mention the payroll for the extra staff members. Definitely not in *my budget*, Mr. Aurell," said Patrick.

"But well within *mine*, Dr. Procter. Elements have been placed in motion as we speak," said Marc.

"Hold on, I haven't said *yes*..."

"Nor have you said *no*..."

The idea of a blank check, new equipment and facilities ran through his mind. He knew Jenny would be his number 1 confidante, really the only one he felt he could trust with all this. But until he talked it over with her, knew that she was onboard, he wasn't going to commit to anything.

"I'll have to talk it over with my head assistant before giving you a definite answer…"

"I am afraid that will not be possible, Dr. Procter. Jenny is, shall we say…*indisposed*…at the moment, perhaps for an *extended* period of time…," said Marc.

It took a few seconds for the words to sink in, and then his whole body went cold. Dropping his cell phone, he ran to his office, rushed in, and grabbed the office telephone, paging Jenny to call him at his extension. Several minutes later, the intercom beeped, and he quickly pressed the speaker phone.

"*Jenny! Where are you? Come to my office right now!*" he said.

"This is Lisa, Dr. Procter. Sorry, but Jenny hasn't been to the office in a couple of days…"

"*Where is she? Did she say anything to anyone? Has ANYONE seen her?*" he yelled.

"No, sir! Not that I know…!" said Lisa.

He turned the speaker phone off just as one of the office outside lines rang. Over the PA system he heard his name to pick up the call. He hesitated, then answered.

"She is in no *immediate* danger, Dr. Procter, nor will she be… *depending* upon your answer, of course," said Marc.

"*You son of a bitch! If you hurt her…*," said Patrick.

"*Aahhh*…ideal threats are quite similar to common opinions, Dr. Procter, a waste of breath and time."

"Okay. Okay! I'm onboard! You can let her go…"

"No, Dr. Procter. Jenny is my *assurance* that you *will* work for me. As long as you cooperate, she will be taken care of quite professionally. I will be in contact, Dr. Procter." The call ended.

It was almost four months ago since his call with Marc Aurell. A message, supposed to be from Jenny, was left on the office voice mail box saying she had to go home because of sickness in her family. Nothing else was heard from her, but Patrick was made aware, through videos of her propped up in a bed, that she was still alive. The building next-door to his office suddenly became vacant; a new health facility opened its doors there. But in the basement was the unlisted annex of his underground partnership with Marc Aurell, with Lisa taking charge of the new staff. Patrick would never find out that Lisa was the one who told Marc Aurell about his new technique, answering a website asking about new and amazing advances. She had learned the technique firsthand from her girlfriend—*Jenny*.

Patrick made his rounds, traveling between both locations, noting the improved healing times generated from his continuing research at the secret recovery rooms. The information he was compiling with the extra surgeries he was doing allowed him to do the procedures not only better but faster. Lisa, having taken the place of Jenny, proved to be a quick understudy, knowing how to do the operation as well as he did. With her knowledge of the procedure, was he even still needed? Would he be able to just walk away from all this, or would he wind up on a slab in the police morgue like half of these poor guys were destined to? And what would happen to Jenny if he did run away? Patrick shook his head, trying to shake out the violent images of what he thought they'd do to her. There was nothing he could do for either of them now.

Lisa, doing double duty just like Patrick, was standing on his left side, waiting for his instructions. He handed the follow-up patient's work the night nurses needed to do, then turned and walked away, deep in thought. After conferring with the night nurses on call, she walked down the corridor, in the auxiliary facility, to her private office. She went in and closed the door. She moved over to the rear wall and pressed two bricks in, just above her head. Lisa heard a soft *clink* as a section of the wall popped back a few inches, and she easily swung it into the hidden room. Jenny was in the bed on the left, IV drip in her left arm. She walked over, checked the medication levels, Jenny's vital signs on the monitors, then leaned over and kissed her lightly on the lips.

CHAPTER 42

Carl Alexander Henderson

Carl shook with the vibration of the Chinook helicopter as it banked to the left, dropping down toward the firebase. He looked up at the other twenty or so guys sitting on the benches, most of them with the same look of...*loss*...on their faces. How in the hell did he get here? *WHY* was he here? It was all still fuzzy, running through his head in circles, making no real sense to him at all. Did this really start with him and Phillip getting drunk, both feeling unchallenged in college and in a total drunken stupor, actually sitting outside an Air Force recruiting office waiting for it to open? He shook his head again, eyes closed tight, quickly opening them.

He thought, *Shit! Still in the helicopter!*

The Chinook continued to bank, slowed, then leveled out, continuing the decent. There was a *thump* as they touched down, then everyone looked up. The flight engineer standing at the ramp in the rear spoke into his helmet mic, hands at the ramp controls on the wall. He nodded his head up and down several times as if whomever he was talking to could see it, then pushed a button. Even over the whine of the main rotors, Carl could hear the ramp motors hum just before it began rotating down, its mating piece folding up to the ceiling. *Master Sergeant Johnson* was up on his feet, standing in the middle of the ramp as the opening grew larger, *M-16* pointing ahead. Before it got all the way to the ground, he had moved up just short of the edge, swiftly moving his head left and right, then jumping out as it hit the ground. The sarge was off to the right, still looking around before he gave them the thumbs-up and waved them out. They all stood, some slower than others, but they all managed to get into a line with their backpacks and gear, moving toward the ramp…

Carl was back at basic training, standing in line, moving past different counters, being loaded up with boots, fatigues, underwear, and caps. He was hurried into a small booth to change, his new mode of dress crisp and stiff, rushed out again into another line, given more clothes from other counters, and finally a large duffel bag to put all those new things in. Now in formation, everyone looked the same, from the short to the tall and the skinny to the fat; they were all dressed in green. Later that day they were all put through their paces. Carl thought of a continuous high school gym course, as their bodies ached and spasm with the unfamiliar routine. Several were sent home that same day; a few more were sent for psychiatric evaluations, only to learn the Air Force doctors weren't buying their sudden craziness and put them back into training. But the majority that were left actually grew leaner, more muscled…and became *soldiers*…

The first three guys made it down the ramp and out; the fourth guy who was directly in front of Carl suddenly jerked backward so hard he make Carl fall back as well into the guy behind him. The guy behind him must have seen it coming and braced for the two of them, but a few seconds later, Carl felt him shake then fall over on top of him. He was suddenly aware of gunfire, close by outside, starting as the guy on top of Carl rocked backward twice, more gunfire; he heard the sarge shouting, *"Drop! Drop!"* More gunfire, bodies hitting the deck inside the helicopter, someone screaming *"No! No!"* over and over again. Carl pushed up, rolling the guy on top of him to his left. Sitting up, he saw the bloodstains on his chest, immediately pressing hard with both hands to stop the imagined bleeding: he *was okay!* Looking down at the guy in his lap, he saw the darkened hole in the middle of his forehead just above his still-opened eyes and thought, *That could have been me, son of a bitch!*

The anger inside of him exploded as he leaned forward, getting his legs under him to stand. The guy in his lap rolled to the right, falling in between the ramp and the helicopter wall onto the ground as Carl pushed up and forward, down the ramp into the open. He caught a flash of light in his left peripheral vision, no more than 150 feet away; he twisted back and to the left, feeling the stream of air as the bullets flew by. Not looking at his *M-16*, keeping his eyes in the direction of the flash, he switched the safety off, clicked into semi-automatic swinging the rifle around, and squeezed the trigger. Five quick rounds followed by another five rounds, continuing until his magazine was empty and the bolt popped up on lock. His thumb hit the magazine release as he pulled a second magazine from his vest, left-handed, jerking the rifle down to expel the empty. As the new magazine was going in, Carl heard more rounds to his right as Master Sergeant Johnson followed his lead, shooting in the same direction. Out of nowhere, a Huey gunship flew overhead fast, both side guns opening fire into the foliage. Carl saw several people drop from the trees further back into the grass line. Two stumbled to their feet, tripping as they tried to get up and run, not seeing the gunship bank toward them, firing short burst from the outboard *M-60*s. Both of them were thrown forward, lifted off their feet, as the bullets literally tore through their bodies. The gunship got within *thirty* feet of them and sent two more burst of bullets into the prone bodies, making them jerk slightly off the ground, then hovered in place as ground personnel rushed in. A third man, close to the tree he fell from, had rolled onto his stomach, crawling to his rifle a few feet away, was stopped short as two soldiers ran up to him, one holding on point as the other kicked him in the side, flipping him over on his back. He was kicked a few more times before the soldier reached down, checking him for other weapons. Carl looked to his left as he saw Phillip cautiously walk down the ramp, *M-16* at the ready. He stopped halfway then walked over to stand next to him.

"*Welcome to sunny Vietnam, Carl,*" he said.

CHAPTER 43

Carl Goes In-Country

Carl settled in. Both he and Phillip spoke little but listened a lot. Two guys coming off the helicopter had died, one onboard tripped and broke his ankle, while three others had jumped down so hard and fast they gave themselves mild concussions. All six were sent home.

A month into his tour, he was given orders, along with thirty-five others, that they were assigned to check out an area *thirty* kilometers to the south, a prelude to setting up another firebase closer to the Viet Cong base of operations. The short time that Carl was there, he had come to realize that no one really knew *where* the Viet Cong, *"Charlie,"* was actually operating from. Some of the villages further south were hideouts for them, and some, not further away, were not. Mostly you didn't know until you were ass-deep in a firefight. Phillip and Master Sergeant Johnson—Alvin was his first name, would be part of the crew—so he knew his back would be well covered.

Two days later, they were on the two Huey troop transports flanked by two smaller gunships. Carl and Phillip, both sitting at an open door, could see a small clearing up ahead, just past the treetops. Their helicopter nosed down into the wide clearing, turning left on its center axis and descended, stopping a few feet from the ground as they all unbuckled, jumping out from both sides. Carl could see the two gunships still high over the clearing as they all sprinted to the nearest tree line. When the last man jumped out, the helicopter nosed down, tail rising high into the air as it quickly moved forward and up out of the clearing. Just as quickly the second helicopter moved in, dropping off its load then up and out like the first one. The troop transports were past the treetops, the gunships lingered for a few minutes, then they, too, were up and out of sight. Everyone was along the tree line as the commanding officer and his second-in-command crouched by the radio operator, talking, pointing at maps on the ground, checking compass bearings, then signaling for the sergeants to come over and join them. After about ten minutes, the sergeants broke off, back to their groups, letting the men know it was time to move out. Alvin came over to Carl and Phillip.

"Word is, this area should be pretty clear. We're here primarily for recon *(reconnaissance)*, but just in case, stay alert. Phillip, you got the *M-60*, so you're on point. Hook up with Dan, he's got the other *M-60*. Be warned about him though, his nickname is *Deathwish*..."

The color quickly drained from Phillip's face as he stared wide-eyed at the sarge, then turned his head toward Deathwish. Dan, down on one knee, had his *M-60* cradled in the crook of his left arm, right hand close to the trigger guard. His head panned from side to side slowly, taking in the area ahead of them.

"Let's move," said Alvin standing up, still within the tree line. He too slowly looked from side to side before moving forward, signaling to his crew to fall in line behind him.

Phillip quickly jogged over to Dan and was just a few feet away when Deathwish stood up.

"Close enough. Let's not make it too easy for them to get both of us, okay?" he said not looking in Phillip's direction, walking away further to the left.

All too soon for Phillip, they were ahead of the others by a good *twenty* yards. He fell into the slow head-panning scan and was surprised to notice little movements all around in front of them: leaves falling, animals higher up in the trees. Monkeys hiding in the trees, then quickly jumping, a short free fall to another branch, then gone again. Deathwish was to his left, about *forty* feet ahead, when he stopped, pointed forward, then pointed to the right twice, signaling Phillip to move up and further to the right. Suddenly Phillip was very aware that all sounds had stopped: *no animal or insect noises, even the leaves weren't moving, nothing at all.* The hairs stood up on the back of his neck as he saw a slight movement to his right further up into the tree line, then he and Deathwish were both fired on. His finger squeezed the trigger as he ran to the right, laying down rounds into the area of the nearest muzzle flashes. Chunks of wood from the trees within that space exploded up and out as he heard a scream, saw a body blown into the clearing, then drop. Out the corner of his left eye, he caught Deathwish running forward firing, bullets hitting the ground to his left, then he was out of sight. He could still hear the *M-60* firing deep inside the trees. Phillip ran forward, aiming higher up into the trees, not wanting to take a chance on hitting him. He could hear screams, more bodies falling to the ground. As he got closer, he saw movement ahead, took aim, but before he could fire, he saw Deathwish fall backward into the clearing, a second body coming into view on his left: *it was the radio operator!* That's who Dan was running for! Somehow he had been moving ahead before the rest of the crew had moved out! Phillip crouched low, still moving forward, and sprayed above the two men, left then right. His *M-60* clicked on locked open as he dropped down next to Deathwish, pulled the lever up to disengage the belt feed from his backpack as Deathwish slapped his own ammo belt feed onto the breach, clicking it in place, the end of his *M-60* barrel split. Locked and loaded, Phillip cut down eight more *Viet Cong* less than thirty feet away from them. He could hear the radio operator yelling out coordinates over and over again as he lay at an angle on the larger unit strapped to his back. Phillip felt Deathwish going for his side arm, unhooking it for immediate use once the backpack ammo was spent. Then to their left he saw rounds being fired into the trees. Again, from his right this time, more rounds. The *M-60* clicked on open, locked again. Dropping it, he went for his sidearm and felt a calf against his back. When he quickly looked to the side, he saw it was the sarge and the rest of the unit were behind them, all firing into the trees…

CHAPTER 44

Got to Be a Hospital...

This time the darkness was total, and strong smells stood out *(Cleaning products, disinfectants...?)*. Stephanie couldn't tell if her eyes were open or closed; it was as if nothing seemed to be working except her nose. Slowly her focus grew sharper, and she could see that it *was* nighttime outside; the room lights turned off. She was in a hospital. Carl, or his *"people,"* must have dropped her off here after knocking her out again. It was an effort to sit upright in the bed, but it seemed to clear some of the cobwebs out.

She was wearing a regulation hospital gown, surprisingly soft and warm. She had an *IV* in her left arm and a monitor clamp attached to her left index finger. A closer look at the bag showed it was simply antibiotics. Another machine was showing heart rate and blood pressure along with other readouts she didn't understand. Looking back at her right leg, she pulled up her gown. A new dressing was over the wound, slightly smaller than the one before. Slowly bending her right leg back toward her, she found it to be stiff, not as much pain but still very tender.

Stephanie's room door opened, and a nurse walked in.

"Good evening, Ms. Caldwell. My name is Robin, one of the night nurses."

Robin scanned the different monitors and *IV* bag then turned back to Stephanie.

"You're in *Christ Advocate Hospital*. And you created quite a *big mystery* for us here."

"*Mystery?* How so…?" asked Stephanie.

"Well, it seems you just *'appeared'* in one of our emergency triage beds, your gold shield lying on your stomach. And with the obvious bullet hole in your right pant leg, we immediately checked you for other wounds. Finding that the wound had already been cleaned, stitched, and dressed, we called the police. They were very relieved to know that you were here."

"*Bullet hole in my pants leg…?* I wasn't wearing…*camouflaged shirt and pants?*" she asked.

"No, ma'am. Black cargo pants, black long-sleeve sweatshirt, and black insulated hoodie. The odd part about them were, they were all freshly washed. The detective responding even said it looked as if your service weapon had been cleaned as well. Do you remember someone finding and helping you?" asked Robin.

The images of the firefight, Carl, and the hotel room all flashed through her mind, but this was information she would keep to herself, for now, until she got more answers.

"No. No. It's all kinda fuzzy, just bits and pieces of images floating in and out. Maybe when I get settled, I'll be able to focus better."

"Well, take your time, Ms. Caldwell. We'll keep you one more day before we release you to go home," said Robin.

"One *more* day…? How long have I been here?"

"Oh…sorry. This is your *second night* with us. You were found last night. If you're hungry, I can send out for something, ask one of the officers outside your room…"

"*There are officers outside my room?*" said Stephanie in surprise.

"Yes, ma'am. The other detective, Alex Smith, said that after being missing for several days and turning up shot, he wasn't going to take any chances. He asked me to call him once you were awake."

For a moment, Stephanie stared at Robin, not knowing how long it had been since she had gotten that message.

"Sorry. Sorry for staring… Yes, please, give Detective Smith a call."

Alex was standing at the closet in Stephanie's room holding her pants. They still had a faint odor of dry-cleaning chemicals, any trace elements from the crime scene long gone. He hung them back in the small closet and walked over to her bed, taking the seat by the window on her right.

"What the hell have we gotten ourselves into, Annie? And what is this *'Carl'* angle in all this? Who are these *'people'* he works for?" asked Alex.

She had filled him in on all the things she remembered, even the part about being sedated twice.

"Well, one thing is for sure. If he was out to kill you, you'd probably be dead and *still* missing. Patrick even said that the stitching done on your leg was very professional, not something done by a *trained soldier,*" said Alex.

Patrick had spoken with her frequently, but she hadn't seen him in weeks. She found it odd, somehow, that he suddenly showed up. And how did he know she was even *in* the hospital? She'd keep this to herself too.

"Whoever these people are, they obviously have a line or connection into the department, especially if they were interested in the mob boss hits from the beginning. Carl did say *Chicago* was one of their main focus areas," said Stephanie. "Maybe that's how he knew where I was when the firefight went down. We need to check out that warehouse that I saw *The Monster* at. Get my car back from over there, if it hasn't been stripped yet."

Alex gave her a puzzled look and shifted his head to the right.

"*What...?*" she looked at him puzzled as well.

"No worries about your car being stripped because it was still in the police *underground lot!* If I hadn't checked the incoming call logs, that message for you would have been missed altogether. And that's why it took us almost *three days* to track down that warehouse lead you got because you didn't leave any notes for me to follow. Yeah, it was empty, *thanks for asking.* But we did find a few rounds from different weapons, including a .9 mm," said Alex.

"No...*NO!* I parked further west, down from that warehouse, and I emptied two clips during that firefight! *What the hell?*"

"Sorry, Annie. I believe what you're saying, but the facts say different. You think Carl could have covered your tracks as well as his? And if so, *why?*" asked Alex.

"It had to have been him. Who else could it have been? As to the *why,* I don't know, I *really* don't know..."

Stephanie flipped the blankets to the right and swung her legs down to the floor, standing up. Almost instantly the sharp pain in her right thigh forced her back down to sit on the bed as she took in a quick breath and closed both eyes.

"Annie, just my opinion now, but I don't think you're gonna get too far in that open-backed gown plugged up to an *IV* and monitors...," said Alex.

She hung her head, breathing in slowly until the pain began to subside.

"Yep...you're right about that, partner. *No more free shows for you today!*" she said in a thick Asia accent. "Think you can find out when they'll be cutting me loose from this place?" Without opening her eyes she heard his footsteps quickly head to the room door.

It was another three hours before they came in to check her vitals, dress her wound, and take out the *IV* needle. With a filled prescription for *600 mg ibuprofen* and a gray adjustable metal cane, it was another *forty* minutes before she and Alex arrived in her apartment living room. She dutifully stood at the door while he went through the whole apartment and double-locked the rear door before giving her the nod that it was safe to sit down.

"I've got officers scheduled to be here, outside, around the clock, until you're back in combat fighting mode," said Alex. He opened his coat, removed a flat carry case, and handed it to her.

"I checked your weapon to make sure it was in working order, it had *already* been cleaned and oiled, and they gave you four full clips in addition to the locked-and-loaded one. Until we find out who these major players are, we *all* need to stay on our toes. Take care, Annie."

As he turned and walked away, she suddenly thought that she should hug him for being there for her but was frozen to the spot.

Stephanie stood there for a moment after the door had closed, wondering where that thought had come from, before turning and heading to her bedroom.

CHAPTER 45

It Is What You Think...

It had been just over five weeks since the firefight at *The Monster's* warehouse, and yet another crime lord had turned up dead in a public place. That made a total of six all together. This case file was expanding with leaps and bounds, she thought. Alex was doing most of the legwork now with the info tech, *Meagan Aymsworth*, keeping her up to date with the latest lab reports and data maps, making sure to copy Alex on everything, passing the messages between both of them.

Stephanie's leg was improving faster than the doctors thought, due in part to her increased exercise routine. At times, when she woke up, it was still tender and a bit stiff, but after a few minutes of walking around, the feeling returned to normal. Her captain and Alex both agreed to continue the round-the-clock police protection despite her protest of being able to take care of herself.

One night she woke from a sound sleep, senses on edge, not knowing why. Her hand immediately went to the gun under her pillow, sitting up and swinging her legs out of the bed. Stephanie quickly rounded the bed, then over in front of the dresser, crouching down looking into the hallway that was faintly lit from the living room windows. Moving over to the door of the bedroom, she took a fast look around the edge and saw a large figure slightly in shadows on the couch. The shape, much bigger than a woman, had to be a *man*. How the *hell* had he gotten past the outside police officers?

Were they even still there? Were they even still *alive?* The shape triggered something in her mind…something familiar…

"You've gotten better with your stealth movements, still not picking up your feet as you move though," said the deep radio-*DJ* voice.

She lowered her gun and walked into the hallway toward the living room. Standing at the end of the hallway, she looked to her left and saw that the front door was locked with the burglar chain fastened. Glancing over to Carl, he was relaxed, dressed all in black, looking out the window. Her right hand held the gun lowered at her side.

"And if I hadn't recognized you, would the hole in your head have been a surprise *before* or *after* you *died?*" said Stephanie.

"Obviously *before*, Stephanie. And I apologize again for drugging you, I needed to keep a distance between us for a while," Carl said, turning to look at her.

His eyes flashed as the light from the window reflected off of them. The hairs on the back of her neck stood up, and at the same time a tingle went through her body. *What the hell?*

"*And now…?*" she said lower than intended but still with an angry tone.

"*Now…?* Now I'll share with you. We work together, this case will be solved a lot sooner."

"Just like that I'm supposed to *trust* you? *After all this?* I've never been able to fully trust men, *period!* Only *one* so far, and that's my partner, Alex, simply because I need him to have my back and he hasn't let me down…*yet!* But the rest of you all promise *shit* that you *half-ass* or *not at all deliver!* I don't know a *damn* thing about you, *Carl!* What would you do in my situation? Tell me, *what?*" said Stephanie, anger in her voice.

"Valid point. I'm really not like the other men that's been in your life. *However* they've hurt you in the past is *not* what I can help you with, but I can promise you that I *won't* be joining their club," he said standing and walked over to her.

"And why the *hell* do you think men have hurt me in the *past?* How'd you come up with *that* gem?" she said looking up at him.

"Because it's present in the *sound* of your voice, Stephanie." He gently took her hand with the gun, looking down into her eyes.

Without a thought, she released it to him, and he laid it on the sofa. Stephanie, finally able to break his eye contact, turned her back to walk away and felt his left arm go around her waist. Suddenly she was aware that all she had on was a long T-shirt as he hugged her to him.

"Do you think about what a man can do *for you* then wait for it? Try thinking about what he *is* doing *with* you instead...," said Carl as he lightly kissed the right side of her neck.

She felt a small heat run through her body; her head involuntarily moved back against his chest.

"His hand isn't just on you, his hand is...*now...a part of you...*," he said, moving his right hand down along her right thigh, gently rubbing the scar from top to bottom.

As soon as he touched it, the tingle she had felt before intensified, making her softly moan. Carl kissed across the back of her neck to the left side, her head slowly bending forward as his left hand traced down her abdomen to the top of her mound, back up again under her shirt, and lay flat against her stomach. The smoothness of his hand along with the heat he generated was like nothing she had ever felt before. She pressed more intently into him, feeling his heat coming through his clothes as well as *his own* excitement!

"Because he's not doing something...*to you*...he's doing *everything...with you...*!" he whispered into her left ear.

Her body stiffened. She covered his left hand with hers over her T-shirt, her right hand tightly gripping the front of his right thigh as a multitude of bright-colored light slivers flashed rapidly behind her tightly closed eyes. The sound coming from her mouth was in short gasps, guttural—nothing she had heard nor felt before! Stephanie felt a sense of falling, floating forward, yet supported. She felt the sides of his face, her lips on his; she had turned toward him (*somehow!*), that sense of floating and moving forward all at the same time... *continuing!* The heat of their bodies joined, grew more intense as her downward motion was stopped by the softness of her bed with the surprisingly light weight of *his* body merging into *hers*...

The sun was just rising outside the bedroom window, casting a soft reddish glow into the room. She saw him looking at her through relaxed eyes, him knowing that she had experienced something totally foreign to her. Stephanie reached up toward his face, hesitated for a moment before she lightly touched him at the right temple, his skin surprisingly soft for a man, then moving down along the side of his face, along his neck and stopping on his chest.

"*What did you do to me...?*" she whispered, another wave of trembling going through her body.

Carl pulled her closer to him, her head bending down to just below his chin.

"Nothing. You...*enjoyed*...me. We...*enjoyed*...*each other.*"

"That...*this*...doesn't ever happen to *me*...with...the *other...men!* I'm usually left...*wanting*... *Why...you?* Why were you...*different?*" she asked moving back a bit to look up at him.

"*Because you heard what your inner voice was finally saying...*" He bent down to lightly kiss her lips.

Stephanie stared deeply into the darkness of his eyes and felt... *safe.*

"*And what was said...what did I miss...?*" she asked in a low voice still looking in his eyes.

"*Hearing...that you're finally safe...*" Moving even closer to him, the unusual warmth radiating from his body relaxed her even more until she had quietly drifted off to a natural sleep.

CHAPTER 46

Forest Hill Inner Office

The dual desktop monitors were showing the latest gathered information from around the world. The private linked network, connected to various intelligence agencies, listed police reports, newspaper articles, on-air news reports, drafts of magazine exposes all collected from search engines based on hundreds of key words helped *The Consortium* operate behind the scenes. *Nicole Alexia Assigani* scanned one screen then the other, highlighting information that she would look at in-depth at a later time, all synced to a smaller tablet she held in her left hand. Her counterparts throughout the world were doing exactly the same thing but more specific to their particular areas. Every third day they would video conference and coordinate information pertinent with ongoing cases to aid operatives of *The Consortium.*

The report from Carl in *Chicago* popped open in a new window on one of the screens, a case she was handling personally. More of the crime lords were turning up dead in public, and he was making headway into sources they had not been able to access remotely. This one detective, Stephanie Caldwell, seemed to be a primary focus in the case, for some odd reason, not to mention the...*attention*...that Carl was paying to her *(An old jealousy popping up...?)*. She made a mental note to check with some of the people on his support team as to how serious this *"attention"* might be. For a moment, she sat back in her chair and thought of how she had been trained, unknown to her at the time, by her father...

Maurilio Bernardo Assigani was an Italian shipping magnate. He had started out as just another hand on a fishing boat, learning the ropes through training from the veterans, in addition to his own trials and errors. By his late twenties, he had become an accomplished merchant marine but was forced to finally settle down after getting thrown from his ship during an extremely rough docking *(a drunken first mate forcibly taking control of the bridge, doing major damage to the dock as well as the ship)*, breaking his left leg and arm when he landed on what was left of the dock. During his recovery in the hospital, one of the therapists helping him to work with his leg and arm was the most beautiful woman he had ever seen. *Kamharida* (I shall not fall) *Abebi* (we asked for a girl child) *Abubakar.* She had left her home in *Nigeria* when she was only fourteen years old, knowing firsthand that her education, if at all present, would be severely limited. During her travels around Europe, she had experienced many things that strengthened her for the world but didn't make her totally cynical about life. Kamharida truly wanted to help people, and after seeing how the doctors, nurses, and the many other people on their support teams treated patients, she was hooked. So when this man, Maurilio, looked at her, she *knew* it was not just with lust but with his heart.

Their romance progressed faster than his recovery, and by the time of his release from the hospital, almost seven months later, she was carrying his child. Two additional children, the last being the birth of *Nicole*, they decided it was time to marry as well as throw themselves into his shipping business that had started from his accident settlement money. Knowing the ins and outs from his travels around the world, Maurilio called on the contacts he made and within six years owned a *multitrillion-lira* international business.

His two sons—the oldest going into medicine and the youngest starting his own construction company, as well as becoming a smart playboy about town—didn't leave them much time to see each other. But Nicole seemed to gravitate to the shipping business. At the age of twelve she began spending a lot of time at the dock offices fascinated by all that was going on. She would drop into the office when her school day ended, asking the people there questions about their jobs and how it fit into the overall functioning of the company. Annoyed but fearful of what their boss would say if they shooed her away, they reluctantly told her most of what they knew, hoping it would be too complicated for her and she would leave on her own. To their surprise, Nicole not only understood the work but offered her own way of doing things that streamlined several operations. At seventeen, she was a full-time employee, even taking online college courses in business finance and administration, becoming her father's second-in-command at twenty. Employees, as well as her father, all knew that one day she would run the company.

Late one evening, after normal office hours, she needed several active files from her father's office. She tried the door; finding it locked, she took her set of keys out, unlocked it, stepped inside. The soft hum to her left immediately caught her attention, thinking it might be his cell phone in his desk drawer. The three file cabinets on the far back wall slid forward smoothly, then stopped. She heard footsteps coming *up...from where?* Then she saw her father walk from behind the cabinets, looking at papers he held in his hands. A few steps away from the filing cabinets, they began moving back toward the wall before he looked up, complete surprise on his face as he saw her standing there at the door. They stood there forever, it seemed to her, before he headed toward her.

"With you being so much a part of my business...*our business...* it was only a matter of time that you would find out...*about this...,*" he said, nodding his head back at the cabinets.

Stunned, all Nicole could do was stare from him back to the cabinets several times.

"It's time, Nikki, that you were introduced to the other part of our business..." Maurilio reached out and took her by the left hand, leading her back to the hidden stairway.

CHAPTER 47

Information behind the Scenes

The room under Maurilio's office was a lot bigger than Nicole had expected. In her mind's eye she had seen a dimly lit room with a few filing cabinets off in a corner, old sagging sofas, a folding table or two with mix-matched folding chairs. But this space, clearly, was designed as the ultimate office. She saw a drop ceiling with fluorescent fixtures, L-shaped workstations with desk drawers and computers attended by a few people wearing headsets with boom microphones, looking at one screen then the other atop their desks, taking multiple notes on pads of paper. Further into the room, several banks of computer servers blinked with small multicolored lights as information was stored and extracted continuously. Noticing that her mouth was open and she was not breathing brought her back to reality. She quickly turned to her father.

"I know, Nikki, I know... Not anything you would have expected, I know... I apologize for not easing you into this '*other world*' more gradually, that is truly my fault, but I was torn if I even *wanted* you in this... '*other world*'...at all!" he said.

"My shipping counterparts here in Europe and the Middle East not only were moving products around the world but information, and sometimes even people that had extremely important effects on whole nations. We all saw, without the slightest hesitation, what we were doing was not only necessary but the means to help the world survive!" he said.

"Soon we had branched out into contacting key people in the police agencies, giving them information that they believed was out there but not having the trust of the informants to get it. Known and *unknown* intelligence groups reached out to test our network abilities, amazed at what we had in our files that they knew nothing of, thus began our entry into *antiterrorism*. And just last month we were approached by the *Americans*, learning of us through their overseas contacts."

Maurilio studied her face as he spoke and saw several looks of disbelief but her intent on hearing him out.

"But the danger to *you*, Father? Who protects *you?*" Nicole asked.

"A small group of ex-military Special Forces, here, around the docks. In addition to a larger squad on the military base just to the Northeast."

"How did you get the military to help you? How can you *afford to pay* for all *this?*" she asked, lowering her voice as she stepped closer to him. He saw the fear in her eyes starting to take hold, and he put his arms around her.

"There are times that the military may need to go into certain *'sensitive'* areas, areas that are not…*open*…to them, areas that a shipping company *does* have access to. A few extra shipping personnel that deliver into those areas are mostly never looked at or questioned."

Nicole looked up into his eyes, feeling the tears ready to flow.

"As far as the payments…*all* governments have *unlisted accounts*, *'black' money accounts*. They dole this money out under the table, recorded in their secret set of books, unknown to all but the agents that set them up. My counterparts and I, *all*, are now part of those *'secret accounts.'*"

Maurilio's heart felt heavy as he watched the tears roll down her cheeks, wondering what he had gotten his daughter into. He felt her arms around him tighten. Even though she had held his gaze for only a few moments, Maurilio felt it went on forever.

"Then, Papa…I guess…*I guess*…I am now part of those *accounts* as well…!" she said, burying her face into his chest, her tears flowing freely.

At first, taking on a part of the information network from her father, in addition to keeping up with the shipping business, had Nicole working late into the night, going back and forth between the two. Sometimes coordinating not only the products being shipped but the *"extra people"* who might travel with it. Very few of these special orders did she follow to the end, mostly just getting the products and people to their locations was where her involvement ended. But some, very rarely, she followed every step of the way, meeting through encrypted messages her doubles doing exactly the same thing from their end. Those people would become lifelong friends, collaborators learning together as they went over every detail of their secret dealings.

It became very personal when she met *Carl Henderson...*

CHAPTER 48

Summer Begins

Summer began with its usual anticipation of increased gang gun violence. Not to disappoint, the first few weeks had people enjoying the mild cooler nights sitting on porches, hanging out in parks, standing in front of their homes, even relaxing in cars with the windows down. None of those places proved to be off-limit *"untargeted areas."*

A young father was shot in the hand as he jumped to protect his small children with him on his front porch, bullets from a drive-by extending past the targeted group of teenagers by more than twenty feet. Several men, just outside of the circle of streetlamp light, all gunned down while trying to make a drug purchase, the sellers intentionally branching out into their rivals territory. And two lovers, embracing in the front seat of a car at the end of what they thought was a perfect date, became violence statistics. One gang, out for revenge, mistook the two lovers car for the one they were after. The police recorded, investigated all the new crime scenes brought on by the rise in temperature. The canvassed areas produced very little leads to go on; a few people stepped forward undercover of anonymity. Parents, loved ones, community groups all had their say; organized rallies went to the news media to no avail. *The investigations barely moved forward; the neighborhood code of silence remained intact.*

Terry was worried that he hadn't heard from Dante, or any of his crew, in a few days, and when he went by the *"shop,"* he saw people inside scrubbing floors and painting walls. Two medium-blue suburban SUVs were sitting out in front, the men inside of them drinking from Styrofoam cups as they scanned the streets. Terry kept driving by.

At the end of the week, he got up the nerve and drove back to the shop. This time the SUVs were gone, customers going in and out, business as usual. Terry parked and went inside. Off to his right was a new sitting area with five tables, four cushioned wooden backed chairs at each. A three-cushion sofa at the far end of the space and another across the front window both had end tables with magazine racks underneath. Several people were sitting at a few of the tables, drinking from coffee cups, reading papers, working on a laptop. A well-dressed man on the sofa, opposite the front window, lowered his newspaper, set his coffee cup down in the saucer on the end table, and stared at Terry. After a moment, he patted the cushion next to him and folded his hands in his lap. At first, Terry was pissed that this guy thought he could be *"gay,"* and his immediate instinct was to go over and beat the shit out of him, but something about the *way* he was staring at him told Terry he better see what the guy wanted. He walked over and sat down.

"Thank you for deciding on the side of curiosity, Terry. I assure you, it will be to your best interest," the man said.

"How you know me? What's this about, man?" said Terry.

"It's *about* you taking over for your friend, Dante. Hopefully you'll be able to follow directions better than him...," said the man.

Terry started to jump up, fist balled, when he felt a hand on his left shoulder stopping him, forcing him back down to the sofa. He turned quickly and saw another well-dressed man had moved his chair over in front of the end table, his hand still on his left shoulder, the pressure of something round digging into his back on the right side.

"He is my associate, his name is Edmond. That is a silenced *.32* caliber automatic...?" He leaned to the right. Edmond nodded.

"Thirty-two-caliber automatic pressed into your back. Any other sudden moves and he will shoot you, several times, then we'll have to ask someone else in your gang to work for us. My name is Stewart," he said.

"Okay. Okay! What? *What about Dante?*"

Edmond slid a manila folder along Terry's left arm, the barrel of the silencer unmoved on his back. Taking the folder and opening it, he saw colored pictures of Dante and five of his crew all in unzipped body bags, Dante's chest soaked in blood. His eyes locked on the images; all he could do was slowly shake his head from side to side. *This son of a bitch was for real!*

"I'll give you the same offer I gave to Dante: *you work for me now, and I'll pay you well for your cooperation.*"

Terry looked up, cold hatred in his stare.

"*No choice, huh, man?*" said Terry.

"Yes, yes, you do have a choice, Terry: *Work with me or join Dante*... That *is* a choice, if I'm not mistaken...?" said Stewart.

"*Yeah, man. Yeah!* What you want me to *do?*"

"Help to clean up the neighborhood, make it a...*neutral territory*...just like this shop has become," said Stewart.

"And how the *hell* do I do that, man?" said Terry, a nudge to his back with the silencer.

"I'll tell you how and when. And please, call me *Stewart*. It upsets my associate when you call me...*'man'*..." Stewart stood and walked toward the door.

Edmond leaned over Terry, closed the folder, and took it with him as he followed Stewart. Opening his right hand, Terry looked down at the puncture marks his fingernails had made in his hand, a few drops of blood beginning to flow. Without a doubt, he knew, Edmond or no Edmond, he'd piss on that son of a bitch's grave!

As they drove away from the grocery store, Stewart went through another manila folder Edmond had given him.

"Very thorough, Edmond. It's amazing that he has this many people he's close to..."

"He probably doesn't think of them as *'liabilities.'* These amateurs rarely do," said Edmond.

"True. True. Forget about his father, he obviously hasn't been close to him since he left ten years ago. Target his mother at home and grandmother in the assisted facility. When he steps out of line, eliminate the grandmother, when he goes to visit would be a good time. Then put a few holes in his mother's bedroom window…just to be on the safe side," said Stewart.

"Will do," said Edmond.

The car radio announcement turned on, letting him know he had a new text message.

"Are you hungry, Stewart?" asked Edmond.

Stewart turned and looked at him.

"Meat lovers or garbage…?"

"*Meat lovers, of course!*" said Edmond.

"Then yes, Edmond, I am hungry."

The second week in July caught the police off guard: *tips pertaining to the shootings began coming in.* Makes of cars, license plate numbers, pointing to individuals that had heard from a friend/brother/aunt/social worker *who was* behind the shots fired. Most of the people in question were caught at home asleep/high/in the toilet when the police were actually *let* into their homes by others present. A few multiple killers were *delivered* to police stations, literally pushed out of moving vehicles, bound and beaten with the weapons they used neatly tucked into their clothing. Most of the investigators decided not to look a gift horse in the mouth, finished the investigations, prosecuted the offenders, and moved on to the next case. But a few others, like Stephanie and Alex, wondered *why*…as well as some of the new local gang leaders.

CHAPTER 49

Neighborhoods Doing Police Work

Stephanie had been out of the office a total of nine weeks, being updated on the progress of the *"crime lord"* cases by Alex and Meagan. Raymond, the medical examiner, called a few times about the face-lifts, said he had something she'd have to see in his lab once she got back. Cabin fever having gotten the best of her, she ventured over to the station. Even if they weren't going to let her go out in the field, at least she could catch up on the some of the other cases she and Alex were working together.

The same old faces greeted her as she entered the building with *"Glad to see you back"* tacked onto most of them. Having heard that she was shot, the various reasons where, why, and how, not even close to what actually happened to her, left Stephanie smiling and nodding her head lamely as she made her way to her desk.

A few notes were at the base of her desk telephone, and her in-basket off to the left was way down from what she remembered when she left.

"Yeah, a couple of our cases walked in the door, solved those in a few hours. I gave several more to other detectives that had their cases delivered to them the same way," said Alex, walking up from behind, sitting down at his desk facing her.

"What's been going on since I've been out? The bad guys suddenly getting a conscience? *Hell* froze over?" she asked.

"Don't know, Annie. Something big went down, we even had a few dropped off with murder weapons *literally* strapped to them!"

"*No shit!* Really?"

"Really!" said Alex.

Stephanie saw the elevator doors open, and Raymond stepped out, walking in her direction with his head down, looking at papers in his hands.

"Hey, Ray, what ya got for me?"

"Hey, Detective. Glad to see you back. Sorry about you getting wounded...," he said with a pained look on his face.

"Occupational hazard, Ray. Comes with the territory... Did you find anything else about those face-lifts? Anything we can work with?" she asked.

"Yes...*and no*...depends on how you look at it," Ray said. "At first I thought it was extra padding, fat taken from another area of the body, as a filler, round out the face a bit. But after I took skin samples, the tissues began to separate in the solution I put them in."

"What do you mean *'separate'*...?" asked Alex.

"Just that—*they separated.* There were actually two *different* layers of skin put together. And I think the upper layer was *symbiotic*, definitely dependent on the lower layer for blood supply. I could see new capillaries in the lower layer that shouldn't have been there," said Ray.

"So explain to us dumb laymen again how this *differs* from a normal face-lift..." asked Stephanie.

"Okay. In a normal face-lift, an incision is made at the hairline, pulling the skin up and back to literally *tighten up* the sagging areas of the face, getting rid of wrinkles, jowls, sagging neck, brow lines, *whatever* the case may be, giving a younger appearance. But in these instances, donor skin was placed *on top of* the facial skin, the incision at the hairline merely done for effect."

"So how many plastic surgeons can perform this type of surgery?" asked Alex, Stephanie looked down with a troubled expression.

"That's just it, unless they've come up with a *new* procedure for *microsurgery*, this surgeon would have to be either *super skilled* or invented a *new unknown procedure*. Technology on this level...*just doesn't exist!*" said Ray.

"*Wow*...sounds like something you should be asking that boyfriend of yours, Stephanie. See if he's heard something on the *grapevine!*" said Alex.

"Yeah...," said Stephanie, looking up with one raised eyebrow. "I'll give him a call as soon as I get home...*for sure!*"

Now she was even more worried about not having heard from Patrick. *Where the hell was he?* she wondered. And with the look on Alex's face, did he know they hadn't been in touch either?

The closed-circuit cameras along the morgue corridor began to roll the images about 2:30 AM. The police officer stationed at the monitors scanning the lower levels was about to call the *IT* tech when the images returned to normal. *Power surge*, she thought, then continued her slow scan of the other monitors at her station.

The uniformed officers came in through the outside access morgue doors, the magnetic card used registering neither on any of the building security panels nor the computer logs. Opening the morgue lab doors the same way, they filed in with gurneys, each group of two going to a different crime lord refrigerated drawer, taking all six out, each body placed in a black zippered body bag. They all rolled out just as orderly and quietly as they came in, loaded the bodies into the waiting dark-gray vans, and then pulled out into the night.

The closed-circuit camera images rolled again; this time she did call the *IT* tech. Just like she thought—*power surge*. *Goddamn* new technology! She went back to scanning the monitors. It was 2:54 AM.

CHAPTER 50

Carl Goes to the Carrier

It was almost an hour before the gunships and troop transports got back to their location. The gunships, six now instead of two, were flying past them laying down rocket and gun cover fire ahead. Most of their ammo was gone by then, and out of the thirty-six men, they had lost eleven: the commanding officer, his second-in-command, the radio operator, and Sergeant Alvin among them. The other sergeant just shut down and had to be lead away from the firefight. Carl, finally giving the order to fall back, headed those left to their prearranged pickup point. Once they were all onboard the transports, Carl wondered why they had run into so many Viet Cong, something he was definitely going to ask *G2* about when they got back to the firebase.

The transports spiraled down to the landing area, and just a few feet off the ground, he saw Phillip jump off the transport in front of his and run toward the *G2* shack, full speed. *Shit!* That wasn't good! Carl was out the door of the transport running after him, a few minutes behind. When he got to the *G2* shack, he heard the gunfire and went through the door. Phillip was moving from desk to desk, shooting people as he cornered them.

"*Why?*" he screamed. "You said it was gonna be clear!" He was shooting through the top of a desk, watching the man underneath fly back on the floor, bumping into the chair.

"*What the fuck!*" he said shooting another man in the back of the head as he turned running into a wall. Several others had pushed furniture into Phillip's way, stumbled, and were crawling along the floor only to be shot at, one getting hit in the neck.

"Phillip! Stop!" said Carl.

Phillip turned faster than Carl thought he could and fired. The bullets skimmed over his left shoulder, deflecting upward off his vest as he was twisted slightly back to the right. The *M16* in Carl's right hand came up, instinctively firing, catching Phillip in the left hip, two in the vest, one to the front of his throat, and another in the center of his forehead, arcing his body off his feet onto a desktop.

For a moment, all Carl could do was stand there, looking at the lifeless body of his friend, left shoulder throbbing, wondering what had just happened. The men on the choppers had all come running at the gunfire, a few standing at the open doorway, the rest at the ready a little further back. Some of them knew they had been best friends; others saw that the shooting was justified. Carl turned without a word and walked back through the broken doorway, the soldiers parting, letting him pass. None of them knew then that they all would stay together, with a few new guys added, and Carl would become their commanding officer...

Almost two years later, Carl, now a *first lieutenant,* his crew numbering thirty men, were being flown to a waiting aircraft carrier after an intense firefight. Just as the chopper was taking off, maybe *forty feet* off the ground, a Viet Cong popped up out of the elephant grass and fired on them. Several rounds hit the cabin ceiling padding, one traveling through the back of his right leg out the front; there was no pain. Without thinking, Carl lined him up with his *Mac10,* getting off five rounds into the man's head and left shoulder; the helicopter continued its bank toward the ocean.

The choppers closed on the carrier, but instead of landing on the deck, they were directed to the flight elevators, setting off a small warning alarm in Carl's head. Maybe they wanted to get him to sick bay quicker because of his wound...*maybe?* When they touched down on the elevator, as the helicopter rotors were shut off, they started the descent, the pilot and copilot flipping control panel switches rapidly. Once on the hangar deck, he saw the second chopper coming down on the other flight elevator to his left. When he turned and looked out the windshield of the chopper, he saw at least eighty combat armed Marines loosely spread out in front of them. Carl stepped down, not sure if his leg would hold him, and maintained a grip on the seat. He relaxed a bit as he saw the gurney being rolled toward him.

The alarm in his head got louder…

Sitting in the captain's quarters, he saw two armed Marines behind him and two more outside in the gangway. Back in sickbay after the doctor had stitched up his leg, clean through and through, he was told that he'd have a slight limp maybe, but definite nerve damage that would get worse as he got older. No more combat missions for him, period. When they left sickbay, with a small bottle of high-dosage pain killers in his pocket, instead of going back to the hangar deck, his next stop would be here, the captain's quarters. The door opened behind him; he didn't turn around. The captain walked past, sitting down at the desk facing him.

"I'm gonna cut to the chase, Lieutenant, you and your crew are here because I have orders to bring you all home," he said.

"With all due respect, Captain, why straight to a carrier instead of a firebase and transport on a Chinook? Or C-130? I, *we*, can't be that important…?"

"Someone higher-up thinks *different*, Lieutenant. The other part of my orders mentioned if problems came up, *extreme prejudice* and *dumping at sea*…," said the captain, eyes tightly fixed on him.

"Clear enough?" he said.

"Clear enough…," said Carl.

"It's up to you, son…"

*****

Back on the hangar deck, as Carl walked over to his crew, he saw that they were all off the choppers and the Marines were now standing a small distance behind them. His second-in-command,

Deathwish, was squatting, *M60* resting in the crook of his left arm, right hand on top of the slide above the trigger. The rest of the crew were in equally relaxed stances, but Carl knew they were all ready to take these Marines out at his command.

"How's the leg, boss?" said Deathwish.

"Stitched and throbbing like hell, *DW*. Got the good drugs, so I'll live…for now."

"So what's the word, boss? What you wanna *do*…?" said Deathwish.

Carl saw his *Mac10* was on the deck in front of Deathwish, perpendicular, clip to the right. There was no doubt in his mind that these Marines would go down in a firefight with his crew, not because they had been stationed onboard but because *his* people *hadn't*. He looked at each one of his men then back at Deathwish.

"We're gonna *stand down*, DW. We're *all* gonna *stand down*… and go home," said Carl a bit louder so they all could hear.

For a long moment, Deathwish looked at him, then put his *M60* down on the deck. Slowly the rest of his crew began stripping their gear, placing it all on the deck as well. A few asked where the *"head"* was; others asked, *"When's dinner?"* Some lay on the deck where they were and fell fast asleep. The tension was gone out of his crew. For a change, they didn't have to be on guard or watch each other's back. They were all going home.

CHAPTER 51

At the Naval Base Stateside

It was almost three weeks before the aircraft carrier arrived in *San Diego*. Carl and his crew were never allowed off the hangar deck during their time at sea. Weapons were all confiscated as cots and other sleeping gear were brought in and the meals were at tables set up just past the helicopters hangar area. Two armed Marines stayed with each one of his men at all times, following them to the *"head"* (onboard toilet), then back to their cordoned-off space. Carl, talking to them all, Marines included, to keep the tension level as low as possible, was periodically called to the captain's quarters for updates on how his crew were handling the *"situation."* The thought that the captain's orders included *"extreme prejudice" (execute them all)* and then dispose of them overboard if they *"acted out"* never left his thoughts for a moment, keeping him on alert the majority of the trip home.

At last they had arrived and were given duffel bags for the clothes and toiletries collected on the ship. Their weapons were not returned. The large dockside door was opened. Carl and his crew were escorted by the Marines down to waiting buses on the dock, to be driven directly to the base hospital, each man to be placed into a separate private room. At dock level, before heading out toward the hospital, a Marine major walked over to Carl. He signaled for his men to load the others aboard the buses but held Carl back, waiting for them all to be out of earshot.

"Lieutenant, I thank you for keeping the men at ease, for the most part anyway. I know that took a lot out of you," said the major.

"I made a promise to myself, Major, that once they put me in charge of these men...*my crew*...I would do everything in my power to get them *all* back home. I didn't see any point in repainting part of the hangar deck *red*," said Carl.

The major twitched slightly, staring hard at Carl, knowing that he was *not* bragging, only stating a fact.

"When the *Pentagon* sent me you and your crew's stats, I didn't believe thirty-one soldiers could do *that* much...*damage, 6,747* confirmed kills...*impossible!* But then I saw you all on the hangar deck... I had *450* combat seasoned Marines onboard that ship, and after seeing them...*seeing you*...I doubted we would have been able to stop you...," said the major.

"I doubted that too, Major...," said Carl.

The blood drained from the major's face as Carl turned and walked to the waiting bus.

As the buses passed by the buildings on base, it suddenly occurred to Carl that they weren't stopping, finally ending up at the main gate. Their escort military SUV driver signed the clipboard handed to him by the gate guard, then they all proceeded past the entry, on down the road. They drove for a few minutes, making several turns until the ocean was on their left. Gradually, they curved to the right moving further inland, just a small sliver of the bluish green water still visible. Looking at his watch, Carl saw that they had traveled twenty-five minutes before coming to a halt. Another fenced entrance, this one more heavily guarded. Again the driver in the escort SUV signed the clipboard handed to him, then they drove forward.

The first thing he was aware of was that the buildings they passed by were all white brick, only numbers on the front, no names on a smaller billboard to list function/personnel of what may be going on inside. Again after several minutes' drive, they stopped at the front of a large, white building, with multiple-glass windows on the upper eight floors. Inside the large lobby, orderlies were waiting to show them to their private rooms; two bearded men seated at a small table to the right of the elevator banks, both wearing glasses, looked at file folders as the men passed them by, jotting down notes. The hairs on the back of his neck stood up, and the warning flags in his mind went flying…

Two months had gone by as far as he could tell. Every third day, they all were let out for fresh air into a vast, open landscaped "yard," a good five-minute walk to the nearest fence. He could smell the saltiness of the ocean on the mild breeze. The doctors, medical and psychiatric, came to see each one of them on a regular basis, mostly small talk, but starting a relationship with the men. By the third month, Carl was ready to go, pacing in his room, antsy from the confinement. He was standing at the window, able to see more of the water from the higher floor level, when the door opened and the nurse walked in.

"How are we doing today, Lieutenant?" she asked.

He turned, looked at her, and then turned back to the window.

"Pretty much the same, *Nurse Candis*. A bit more *'antsy'* from the confinement, but I guess that's understandable…," said Carl.

"Ooh…? Yes, I guess it is understandable, *especially* after being cooped up for a while. Is there anything I might be able to do or help you with?" she asked.

He thought for a moment, choosing his words carefully.

"No…*no*, Nurse Candis. It's simple to put into words but not something I'd want to or feel…*comfortable*…telling you. I'll just simply say, *'it's a guy thing,'* without a doubt…!"

"Oh. *Oooooh! Then I truly understand, sir!*" she said.

The click of her heels on the floor told him she was walking away slowly, toward the door, as if trying not to make any sudden moves or loud noises. He sighed when he heard the door lock and hung his head a bit lower.

Now they're locking me in…wonderful! he thought.

Turning around, to his surprise, he saw Nurse Candis still standing in the room. She had taken her cap off, tossed it on the bed, a portion of long blond hair hanging down in front. Unzipping her dress, she tossed that too on the bed. Walking toward him in white lace bra, white lace garter belt, no panties, white lace-top stockings, and five-inch white stiletto heels, all he could do was stare, suddenly becoming aware as to how *truly beautiful* she really was! How had he missed this, *missed her*, all these months? He couldn't move as she embraced him, going up on her toes to kiss him lightly on the left cheek, then over to his lips, softly licking them with her tongue as she pulled slowly away. The heat from her quickly seeped into him, taking him over as she moved them both backward to the bed, easing his head down for a deeper, wetter kiss. His nervousness was completely forgotten…

He was back in basic training on the Air Force base, sore arms hanging to his sides from all the pre-overseas shots. Now sitting in the psychiatrist office answering questions about his childhood, family members, likes, dislikes, hobbies. Was he gay, straight, engaged in bisexual play? What type of woman did he prefer…*the type of woman he preferred…! Blond! White lace underwear! White stockings! White five-inch stiletto heel shoes!*

"*Shit!*" he said out loud, sitting up in the bed.

Candis jumped beside him, moving back toward the head of the bed.

"*How did you know? HOW DID YOU FUCKIN' KNOW?*" Carl screamed at her.

"*What? KNOW WHAT? I don't know what you're talking about?*" she said, her eyes wide with fright.

"*WHY WERE YOU DRESSED LIKE THIS?*" he said, grabbing her by both arms, beginning to shake her hard for emphasis.

Carl felt the small needlelike pain on his back, just below his right shoulder. He turned and looked to the door at the orderly holding the dart gun just as the second dart hit him in the right pectoral muscle. His vision began to swim as he fell forward toward Candis. Catching him by the shoulders, she gently eased his head down toward the pillow, removing the dart from his back before laying him flat. As his eyes, still with an angry questioning look, slowly closed, he began to breathe normally.

"You know he'll have questions," said the man's voice.

"Yes, I know. All in due time. All in due time...," said the second man's voice.

Carl heard them as if he was in an echo chamber, head barely able to move, slowly looking around the room. He *wasn't* in his room, an *operating theater...maybe?* Two *IV* bags were hanging on his right, the drip line going into his right arm.

"He's awake! He can see us!" said the first man's voice.

"Yes, but not clearly. At best, he'll think it's a dream. If not, we'll just implant those thoughts, maybe erase this memory completely...we'll see later," said the second man's voice.

"He doesn't seem to be having the same reactions that the others had. Do you think it's finally working?" said the first man's voice.

"Maybe. Maybe... This one might take. Maybe...he'll be all right," said the second man's voice.

Carl began to feel very warm all over his body. Even his hair felt warm, then he quietly passed out again.

A warm breeze blew across his face, the start of a nice day outside. Carl sat up in bed, fully rested, totally aware of his surroundings. It seemed to him that everything in the room was in sharp focus; details he hadn't noticed before appeared closer than what they actually were. He swung his legs out the bed and stood up. The sharp pain in his leg caught him off guard, making him almost fall to the right, but just as quickly as it came, it was...*gone!* He could stand, even stomp his right foot without the sharp pain! He felt...*stronger.* The door to his room opened, and the nurse walked in.

"Good morning, Lieutenant. How are you today?"

"I'm fine, *Nurse Mia*. I just had a very sharp pain in my right leg, but it went away almost as soon as I felt it," he said.

"That's understandable with that type of bullet wound. Usually, nerve damage is involved, sometimes making the way for *arthritis* earlier than normal," she said, walking over to him.

Carl had always been attracted to *Asian women*, even as far back as elementary school he had thought they were extremely beautiful. Today it was as if he was seeing Nurse Mia for the first time. She gently touched his abdomen, moving him back onto the bed in a sitting position, lifting the bottom of the white boxer shorts up. She began to remove the front bandage from his wound. Her thick pony-tail, super-shiny black hair, in stark contrast against her bright white nurse's uniform made him think of his girlfriend back in college, also *Asian*. When she stood up, their eyes locked, a silent conversation taking place as they both leaned forward, stopped only by her hand on his chest, easing them slowly further apart.

"After taking care of you these past few months, I've…I've grown very close to you, Carl. But I know you'll be gone in a while, and I'll still be here, alone. Will either of us ever know…*what happens to the other?*" she asked.

He covered her hand on his chest with his, still looking into her eyes, knowing she was right. She leaned in and kissed him on the cheek.

"I'll get fresh bandages…," she said as she walked away, a small smile on her face, pleased with the performance.

Carl watched, her *sweetheart* nurse's shoes making low, squeaking sounds on the floor.

"It appears our memory 'suggestions' have taken," said the first man.

"So…he shouldn't remember the last five weeks either?" said the second man.

"No, but eventually he will, and then it'll be the devil to pay…," said the first man.

"And we're possibly looking at that devil right now…!" said the second man.

C H A P T E R   5 2

Warehouse Moving Day

Eddie had stacked five cardboard boxes on the two-wheel dolly, angled them back, then turned and headed for the panel truck at the loading dock. A bunch of other guys were doing the exact same thing, even had a few guys together stacking the boxes on skids then going around them with plastic wrap, to keep them from falling. A forklift would roll over pick up the skid and head to a trailer truck. *Big-ass operation!* His girlfriend's cousin, *Junebug*, had told her about the gig, asking if she knew anybody that wanted to help move a lot of stuff out of a warehouse. At first she was kinda suspicious, figurin' that there had to be something illegal about it, you know that word-of-mouth shit that gets people shot or killed. But when she heard that these people were paying five bills a day, she immediately told him, illegal or not, the money said it all. What her cousin *didn't* tell her was that they would be working twelve to fourteen hours a day and they couldn't go home, no choice but to stay! And with the muscle and firepower they were showing, you sure as hell didn't ask twice. They had brought in rollaway beds to sleep on and food, *lots of food*, all kinds, even lunchmeat to make sandwiches! He was pissed they took his cell phone but said nothing and went right to work. And the way they were being rushed, Eddie just knew he had gotten into something that he was gonna be looking over his shoulder for a while...*if they let him walk out of here!* He didn't like it. Nope, didn't like it, not at all...

During one of the breaks, this time they had brought in pizzas and ribs, he noticed this one brother eating a slice, leaning against the outside wall. He was tall, easy six feet or more, and well built. Something about him was kinda out of place, 'specially the way he was lookin' 'round at everything. Maybe he was one of the guards working with them to see that these ghetto niggas didn't take that *"five-finger discount,"* or maybe he was just nosy. Either way, it wasn't his business or problem. Eddie really didn't care what the hell was in these boxes; all he wanted to do was get his money and get out! The big brother had finished his slice of pizza and walked over to one of the forklifts, got on, picked up a skid, and started driving in his direction.

"Hey, the boss man wants me to get you and a few others to load this skid. Follow me and finish eating on the way. Name's *Dwayne*," he said, reaching over to shake hands.

First thing that hit Eddie was his voice. *This brother should be on radio or TV!*

"Damn, brother! You a *DJ*? If not, you should be!"

"Naw, I get that a lot though. Maybe I'll look into it..."

"Yeah, man, you should. That can be some tall dollars you get a *'list'ner base'* goin'! Easy five to six large a week!" said Eddie, popping the last bite of pizza in his mouth.

"That much, *huh?* A lot for a brother...*yeah!*"

Eddie got close to the forklift and lowered his voice. "But that's chump change to dealin', bruh," he said looking around.

"*Dealin'...?*" Dwayne leaned down closer.

"*Slingin'*, brother! This *shit* we movin', three to four large a *day!*"

"Come on, man! This ain't no *dope shit*! *You crazy!*" Dwayne said, jerking back.

"And you *stupid nigga!* We gettin' five bills a day, all we can eat, movin' boxes? What else *can* it be, *huh?* All this probably was *The Monster's* stash! Why you think we *movin' it?*" said Eddie.

"*The Monster?* He dead, man! How the *hell* he gonna move his *shit* if he *dead?* You the *stupid nigga!*" said Dwayne.

"Could be, but that don't mean his *number 2* ain't takin' over. *Look at this place!* How much *shit* is in here? *Millions? Billions?*

Somebody got this! And they *changin'* places to put the other folks off! *Believe it!*" said Eddie.

"*What y'all talkin' about?*" said the loud, stern voice behind them.

They both turned and saw a man in a long, black overcoat, unmistakable bulges under each arm.

"*Nothing, boss!*" said Eddie.

"Then keep that *nothing* to yo' *goddamn self!* Get yo' asses over to *bay number 11*, and load up that skid! *Now!*" said the man.

Eddie quickly turned and took off in a trot, not knowing where *bay number 11* was.

"To the right, *nigga! Yo' uh'tha right, nigga!*" said the man.

Eddie abruptly changed course, in the opposite direction, moving even faster.

"What the *fuck* are *you* waiting for…*Christmas? Move your ass!*"

Dwayne had looked at the man longer than he should have, turned the forklift in Eddie's direction, and moved forward after him. The man in the long, black overcoat felt the hairs on the back of his neck stand up, something about the way that big guy on the forklift had looked at him. Did his eyes really turn darker, or was that just a trick of the light? A chill ran down his spine just thinking he might have to see him again.

CHAPTER 53

Carl: Back into the Workforce

Carl had been discharged from the hospital with *"no paper"*—meaning, all his time in service was erased, not just because of what he and his crew had done over in *Viet Nam* but primarily due to his age, turning eighteen just one month after his discharge. The two APs *(Air Force police)* had walked into his room carrying regular suitcases, unpacked his duffels of military issued items, tossing those things on the floor and putting what was left into the suitcases. They handed him a brown paper bag with street clothes and shoes; even the underwear was nonmilitary issue, only saying to him, *"Put these on...now!"*

Twenty minutes later, he walked out of the bathroom dressed in civilian clothes and saw a heavyset colonel, all muscle, standing over by the window. He was easily five or six inches taller than him, hands behind his back, looking out across the base. The two APs and his luggage gone from the room.

"Son, you and your crew did a *hellava* job for your country in *Nam*. No other unit had y'all's numbers. But we missed *yo'* intel (information) son, the fact that you was *'underage'* for us is a *big-ass embarrassment!*" he said in a thick Southern accent.

"The charges they could bring us up on is a list longa then mah arm, and no matta' what you done, I'm not *'bout* to go through that shit fo' ya! Yo' choice, Juna', is simple: carry yo' ass home, or we put yo' ass in prison and forget ya there...!" He turned and looked at Carl with stern eyes, hands still behind his back.

"That's a choice...?" asked Carl.

"For y'all, son, yeah...!" the colonel said with a smile.

Carl walked over to the door and put his hand on the doorknob.

"Then...I guess I'll go home...*asshole!*" said Carl.

At first the colonel stood there, the smile slowing fading from his face. Then he seemed to move in slow motion as he charged toward him, hands coming up, outstretched in front of him. It was like he was moving in water, forcing each movement to get to him. Carl stepped to his right, his right hand, palm open, pushed against the inside of the colonel's right arm, moving it outward and up. Making a fist and bending his forearm back to his upper arm, his elbow caught the colonel in the chin then slid down hard into his throat. Seeing the colonel's eyes widen, bulging out as he swung his fist down into his midsection, he surprised himself at his own strength and speed. Equally as fast his right hand came up, palm open, he grabbed the colonel, thumb on his neck and fingers behind his left ear, and pushed his head into the wall next to the door. The drywall cracked a bit as the colonel's eyes rolled up into his head, quickly sliding down the wall, leaving a thin blood streak toward the floor. By the time he hit and settled on the tile, Carl was back opening the door. The two *AP*s looked at him then at each other.

"I guess you two are my ride and escort to the airport. Which of you has my plane ticket home?" said Carl.

The *AP* on his left reached inside his jacket and handed him the one-way ticket back to his hometown. Walking off, the *AP* on his right picked up his luggage, and they both followed him out to the waiting car.

Carl was finding it very difficult adjusting to life outside of *Viet Nam*, unsure of how to relax his guard or whom to trust, even to talk with. He remembered, only after a few days being over there, the vets had told him not to eat or drink anything handed to him by the *Vietnamese* because you couldn't tell if they had put something in it. Finely ground glass, bamboo slivers curled into spirals, feces, just to name a few things, causing sickness, internal bleeding, or even slow, painful death. Having seen children of all ages run into groups of military personnel blowing up themselves and the soldiers as soon as they made contact, these images stayed vivid in his mind. It became very evident that not knowing who was friend or foe got people killed in a guerilla war American military, and their allies were not trained to fight...*and they lost very badly*. Now, back at home, he didn't have anyone to tell him what to do or not to do, what to expect, *period!* It would literally take him months before he could sit down at the dinner table and eat with his family. And that only happened because he finally told his mother *why* he couldn't eat the food she had prepared for him or be in a *"group"* setting. After that, she made it a point that when she started to cook, she would call Carl in the kitchen to help her, just the two of them.

When Carl finally got the nerve to look for a job and go out to interviews, simply riding the bus turned into a tense ordeal for him, not knowing what straightaway or turn around a corner would result in an ambush, killing him and everyone with the misfortune of being nearby. It was so awful those first few times out that after only a few blocks, his paranoia would force him to get off, anxiously looking for a deep shadowy doorway or alley to hide in until his nerves calmed down enough so he could continue on or go back home. Fifteen months later, he finally landed a job as a construction laborer. He found he had a natural ability for reading printed floor plan sets and was able to explain those sets to his fellow laborers, making their work more efficient and faster. Soon he was made crew leader then, a few months later, crew chief, given responsibility for eighty-three men and women. Before long, he and his *"new crew"* were five weeks ahead of their schedule, most time wandering around the site doing busy work until the other subcontractors asked them for help.

When the lead architect came for a site visit, he was well aware that the reason for the project to be several months ahead of schedule was directly due to Carl's leadership and knowledge of the construction timeline, not to mention his interactions with *all* the subcontractors. After touring the site with Carl for the better part of the day, the lead architect was convinced that he was going to be his construction manager, not just for this project, but for all the future projects in their company's agenda.

The new promotion came with the condition of Carl having to be in the office, and once settled in, the first project behind him, Carl was introduced to computer drafting, enabling him to see the completed construction set of drawings on the large-size computer screen. Being in the small cubicle and darkened *CAD* drafting area greatly calmed his nerves, and he quickly advanced in using the program, going on to take the updated classes for *CAD* as soon as they were available. A year as construction manager and part-time *CAD* operator rolled by, and he had even learned to ride public transportation from home all the way to work downtown, the infrequent flashbacks making him uneasy but not enough to get off the bus anymore.

As usual, Carl had stayed late to finish a few pages of redlined markups for one of the company's projects, leaving well after dark. Stepping out of the elevator onto the ground floor lobby, his eyes were immediately drawn to the two men in suits at the end of the long information desk. Moving his eyes back to the seated guard, he saw them turn from facing him and slightly nodded to them, then looked down at the desktop. Angling toward the exit door, he slowly walked across the lobby, keeping his eyes on the two men as they moved to intercept him. Getting closer to them, the unmistakable gun bulges under their jackets stood out, so he turned and walked toward them. They both stopped, looked at each other, then back at him. At about twelve feet away, they moved their jackets to the side, clearly showing their *Federal Marshall* badges and *.38* automatic holstered pistols. Carl stopped, cocking his head a bit to the right.

"And your *point*, gentlemen...?" asked Carl.

"A clear understanding, sir," said the officer on the right.

"Are you *Carl Henderson*?" said the officer on the left.

"That was obviously already confirmed by the security guard and the photo in your upper jacket pocket."

The officers flinched, and the security guard quickly looked up, wide-eyed, and then slowly rolled her chair to her left.

"What can I do for you, officers?" Carl asked.

"The *FBI* would like to speak with you..." the officer on the left said, still holding his jacket back.

"Because of *'national security,' right…?*"

"Yes, *'national security,'* sir," said the officer on the right.

Carl stood for a moment, turned to his left, and headed for the glass exit doors. Both officers tensed, not knowing what to do as he walked away.

"Meet you at the black, four-door Crown Vic parked in front… *right?*" Carl said, walking through the doors.

Still holding their jackets back, the two officers followed him out, maintaining a slight distance.

The late-night roundups, every five or six months, would continue for the next twenty-five years. The program, started at the *San Diego* military base, would update their records on the progress of Carl and his surviving crew members *(the two days away wiped from their memories)*…until *"they"* would give Carl his first mission, conveniently removing it from his memory.

CHAPTER 54

Carl's New Running Buddy

The sun was just coming up as Carl was doing his early-morning stretches in the park. The thoughts of what had happened to him after the marshals had picked him up the other day were still a blank. Regardless of the time of year, they always showed up on a Friday evening; whether he was at work or home, they'd find him, returning him back to the place they picked him up early on Sunday morning. He always felt fine, rejuvenated really, but if his life depended on telling someone what had happened to him during those last two days, he'd be a dead man. After twenty-five years of the same routine, those days were always left blank. A few times, quick flashes of an exam room, running on a treadmill, even wearing a breathing analyzer mask popped into his mind, each time becoming quickly confused with memories of past physicals he had taken during complete medical workups. Were they actually fragmented memories from those lost days? He really couldn't tell. Standing up straight, looking ahead, he was about to put his earbuds in to listen to his *"smooth jazz"* recorded tracks when he decided to speak instead...

"I doubt an *'old man'* like me would be of that much interest to a *'young woman'* like you...unless, of course, you're just waiting for me to keel over during my morning runs...?" said Carl, turning to his left, looking at the young lady off to his side.

Bent at the waist, she quickly stood up, startled that he had noticed her staring at him.

"*Old?* You look *too* good to be an *old man!* No! *No!* I mean *fine-looking…!* S*HIT!*" she said then turned, put her head down and, sprinted away, obviously not running fast enough to hide her embarrassment.

Carl smiled as he watched her run away. He was still trying to get used to the way these younger women dressed in public: at odds with the creator of *"leggings"* and women's active sportswear, not knowing whether to hate them or praise them. In the case of the young lady who just took flight, it would definitely be the latter. Because of *how* he looked, people thought he was in his midtwenties instead of his actual late forties. Many a day, young girls would ask him what college he attended, some being so bold as to ask if he was seeing anyone special. Most times he would just smile and walk away. But a few times, depending on how forceful they confronted him, he'd say he had clothes older than them before leaving their mouths open in surprise.

But then, his suspicious mind kicked in, and he wondered why she was really staring at him. This young lady he had first noticed about a week ago, the kind of woman that would *stand out* in a room *full* of beauty contestants, too beautiful to be *natural* or *real*. She was tall, easily five feet, ten inches, with long, shiny pecan-brown hair with dark-honey blond highlights. The body of a runway model that ate on a regular basis but remained athletically toned. Her golden skin color *(not an artificial tan)* said she was of mixed-race parents. And from the sound of her voice just now, European—Spanish, probably Italian. *Curiouser and curiouser*, thought Carl. He put in his earbuds, started his *"smooth jazz"* tracks, and began his run.

Stopping a few blocks away, *Nicole Alexia Assigani* couldn't believe what she had just done! Bent over, hands just above her knees, she was breathing hard from her flat-out run. She had read Carl's bio, her researchers digging deeper into his background to uncover what the military had done to him and the men under his command; she knew it was time for him to be made aware of his past. But she wasn't prepared for the way he actually *looked*, sounded, with that deep, professional voice, making her feel like some airhead schoolgirl! A week ago, when she first came out to the park to *"see"* him up close, she was amazed at his appearance. This man *couldn't* be in his late forties! Their information had to be wrong; that first day of observation left her rooted to the spot as he started his daily run. And today when he spoke to her, the reply she gave left her no choice except to get away as fast as possible. But that wasn't her mission: Could he be persuaded to work for *The Consortium*, without the implanted mind triggers? And once he knew the truth, what would he want to do, what would he be *capable* of doing to those people responsible? To those people *around* him? All the tests he had taken over the years proved that he had been enhanced: reflexes, body, even his mind, but what about his *temperament?* Would he be prone to uncontrollable violence once he learned the truth, or could he handle it, able to channel that rage into productive energy…*working for them?* Too many questions unanswered. *Hell!* She didn't know anything about the man except for what she had read, and that didn't tell her how he *felt!* Taking a deep breath, Nicole knew she had to go back. At the least she would tell him what the military had done. At the most… *who knew for sure?* She stood, made a shape U-turn to start jogging back, and ran directly into Carl's chest!

Nicole's forearms were flat against his upper body, her hands balled into fist just above his pectoral muscles, feeling their physical contact down to her knees. His arms wrapped around her, hands flat against her lower back as they both stared into each other's eyes.

"We *really* have to stop meeting like this, people are beginning to *talk*…," he said.

Nicole was at a loss for words. She knew he had been jogging, but the warmth coming off of his body was like nothing she had ever felt before.

"I'm…sorry… Why…why are you…*so warm?*" she said, surprised at her choice of words but unable to break eye contact.

"Because I'm not *from* this planet. I think it has something to do with your *yellow sun!*" Carl said with a slight smile, holding her a bit tighter.

She opened her hands, moving them behind his neck. A feeling of comfort came over her, and she knew he could not, would not hurt her in any way. Nicole gently pulled his head down as she went up on her toes, kissing him softly on the lips. Standing back down, she looked him in the eyes again.

"*I don't know why I did that*...," she said in a low voice without embarrassment.

"I don't know why I *let* you do that...but I won't be upset...if you do it...*again*...," he said with a curious look on his face.

The second kiss lasted longer, more intimate as their embrace tightened, while other runners and bicyclers smiled at the two lovers on their way past.

CHAPTER 55

Carl's Memory Is Returned

Nicole, sitting naked in the club chair facing the window, wondered what had happened. How did she end up in this man's bed that she was sent to hire? Or worse, *kill*, if he proved to be too unstable? She heard Carl shift in the bed and turned to look at him. Lying on his right side with his eyes open, he was looking at her. That slight smile on his face again, making her feel warm and comfortable. She stood and walked over to the bed, sitting down on the edge away from him.

"Seeing that this isn't a TV soap opera or some traditional romance novel, why are you *really* here?" asked Carl.

Nicole studied his face in the fading sunlight, noting how smooth his skin was. Reaching over, she lightly touched his cheek, trailing her fingers down under his chin then sat back.

"My name is *Nicole Alexia Assigani*, and I am part of a group that helps law enforcement agencies around the world with information. Sometimes this information can't be made public, because of how it was obtained, but nonetheless still valuable to their cases. Infrequently, we find information that won't be pertinent to a *'particular case'*…but very important to a *particular group*…or *person. You* are one of those people, Carl," she said.

He raised up, propping his head up with his right hand.

"The visits by the *FBI*, I take it. I can never remember what happens to me during those days they have me," said Carl.

"Yes. Can you remember when it started?"

"A few years after I was discharged, cut loose by the military… *after Nam*…easily a good twenty-five-plus years ago," he said, memories of his two months on the *San Diego* base sharp in his mind.

"How long were you and your men at the *San Diego* base before they sent you all home?" Nicole asked.

"Maybe two months, a little bit more…*maybe*. I'm not sure. I was never told anything about my crew after I was sent home either," he said with a questioning expression on his face.

Nicole looked down at the bed before she spoke.

"You were there just over *ten months*, your men, the ones that survived…*almost a year*."

"What do you mean '*survived*'?" Carl said, sitting up fully.

Looking up quickly, Nicole was suddenly aware of her literal nakedness and beginning fear as she moved back a bit.

"You all had been…*given*…*experimental drugs*…to *enhance* you, physically, mentally, some things they were unprepared for, that happened after the treatments. Some of your men lapsed into a coma and died. A few began to age rapidly to such a degree they were dead of '*natural causes*' within a few weeks. Most of them though, their immune systems were heightened to the point that they, to this day, have never gotten sick regardless of what they were exposed to," she said, watching him even closer now.

"But you…*you and four others* went *beyond* their expectations: your aging slowed, muscle tone and mass increased, reflexes and vision tripled. Even your *night vision* was enhanced. They were finally on the verge of that so-called '*super soldier*' that all nations have wanted." She saw the anger on his face, moved back a bit more, but knew she could not stop talking…

"*And the other four like me*… Are they still being *watched*? Studied like *lab rats?*" Carl asked, hands clenched into fist.

"One, while on a base for follow-up exams, went…*berserk*… killing twenty-three soldiers before they killed him. Another was found in his apartment, overdosed. The note he left said he couldn't handle the missing time, equated it to alien abduction, and didn't want to be taken again. The third one, after *his* implanted trigger release was spoken, went to work for the *NSA* collecting information that their average team of agents usually took months to obtain."

The room fell silent; muffled outside sounds seemed to get louder as the seconds ticked by. Nicole, now totally afraid of the next questions she knew were coming, was unable to move.

"The fourth! *What about the fourth?*" Carl asked through clenched teeth.

"Unknown…*unknown*… He's been out of surveillance for several years now. A few pieces of information have surfaced…but all dead ends."

Now the last question. The one that could possibly kill her because she let her guard down. Or by some quirk of fate… *Could she kill him…?*

Don't answer. Don't answer. DON'T ANSWER! she kept repeating in her head.

"*What are MY trigger words?*" he asked, looking down at the bed, knuckles white on both hands.

She watched him, felt the tears run down her cheeks, and was compelled to speak the words regardless of the outcome.

"*Citizen Kane's secret was Rosebud.*"

If she had just spoken *"Rosebud,"* his mind would have gone into an open mode: taking in commands, performing them without question, what the military doctors said to him while doing testing. Speaking *"End Rosebud"* returned him to *"normal"* with a time delay of sixty minutes so he would be far enough away from their location without him seeing any locating landmarks of where he had been. But speaking *"Citizen Kane's secret was Rosebud"* would release all those buried memories, erasing them as they came up until they were completely gone, returning him back to normal again, all implanted triggers erased as well. But what the military doctors didn't put in their files, afraid to even mention it among themselves, was that all those memories would come flooding back *all at once*, in theory, giving them a mental overload, brain damage similar to a massive stroke, shutting them down completely. That was the military's *fail-safe* in case the memories surfaced on their own, making sure that they would not be able to testify against the military doctors. But when they tried it on the first soldier, it produced that violent reaction instead. He took forty-three rounds, the last four directly to his head, before he stayed down. The official records stated that a brain tumor went unnoticed, causing the deadly outbreak. From that point on, all subjects had unnecessary brain scans, photos included in their files, each time they were brought in for the updating exams.

That was what Nicole thought would happen, what she believed from the files. It didn't happen...

Carl's head jerked up, his mouth open in a silent scream as his right fist crashed into the wall above the headboard, denting it. Nicole was up and off the bed as Carl twisted to his left, falling to the floor hard. She sprinted around the foot of the bed toward the bedroom door, but he was up on his feet, swinging his arms wildly, catching her in the left jaw with his left fist. Rolling with the blow, she turned her right shoulder into the mattress, kicking him in the head with the heel of her left foot. Falling to his right, Carl went down on his right knee, the momentum bringing him back up flat against the wall. This time she heard the scream as he slammed his head back hard, punching a hole in the wall. Almost as if he was pulled by an unseen cord, he was flying at her on the bed, only to be met by her right foot to his face, bending his body back in an arc. With his knees still touching the edge of the bed, Nicole bounced up on the bed, turning *180* degrees as she brought her weight down behind the punch to his midsection. Carl folded, stumbled back into the wall. Looking up, he saw Nicole float off the bed, landing on her feet between his legs. Both of his arms shot backward, elbows knocking more holes in the wall, building up to hit her with both fist, but Nicole pinned him to the wall with her left forearm and body weight as she continuously punched him in the sternum with her right fist. His arms sagged, only able to punch her in the left side once. She had never been hit that hard in her life but knew if she went down now, she would die! Turning her left side away from him and planting her left foot on the floor, she hit him again as hard as she could, then brought her right knee up into his testicles. Carl's eyes bulged as he coughed blood into her face. His right arm came up fast; she blocked it with her left, bringing it down slightly before swinging her right fist up into his chin. They both rolled to her left as he twitched, slamming his face into the wall, finally sliding down to the floor. Nicole, arcing onto the bed, landed on her side, seeing spots before her eyes from the pain. She slowly lifted her head and looked down at Carl; he was still out against the wall. Trying to sit up, thinking she had to get out while she could, the spots in front of her eyes grew brighter until they faded to black.

Nicole felt the warmth on her face then the dull, tender ache in her left side. Obviously, she wasn't dead if she still hurt, but then, with some of the things she had done, this *could* be hell. Opening one eye, she saw she wasn't in Carl's apartment anymore, nor was she in a hospital. *Of course...!* After not checking in, her people would have come looking for her. She had to blush, thinking of what whomever had found them thought, seeing them both naked and battered in the bedroom. This would definitely take some time to live down. Taking a while to dress, she finally made her way downstairs. One of her assistants, *Eduardo*, was waiting in the common area.

"*Buon giorno, bella!* Are you sure you should be up and around, Nikki?" he asked gently hugging her, kissing her on the cheek.

"Still a little tender, Eddie, but able to function," she said.

"That was some...*event*...you *both* went through...!" She dropped her head a bit, hoping her cheeks weren't blushing red too brightly.

"Yes! Unfortunately, we need to dig into those trigger words a little more. It seems when I said the phrase to bring his memories back, it made him go crazy. We missed something, we had to have...," she said mentally going over her notes.

"Were you able to recover him...*safely?*" she asked. "I felt badly about what I had to do to him, but I think if I hadn't, you would be sending condolences to my parents..."

"He appears to be well. I mean *very well!* As soon as he regained consciousness, he asked if you were okay, even though he himself was badly injured," said Eduardo.

"Really? Which room is he in upstairs? Can I see him?" she asked.

"Unbelievably, Nikki, he is *downstairs*, in the exercise room this moment! *Amazing!*" he said.

She looked at him with a puzzled expression. Knowing what she had done to him, how could he be *exercising?* Slowly turning, she made her way to the stairs, going down faster than she should, feeling the pain grow in her side. As she neared the exercise room, she could hear the weights on the wall-mounted arm pulls clinking together rhythmically. Nicole stopped at the open doors to catch her breath and peeked around through the opening.

His back to the door, Carl was sitting on the workout bench, the weights set for *two hundred pounds*. How could he be lifting that much weight after being hit repeatedly in the sternum? Let alone what she had done with her knee! The weights clanked to a stop, and he leaned forward, taking deep breathes. He reached for a towel and dried his face.

"I'm having a tough time getting up the nerve to stay here, not to mention ever looking you in the face again... I hurt you, Ms. Assigani. *I can never apologize to you enough!*" he said.

Startled, she stepped into the room, not knowing if he sensed or heard her coming.

"I heard you, and *no*, I don't read minds. It seems the older I get, the more *acute* my hearing becomes. I can sense people around me at some distance, but that really works better outdoors."

"I let *my* guard down, Carl. After what...*happened*...between us, I didn't think you could ever hurt me, nor I, you...," she said walking into the room further. "But those doctors...who did this to you...probably didn't know it all either." Now she was standing directly behind him.

"I remember it *all*, Ms. Assigani—the labs, the infusions, and the way the drugs made me feel when I started...*changing*..."

She touched his shoulder, the warmth from him that she felt in the park flowed into her hand. Bending down, unable to stop herself, she wrapped her arms around his neck and kissed him lightly on the cheek. Nicole stepped around in front of him, hesitated for a moment, then sat down on his lap. Carl hesitated, fighting the urge to gently move her away and leave the room. When she laid her head on his shoulder, snuggling close to his chin, he slowly folded his arms around her, careful not to press down on her left side.

"Promise me you'll *never* go out into the field again, Ms. Assigani… Leave that to the expendable ones…*like me*," he said. He felt her kiss him lightly on the neck.

"I'll stay out of the field if you call me *Nikki*. And you are *not* expendable, *bella*. You *never* will be…*not to me*," she said.

Feeling the warmth of him all over her body, she drifted off to sleep.

Eduardo turned the monitor off, satisfied that she would be in good hands around Carl. But deep down inside, he knew they would one day have to deal with that *"fourth subject,"* and for now he would keep his identity…*and location*…out of the stored database.

CHAPTER 56

Captain's Tension at the Station

Captain Donaldson looked at the video records for the fourth time, seeing nothing that gave him any clue as to how six bodies had walked out of his morgue in the middle of the night. Stewart had called him at home, several days ago, letting him know that his *boss* wanted to take the crime lord bodies out of the station. They had given the appearance of internal tensions for their respective businesses, a violent control shift for whatever the reasons, but now it was time to get rid of the evidence, not let his detectives or medical examiner get too close to what actually happened. The cover story of *Feds* moving onto the investigation was in the works. They needed to move all the accumulated files, information collected, including the bodies, to their labs at Quantico. Obviously, once out of the station doors, everything would disappear, no one the wiser.

But now, when he got the go-ahead for the transfer to happen later on today, he had made it a point to check on the things to go firsthand. The blood drained from his face when he couldn't find the bodies! If Stewart's people were responsible, he would have been told. He would have watched as they were all taken out the doors, then he would have signed off on the transfer. Now he was afraid to even contact Stewart, having heard what happened to those people that screwed up...

"Captain, you have a call on line 1," said the voice over his desk telephone intercom.

"Can you take a message please, Kelly...," he said.

"Sorry, sir. He said it was *Commissioner Matheson*," said Kelly. Without hesitation, he picked up the receiver.

"Captain Donaldson, sir. How may I help you, sir?" he said.

"How professional, Captain Donaldson. Have you uncovered the methods used to extract the crime lord remains from your facility?" said the male voice.

"*What...? How did you know...?*"

"I am one that does not appreciate surprises, Captain Donaldson. I pay quite well to stay informed. I take it that your perusal of last evening's video recordings have yielded nothing of consequence?" said the male voice.

"No. No, nothing that I can see... I'll have my *IT* tech go over it in closer detail," said Donaldson.

"That will not be necessary. My technicians have just this moment received a duplicate file. Your *inept* services will no longer be required," said the male voice.

"*Inept? INEPT? You don't even know me!*" screamed Donaldson.

"*Nor you...I.* Yet you have admitted to a '*voice*' over the telephone of losing pertinent evidence in several major murder investigations...? Good day, Captain Donaldson." The call ended.

For a moment all he could do was sit still, holding the telephone. He had no idea with whom he had just spoken or even if he had been recorded. Whomever it was knew a lot more than he did.

Hanging up the receiver, he turned off his computer. Captain Donaldson leaned back in his chair.

Time to go, was all that popped into his mind. He stood and headed for the door.

"Kelly, I'm heading downtown for the rest of the day. If you need me, you can call me on my cell," he said as he passed her desk.

Captain Donaldson, down in the garage, unlocked the driver's side door of the Ford Taurus. He thought for a moment then turned and went to open the trunk. He took off his uniform jacket, folded it, put it in off to the right side, and reached for the bulletproof vest. Putting his head through the opening, standing up, and flipping the vest down, he thought he had caught the vest on the edge of the trunk lid until he felt the burning sensation passing through his body on the right side. *He had just been shot!* The gloved hand, holding him by his shirt collar, held the back of the bulletproof vest up, the silenced barrel of the gun sliding up to the middle of his back, firing again. Quickly moving up to just under his left shoulder blade, firing again. All the bullets hitting the front inside of the vest as they exited dropped into the trunk of the car. Donaldson's lifeless body tipped forward into the trunk, headfirst, landing hard. Edmond grabbed his legs, bending them up, then inside, as he brought the lid softly down to close. Taking the keys from the lock, he calmly walked to the driver's side door, got in, and drove out of the police station garage.

CHAPTER 57

Detailing the Unknown

The *IT* tech Nicole had placed in Stephanie's police station had written the program that allowed Eduardo and his people access to the morgue without a trace, erasing itself after they left. The bodies, once loaded into Danny's van, were delivered to the airport where a waiting *Consortium* jet flew them to *New York*. Her medical and science personnel were running test on them almost from the moment they were brought into the facility. Finding out how this plastic surgery was done would definitely lead to advances in medical science but also new ways to help their people get into other organizations and cover up the sudden disappearance of those individuals necessary to *The Consortium*.

Nicole had been studying the dossier on the events going on in *Chicago*, the amounts of cash and payouts moving about were well hidden but after a while brought to the forefront by her forensic accountants. *Robert Stevens* was extremely good at manipulating accounts, setting up *almost* totally legitimate businesses that funneled into existing companies. Some of the layers went as far down as ten or eleven branches from a parent enterprise before exposing a relative or associate of a known crime lord. But this case was very different. Usually, within a few months of *The Consortium*'s investigations, no more than five or six, they'd have several leads pointing to who started what and when. This case, the money trails were from multiple sources, information streaming out of a suburban law office directly into multiple sources, but *no one, no name,* except *Stewart Jamessen* popped up. His track record showed that he had the brains to put something like this together, even the *"persuasion techniques"* to keep the people in line, but *not* the *cash flow.* Tens of millions had been provided, even more millions coming in from the organizations *"he"* already controlled, being laundered by Robert. Someone else was pulling his string, but to what end? Control crime on the *North* and *South* sides? Control the city? So far the gun violence in *Chicago* dropped by *17 percent* in the past eight months, and gang members *(as well as their locations!)* were being handed over to the police almost as soon as the crimes took place! There was a larger agenda here, and these crime lord killings were definitely a major part of it. Her desk telephone rang and went to hands-free answer.

"Hello, Ms. Nikki, this is Milo in the lab," said the male voice. "So far, it appears donor skin has been placed over the recipient skin, creating a symbiotic union," he said.

"Is this something you can *recreate*? Or is this technology beyond our ability at this time?" she asked.

"At this time, *no.* The bonding agent, even the microsurgery are techniques unknown to me or my colleagues here," Milo said.

"But you *are* sure of the microsurgery aspect? *A symbiotic union?*" she asked.

The dual monitors on her desk came to life. The left monitor had several open windows showing skin samples in various magnifications, the right one displayed referenced notes to the open windows describing what she was seeing. One open window on the left monitor caught her eye.

"Are those *capillaries*…?" Nicole asked surprised.

"*Yes! Che grande!* (How amazing!) Whoever did this is a *genius* or came upon this unexpectedly…! Either way…*che grande!*" said Milo.

"Yes, Milo, it *is amazing!* I'll make a call and ask that this be looked into. *Ciao, Milo,*" said Nicole. The call ended.

Looking at the open windows and reading the notes increased her determination to learn all she could about how this plastic surgery took place. Without turning her attention from the monitor, she spoke aloud, *"Call Carl, cell phone."*

His cell phone only rang twice before he answered.

"*Ciao, bella...* (Hello, dear one)," said Carl. His voice still gave her a warm feeling, thinking of things past...

"*Ciao, bella...*how *are* you?" she asked.

"Well, Nikki, well. What do I owe this pleasure to?"

"That is good, Carl. I'm pleased. I was looking at the lab reports, the plastic surgery in detail. Are you aware?" she asked.

"Yes, I was sent the audio-video from the lab here and found it very interesting," he said.

"Any thoughts? Any possible leads you may look into?"

"A few... I have our people running down some things that I found...*odd*... Maybe ask a question or two to the detective, get her thoughts on this as well," he said.

"This technology is unknown, quite unheard of too. The people...*or person*...responsible for it should be *invited* here for an interview. We would truly like to hear what they have to say."

"Understood, dear lady. I'll put that on the top of my *'to do'* list. In the meantime, get up and walk away from those monitors on your desk. They can't be good for your eyes!" he said.

She could almost see the smile on his face and smiled to herself.

"Thank you, *mio amore* (my love), I will. *Ciao*," said Nicole. The call ended.

She had faith that Carl would find the surgeon and bring him, *or her*, here. For a moment she was saddened because she knew that whomever that person might be, they would be here a very long time...

CHAPTER 58

Marc Aurell Has Questions

After the telephone conversation in Marc Aurell's borrowed offices, Stewart had begun wondering who he really was. Not meeting his employer in person was something that he had never experienced before, *very much* out of the so-called *ordinary* criminal protocol. The few calls he received from Marc Aurell weren't long enough for him to trace but long enough for a voice analysis. Hearing the man in the office posing as Marc and then hearing the voice over the office loudspeakers was *too* exact a match—the telephone voice obviously synthesized to match the living person. His cell phone rang.

"You may not be aware, Mr. Jamessen, that the duplicate crime lord bodies have been removed from the police facilities…?" said the voice of Marc Aurell.

"No, I had not been made aware of that information, Mr. Aurell. Is there anything that will help me trace their whereabouts?"

"Unfortunately, no. Review of the video surveillance provides only images of empty corridors and vacant outside loading areas," said Marc.

"*That* would appear to be evidence of *deliberate* erasure or the cameras being paused…?" said Stewart.

"A possibility, Mr. Jamessen. Another conclusion, more so to the point, may be the placement of a mole *within* the facility," said Marc.

Stewart began to wonder about Marc Aurell's paranoia being raised again.

"Why, let alone *who*, would have the resources to accomplish something like that?" he asked.

"There are organizations in the world that...*observe*...certain forms of activities that may not be to the benefit of the public or law enforcement agencies. What I...*we*...are in the process of engaging upon truly falls under that, as well as their, scrutiny," said Marc. "I surmise, our crime lord duplicates may be under examination, as we speak, by one such organization."

Stewart had heard rumors about secret or shadow organizations that were well funded and seemingly untraceable. Maybe Marc wasn't that paranoid after all...

"*Soooo*...our doctor may be in jeopardy? And if so, is he...*expendable?*" asked Stewart.

"*Somewhat* in jeopardy at the moment, most *definitely expendable* for the duration," said Marc. "For the present, we will continue our agenda. There *is* a second person that is aware of the doctor's procedure to step into his place, if necessary. I will have someone look into the possibility of a mole and, if so, deal with that as need be," Marc said.

"Then I will leave that to you, Mr. Aurell," said Stewart. The call ended.

He stopped the voice analysis program running on his laptop and clicked on the review mode. The screen displayed multiple bar graphics showing the results. It was verified to be a human voice but *100 percent synthesized*, the dialog *not* computer-generated either. Whether it was a male or female speaking was undetermined. Stewart sat back in his chair, still staring at the computer screen.

Who are you really, Mr. Aurell? And why do you want to control the city? And will that be enough for you...? he thought.

CHAPTER 59

The Gangs Call a Truce

Roy was sitting in the park watching his children running around laughing, enjoying themselves. This area was a safe place that they *all* could relax in, let their kids play in peace. He had heard that Terry was now running Dante's crew, without anyone knowing what had *happened* to Dante. Why wasn't Dante *still* in the picture? And this *prick* Stewart was going around trying to recruit *all* the gangs to work for *him!* This stank! *Really stank!* He was thinking about putting out some feelers, maybe even asking some other gang leaders to meet with him, on neutral territory somewhere, find out what the *hell* was going on…? Luis, one of his lieutenants, walked over to him on the bench.

"*Jefe* (boss), word is Dante and some of his boys, *all missin'!* Some of us tight with them said they mama's been askin' 'round if they been seen," said Luis.

"*Our* crew hear anything more? *Seen anything?*"

"*Nada* (nothing), *jefe. CC,* a couple more hypes, all with *5-0* after Isaac got hit. Ain't seen *them* after that," said Luis.

"I don't like this, Luis. *Don't like it at all!* Maybe we need to talk with *everybody…* Yeah, Luis, EVERYBODY!" said Roy. Roy knew it was what they needed to do, but would the other leaders see it that way too? He had to take the chance.

"Truce, *hermano* (brother). Tell them *truce…*"

*****

Later that week, the word was put out on the street to all the gangs: *Latino, Irish, Asian, Black, White,* all the major players in the city, even the major female gangs. At first they were skeptical about the sudden interest in talking, but when they were told *"truce"* and had the disappearances of *other* gang members confirmed, they were willing to listen. Much to Roy's surprise, most of them had been approached by Stewart with the offer to work for him, follow his orders, with that implied *"or else"* hanging in the air. A few decided to go along and found that the money starting to come in was close to triple what they had been receiving. While rumors also began to spread about the gang leaders that said *no* to him, more than twice, were replaced by their second-in-command, the previous leaders seeming to have fallen off the face of the earth. The new leaders refused to come to any meeting not requested by Stewart, even though it was very evident that the sentiment about him wasn't a good one, they didn't want to take a chance of disappearing as well.

After a few weeks, an abandoned factory on the lakefront, out past 137th Street, finally got the okay for the meeting, members of each gang sending an advance group to check out the location. Inside, a three-story open area was littered with trash, remnants of squatters, and their cheap rooms for the evening's activities. A heavy smell of damp earth throughout hung in the air. Several lights were strung along the walls, giving the space a somewhat official *"town hall, air your grievances"* feeling. Close to *ninety* people were standing, giving each other their personal space; the area was dead silent as Roy stepped forward, Luis by his left side.

"Gonna get right down to it! *El cabron* (this asshole) steppin' into our territories trying to make us work for *him?* Making our crews *vete* (go away)! What have *you all* heard about this *pendejo* (dumbass)?" asked Roy, looking around the room.

"Yeah! He offered us money if we *hooked* up with him! Said *'that's the new way to go'?*" a voice from the crowd said.

"Told *me* it was gonna be *easier* on me if I went along with *him!*" said another.

"But always, man, *always* that *'or else, shit, if you don't'*…just *hangin'* in the air!" said another man stepping forward.

"This for *all,* y'all?" asked Roy, looking around.

"Yeah's," coming from around the crowd.

"I *know* that *fucker capped* Dante and his crew! Ain't heard from *none* of them brothers in *weeks!"* said another angry Black man.

Roy put his head down for a moment, thinking to himself, *This Stewart was moving through the gangs fast!*

Why does he want to take us all over? he wondered, *that's muy loco!* (Very crazy!)

"We *gotta* move on this *pendejo* before we *all gone!* Truce! TRUCE! Until we get him *outta* here! We work *together, no?"* asked Roy. The room fell silent.

An *Asian* man stepped forward.

"Only *until* he's gone!" he said.

"Then…we're *all* done! Back to our *own* business!" a White man said stepping forward.

"Okay…," said Roy.

"Okay."

He turned to the left and looked at Luis, wondered why there was a small red dot on his forehead. His head jerked back from the impact of the bullet as it forced its way through, blowing out large chunks of brain and bone. Before he could even turn around, Roy felt something slam into the back of his head, his chin pushed hard onto his chest, almost flipping him over as his lifeless body continued to the floor. A few people managed to get their guns out before being shot several times, dropping quickly to the ground. As the main group ran to the outer wall shadows, the *mini gun* let loose, spraying across their upper backs, sending them flying forward, then crashing to the floor, landing awkwardly among the trash. No one was left standing. A dozen men, all dressed in black, methodically moved through the bodies on the ground, single shots fired here and there as they passed.

Stewart stepped forward from the shadows on an upper level, watching as the men below finished their task. He held up his hand and waved it forward toward the railing he was standing at. Terry and several other secondary gang leaders stepped into view behind him, four or five men behind them, dressed in black with automatic weapons, still slightly in the shadows. He looked down at Edmond in the middle of the room. He turned, looked up in Stewart's direction, and nodded. Stewart placed both gloved hands on the railing and turned his head slightly to the right.

"Are there any *questions* you might want to ask? Now would be a...*good time*...to bring them out into the open," he said.

The people behind him all remained quiet, not really believing what they had just seen and heard. But they all knew there was no other choice *but* to do what this man told them to do.

"Very well. You'll all be returned to your respective...*'territories'*... I wouldn't want *any* of you to be the victims of random *'gangland violence'* on the way home... Good night, everyone. *Travel safely!*" said Stewart.

The men dressed in black directed them toward the stairway leading down to the waiting *SUVs*. As Stewart watched Edmond walk around among the dead bodies on the ground, he saw him take out his cell phone and place a call. No doubt, in his mind he knew: *Edmond had probably just placed a pizza order...*

CHAPTER 60

A Friendly Conversation

Jerry had not taken any time off after Warren was murdered, too afraid at what might happen if he was away from the gaming house for a long period of time…*any* period of time! Danny and his cleanup crew had come in; Mike and his partner, Mel, had supervised the removal of the bodies. A doctor connected to Danny had come along and treated his wound in the back of one of the panel trucks. The two pills the doctor gave him stopped the pain almost immediately but knocked him out for the better part of a day and a half. He woke up on the couch in the gaming house office, stiff and in need of a shower and shave. He sat up, trying to clear some of the cobwebs out of his head, when the door opened and Mel walked in, then he knew for *sure* it wasn't a really bad dream…

That was, unbelievably, over seven months ago. He had told the workers, only the ones who asked, what happened to their *boss*, that Warren had gotten to be too much of a target on the police radar and had to lay low for a while, probably a *"very long while."* But the money kept flowing in. Even out-of-town players started showing up, having been told by *"a mutual friend"* that the gambling and entertainment experience here was second only to the *French Riviera*! Checking the books with Robert, he could see the increase on paper, as well as the balances of the multiple accounts, with an off-the-top negative *15 percent* going to the unseen *boss* of Stewart's.

Jerry revamped the security in the main entrance, several high-definition, closed-circuit cameras equipped with night vision, thermal scan, and separate power source. He widened the four hidden escape tunnels *(two on each level)* and added heavier firepower to the guards' armory closets. Jerry felt it was like locking the barn doors after the horses ran away, but he sure as hell wasn't going to lose any more horses!

"Heavi' thoughts goin' on insida' yo' head, dear boy? Wha' got ya so worri'd?" the deep Southern voice beside him asked.

"Business, Mason, business. And how *fucked up* life can be!" said Jerry.

"Ah' take it tha' biz'ness has a' bit ta' do with... *Warren?* Ah' haven't seen him buy' mah' estab'lishment as of late...," said Mason. "Quite ah whil', as a' matta' of fact."

"Yeah...yeah, Warren...," said Jerry. "Don't know where to begin, Mason. Too much *real crazy* been going on!" said Jerry.

"*Weellll*...maybe we give it a' start in yo' office, ova' a coupla' shots of tha' twenty-five-year-ol' brandi', dear boy," said Mason.

Down on the lower *VIP* level, with the office door closed, the outside noises were barely a whisper. The couple of shots had turned into two-thirds of the bottle being emptied. Except for the deaths of his people, the invitation from Stewart to join this mysterious "*boss*" was identical.

"Sounds lik' ah' def'nit' move ta' takeova'. They hittin' all tha' mayja' playa's, tryin' ta' put them in line," said Mason.

"The money, I can understand, even calling the shots for all these *businesses* they're talking to. But all this killing is *waaay* beyond me!" said Jerry.

"Powa', Jerry. Tha' powa'! *Ah'm not gonna just tell y'all wha' ah' wont' but sho' ya too!* Ah dead bodis' saiz' a lot mo' than just tha' *words!* Lots mo'...!" said Mason.

"Who the *hell* is this guy, and what are we going to *do* about him?"

"Bide our time, dear boy. Bide our time. 'Til then, jus' don't die' own me, 'kay?" said Mason.

"Okay. I'll do my best," said Jerry.

On the way back to his townhouse, Michael was driving. Mason wondered in silence just how many people were involved in this affair. Was this a bid to take over organized crime in the city, or did it include the suburbs as well? Obviously city officials, maybe even government officials, would be pulled into this scheme, if they weren't already, then what? How far would it all go? Better yet, how would this all *end*? And why didn't he share the name *Marc Aurell* with Jerry? Why indeed…

CHAPTER 61

Patrick Has Food for Thought

He had expanded his technique faster than expected with the additional business from this Marc Aurell. The new facility was equipped even better than his legitimate offices and operating rooms. The procedure, so easy now he could do it in his sleep, yielded data he collected privately, knowing that he could never share any of this with his business partners. His new operating nurse, Lisa, knew almost as much about it as he did; no doubt she could do this all on her own, without him. But not knowing what had happened to Jenny weighed heavily on his mind, along with her unknown whereabouts or even if she was still alive gave him nightmares. Some of the money that Marc Aurell was paying him personally, he used to buy several new pieces of needed equipment for his *shared* office space, telling his colleagues that a grateful *Norma Roberts* had donated the funds, profoundly pleased at the reconstruction surgery he and Jenny had performed.

Because they had taken Jenny right from under his nose, Patrick made it a point to stay away from almost everyone he knew, *especially* Stephanie. They had already shot her up, tried to kill her. Obviously, her investigation was getting too close to the truth of what was really going on with these crime lord killings. No, he wouldn't risk putting her in any more danger than what she was already in now. Or did his staying away from her even matter? Would they go after her if he stepped out of line? He had to talk with her... *but he was afraid.*

During the construction of the new facilities, Stewart insisted that he should be available, at a moment's notice, to come over to the work site, giving his input on where equipment, storage cabinets, even where the lighting final placements should go. When the computer system was being installed, Patrick thought it very odd that Stewart wanted him to personally speak with the *IT* tech installer, *Evan*, discussing almost all the programs installed, a few times sitting in on the system diagnostics with him.

Finally, it was all done—everything up and running, new staff all briefed, in place. Patrick was called over to the new facility by Stewart.

"Mr. Aurell felt it was necessary for you to meet your new staff. Not only for you to get acquainted with them but for them to find out something about the man they would be working for," said Stewart.

"I'm sure they really *don't know* what type of work they'll *actually* be doing. And I *doubt* that they know who the *real 'boss'* is…!" said Patrick, looking Stewart in the eyes.

"Yes, this is true, but with the money they're getting paid, I really don't think they'll ask any of those questions. So for all intents and purposes, *you are the 'boss'!*" said Stewart. "Now let's go join them for a *'meet and greet'* meal… *Shall we?*" He turned and walked off toward the staff break room.

Patrick stood for a moment, debating whether to follow or go back to his *"real"* place of business. When Stewart stopped, turned, and looked back at him, it was made very clear by the expression on Stewart's face what he should do… Patrick slowly walked forward to meet his new staff.

Patrick Runs Away

Patrick felt like he just finished running a twenty-six-mile marathon. His entire body was...*tired*. His breathing was shallow, labored; he literally could not move. But most surprising...*his face hurt!* After trying for several minutes, he was able to begin a twitching of his arms, then his fingers, gradually making fists. Fighting to open his eyes, he saw dimmed *LED* ceiling lights. *Why was he in one of his recovery rooms?* Painfully turning his head to the left, he saw Lisa check the flow of an *IV* drip, then the heart rate and blood pressure monitors. Patrick looked as the blips traveled across the face of the screens, knowing there should be sound but heard nothing. Lisa noticed him looking at her, smiled, and began to speak. As if someone were turning the volume control up, the sound of her words finally began coming through.

"...to the living, Patrick!" she said. "How are you feeling?"

He tried to shake his head but only managed to slowly roll it from side to side. He cleared his throat with difficulty and exhaled.

"*Whooooaaa...*" came out hoarse. "*Ooookay...what... hap-pened...?*"

"The doctors say it was a *mini stroke*, slight paralysis, but that appears to be wearing off."

He reached up, like moving through syrup in a bad dream, and felt the bandages on his face. Lisa gently placed her hand over his and moved it back down to his side.

"You were leaving the dinner with the new staff when it hit and you fell into the glass door. Mostly minor cuts, a few deep ones, but they'll all heal to hairline scratches. Give you a bit of character, definitely a conversation starter for sure!" she said smiling.

"*Been...out...long?*" he asked.

Lisa looked away then turned back.

"Five days... We kept you in a coma for the healing, and they haven't seen any signs of brain damage. They decided today to bring you around."

"*The group...knows...? Stephanie?*"

"The group only knows that you were at a dinner with a client when the stroke hit. *They* did the work on you, called in your buddy Larry as well for a consultation."

"*And...Stephanie...?*"

"No. No... With all the news about the crime lord bodies missing and their captain disappearing, they felt she had enough on her plate to deal with." Patrick exhaled deeply this time, grateful they had the sense *not* to involve her. She didn't need to be made into a bigger target. He turned his head toward Lisa and closed his eyes.

Checking the equipment and *IV* drip one last time, she walked out of the room, closing the door softly behind her. Patrick opened his eyes and began taking long, deep breaths, clearing his head. He managed to sit up, threw the covers off as he eased over to the edge of the bed by the monitors, and swung his legs over the side. Opening the bedside table top drawer, he pulled out the small mirror and surgical scissors. Cutting through the right side of the bandages on his face by the jawline, he felt the hair growth and pressed harder to feel the skin beneath. It was smooth but uneven; further along by his chin was the same uneven pattern. Cutting the left-side bandages, feeling underneath them, he found his skin felt the same as the right. Taking the bandages off completely, dropping them on the floor, he picked up the mirror and looked. The lines had begun to fade; there were small spots all over his face, almost hidden by the beard and moustache growth. No mistaking it—*his face had been harvested.*

Patrick waited until the night nurse made her rounds before he got up and checked the closet in his room. His clothes, wallet, and cell phone were there, and he dressed, placing the *IV* into a glass, not interrupting the flow. The finger clip for the vitals monitor, he quickly took off and replaced, hoping that the nurses would only see it as a momentary glitch. He rolled the monitor to the door and eased it open a crack and saw that the room was directly across from the stairway next to the outside exit, the alarm disabled for the staff smoke breaks. Not hearing any movement, Patrick turned the monitor off and rolled it over to the side of the door. He quickly walked across the hall and opened the stairway door, down the short corridor, and out into the night.

Stephanie's Late-Night Meeting

The doctor had finally cleared Stephanie to go back to work with a stern warning not to attempt *any* field excursions, PERIOD! Her and Alex's caseload had been reduced drastically by the sudden *"help"* from the neighborhood residents and the local gang *"new"* leaders. Their *CIs (confidential informants)* told them that the known gang chiefs for almost all the gangs had not been seen in a few weeks. Rumors spread that somehow they were wiped out at a hidden location during a *"neutral meeting"* somewhere further South along the lakefront. What the detectives were really surprised by was that the new leaders who replaced them were not making any moves on each other in retaliation.

One of Stephanie's *CIs* called her cell phone. He had pinned down an area that could be the possible location of the meeting. She saw the area in her mind's eye, remembering an abandoned factory on the *Eastside* sitting right on the lake.

"It's been a *looong* day, partner. All this sitting and typing reports has me worn out. I'm gonna call it a day. Maybe stop for something to eat...," she said to Alex.

"No worries, Annie. Get some rest... Just call me when you make it in, *huh?*" said Alex.

"*Will do, Dad!* I'm surprised that you don't want to *'tuck me in'* tonight?" she said.

"No, *no!* Remember, I saw you in a hospital gown…*things you can't unsee…!*" he said, rubbing his eyes, head down.

"Yeah…*right!* Wish you had *taken pictures…!*"

He looked up to the right, a blank expression on his face, mouth slightly open. For a moment she thought he was trying to come up with a something smart to say but held the position a bit too long.

"Al? You okay…?" she asked.

He shook his head and turned to her with a sheepish grin on his face. "Sorry, Annie…I had *an image* there for a moment…"

She threw a balled-up sheet of paper at him and got up from her desk.

She stopped by her locker for a warmer jacket, then headed down to the parking garage. When she reached her car, she saw Alex leaning against the passenger front fender, bulletproof vest hanging open on his shoulders, pump-action riot gun held under folded arms. Off to the left were two patrol units with two officers each standing outside of them, all ready for a fight.

"I guess we *all* decided to call it a *day* as well, Annie…," he said with a shrug of his shoulders.

She dropped her head smiling; a warmth came over her she only felt around family. These guys *were* her family, she thought. Looking up, Stephanie walked over to the trunk of her car, opened it, pulled out her own bulletproof vest, and put it on.

"*I'm driving…,*" she said.

The abandoned factory could be seen off to the left from the expressway. Taking the closest exit, they crossed back over and drove a few blocks north until they reached the access road to the parking lot. It was weeded over in many spots; some areas showed recent multiple vehicle traffic. They stopped away from each other, leaving room for maneuvering space, if necessary. The main doors were open, most of the glass broken out long ago; they cautiously walked in. Trash, littered along the walls, showed that many people had used this place for whatever purposes many times over. After a few minutes' walking down the corridor, they finally got to the three-story open-space area and fanned out along the interior wall to the left and the exterior wall on the right. Further into the open space, they all stopped, looking down at the concrete floor; dark-brown patches were in a tight arc toward the center, smaller dark-brown patches closer to the exterior wall. One of the uniformed officers walked over to the exterior wall columns, shining her flashlight at the multiple holes in them, mid-torso high. As she moved the beam of light to the left, most of the sixteen columns along that wall had the same type of multiple holes. Stepping back, she turned to the detectives.

"Whoever was in here, they didn't stand a chance. This looks like what a *'mini gun'* would do…," she said. "And look, no trash in here…" They all looked around, shining their flashlights along the floor.

"Military firepower *and* cleanup crew? Who has that kind of arsenal and personnel? Locally? Don't think so. Out-of-town contractors? Probably, probably…," said Alex.

"This wasn't a gang war, *couldn't* have been," said Stephanie, shining her flashlight around the room. "This was a *'message'* to the gangs." Another officer walking further into the open space turned in her direction.

"If this was a message, what were they trying to say? *'Death to gang members?' 'We're coming for you?' What?*" he asked.

"Very loud, very clear: *'You don't run* anything *now. I do…!'*" said Alex.

"*Hellava message*…," said Stephanie, still shining her flashlight around the open space.

She dropped Alex off in front of the station so he could pick up his car. This time she really was going home, running through the list of food places in her mind that were still open at this time of night.

"And *yes*, I *will* call you when I get home, *after* I get something to eat…," she said as Alex looked over his shoulder getting out of the car.

"Okay, Annie, I believe you. I'll put in a request for the *CSIs* (Crime Scene Investigators) to get out to that factory. It may be cold after all this time, but you never know what they'll turn up. Safe travels, Annie," said Alex.

"Safe travels, Al," she said.

Turning right at the end of the front entrance drive, Stephanie noticed the pearlized medium-blue *Maybach* parked several car spaces down on the right. She pulled in behind it and got out. Melissa, standing outside on the passenger side, opened the rear door for her.

"Hey, *doll…!*" she said.

"Hey, Mel. You're up late…"

"So are you, *beautiful*, but the *'boss'* had you on his mind…" Melissa said, nodding her head toward the inside of the Maybach. She got in, settling down on the plush leather seat.

"Ah' see tha' ra'ports of yo' de'mise has been grate'ly *ex'sagger'rated*, darlin'," said Mason.

"Sorry for your loss, Mason. I know how close you and Alan were. But what can *I* do for you?" she asked.

"Thank ya kind'ly, darlin', but it's all parta' this own goin' play. Ah' can giv'ya' a'notha' vic'tum an'a few names, y'all might not hear'da yet…," he said.

"How do you figure in this *madness?* This is much too…*brutal*…for you or *your girls!*"

"This is true, butt nonetha'less mah' biz'nuss is a par'ta tha' cash flow fa' one *Marc Aurell*. He's tha' one pullin' tha' strings," said Mason.

"What's he got on you, Mason? How'd he pull you in?' asked Stephanie.

"By *killin'* Alan…tw'ice! An' threat'nin' mor' mah pe'ple!" he said.

"*Twice?*" she said, truly surprised.

"Tha' Alan in y'all d'raw is face own'ly, ah' copy. Tha' real Alan was shot at tha' homes up Nor'th buy Aurell's stooge, Stu'wurt James'sen. An' *his* stooge Ed'mond David did tha' shootin'!"

So it wasn't really plastic surgery after all. Some type of mask, human mask at that, placed over a stranger's face, just to throw off the investigation! thought Stephanie.

"Who could do that type of surgery? And who was the other victim you mentioned?" she asked.

"Ah' don't know tha' doc'ta, auh' high price'd one som'wheres downtown. Butt tha' o'tha' vic'tum was War'ren Bent'ley."

"The gambler up North? *Why?*"

"Rev'va'nue, darlin'. Rev'va'nue! Ta'ken ova' tha' game'min' house was auh' gol'mine! Folla' tha' money, an' y'all might fine ah' Marc Aurell…," Mason said.

"*Marc Aurell?* Who the *hell* is that?" she asked.

"He's the one tha' called me. Auh' think he's tha' one tha's pullin' tha' strangs, darlin'."

"What does he look like? Anyone you've seen before? Heard about?"

"Naw, Sugar. Own'ly a' voice ova' tha' 'fone. Neva' met 'em," said Mason.

Now she had a name at least, one that didn't ring any bells but still something new to look into.

"Why are you telling me all this, Mason? What's in it for you?" Stephanie asked.

"Nu'thin'… Nu'thin' butt ra'vinge! Bring tha' som'bitch down, hun'ny. He *gotta'* go down…," he said, a faraway look in his eyes.

Sitting in her car, Stephanie watched as the Maybach pulled away into the night, all the information swirling around in her head. Where did this Marc Aurell come from? Stewart Jamessen sounded familiar, and his muscle, Edmond David, was a shooter. Maybe Edmond was the one that got rid of the copies. If so, that would make Stewart the go-between for this Marc Aurell. When she got home she'd record all this, not to leave anything out when she talked to Alex later in the day. Stephanie pulled away from the curb, not the least bit hungry anymore.

Edmond pressed the Stop button on the digital recorder, having picked up the entire conversation between Mason and Stephanie with an array directional microphone. He had changed the license plates on the captain's Ford Taurus at Danny's when he unloaded the body from the trunk; Danny's people did an excellent job cleaning up the bloodstains and odors. He'd let Stewart know about the conversation later when they met. Without a doubt, those two were added to his "*elimination list.*" It would be just a matter of time before she and her partner started to put all the pieces together. Taking a bite of the last slice of cold pizza, he found it was even tastier with the almost-solid cheese covering the different meats. He would definitely have to set up a way to get these pies to *New York*.

CHAPTER 64

Edmond Tried Too Hard

As a child, *Edmond Assan Davidovich* could not remember being interested in anything. With a Croatian/Slavic ancestry, raised Muslim, he would listen attentively to his parents and learned at an early age not to question either one nor give his opinion on their beliefs. Once they were forced to come to America, he heard and saw things he had no idea even existed, and that, *actually*, piqued his curiosity, while his father, still telling him to be on guard, warned him to always expect the *unexpected*. As Edmond grew older, he gravitated to physical training: boxing, martial arts, survival techniques. But he was actually surprised when his father began teaching him how to shoot, rifles as well as pistols. Practicing calming himself, following the target, slowly pulling the trigger to not throw his aim off, Edmond was taught how to make a complete shell, normal loads in addition to hot loads. Taking the weapons apart to clean them, putting them back together under varying conditions, even while blindfolded, was also included. One day when he asked his father how he had learned these skills, a dark expression came over his father's face, head dropping slightly. Finally the only answer given was that it was…*necessary*. Edmond never asked again.

After he turned twenty, he witnessed an argument between his father and one of his father's friends. Almost coming to blows, they both went their separate ways, giving each other lewd hand-and-arm gestures as they parted. Somehow, not really angry, Edmond began following him, noting in a small spiral-bound notebook places and times of his whereabouts. After six days, Edmond chose the parking lot of his workplace, where the man parked at the far end of the lot, the beginning of a darker area. Lying down under a bush, Edmond waited until the man got into his car, the driver's side door about to close, when Edmond fired the rifle. He was startled by the loudness of the shot, but the bullet still hit its mark: right behind the man's left eye, angling up through his forehead and exiting out the windshield. The driver's side door hung open as the lifeless body hit the steering wheel. The car horn did not sound. Inching backward, keeping low to the bushes Edmond made his way through the shadows, keeping the gun close under his coat until he reached his car a few blocks away. Before standing up, he eased the trunk lid open a bit and placed the rifle inside. As he settled in the driver's seat, he looked over at the pizza box on the passenger side and two colas in a cup carrier on the floor, his excuse for going out that night. Reaching inside, he took out a slice, garbage pizza, and pulled out in traffic. He had no thoughts whatsoever about the man he had just killed...

*****

Sitting on the rooftop across from Stephanie's six-flat apartment building, Edmond looked through the telescopic night scope into her living room and watched as she went back and forth fixing her something to eat before settling down on the couch to look at television. He adjusted the vision range; a close-up of her head came into view, his target: *her right temple.* The rifle slid down the parapet wall as he swiveled to his left, crouched, the dual-edge stiletto knife popping easily into his left hand. He hit the man behind him in the upper left thigh, cutting upward across his abdomen into open air. Within the blink of an eye, he saw that the blade had no effect, not even cutting the material. Almost as a continuation of the same movement, the *.380* silenced pistol appeared like magic and shot the man in his left knee, forcing the man's leg away and down. Still pulling the trigger, he fired another round into the man's upper thigh, left side and back, swinging the man's body further into an arc. The

.*380* was knocked out of Edmond's grip by the man's right elbow as he continued to spin around, catching Edmond's left hand by the wrist, twisting it around until a muted snap was heard, the knife falling to the rooftop. Edmond flipped his right wrist toward him, bringing it straight again as another smaller gun popped into his hand, only to have it stopped with the man's left hand, forcing it up and away. In that brief moment, he saw the light glint off the eyes of the man in front of him: *Carl!*

Carl's right fist hit Edmond in the side of his head in line with his left eye; even though he rolled with the punch, it brought bright colors into his vision, intensifying as a second blow landed almost in the same spot. Edmond, knocked back along the parapet wall, freed his right wrist and leveled the gun at Carl's chest, firing seven rounds; the gun locked open on empty. Carl, falling back from the repeated impacts, landed hard on his right shoulder, rolled onto his stomach, pushed himself up, and rushed at Edmond. Sitting up, his vision clearing and dropping the gun, Edmond turned his right hand, palm up, another dual-edge stiletto knife popped into his hand, this time stabbing Carl in the left shoulder all the way to the handle. Carl's body arched up, away from the blade, pulling the knife with him, his right hand scraping down the wall. Edmond moved his head out of the way at the last second. Immediately bringing his knee up into Carl's midsection, grabbing him by the neck of his hoodie, Edmond flipped Carl over his head. Still holding on, he brought him down hard on his wounded shoulder. Carl let out a loud grunt, breathing out hard. Edmond rolled over, up on his feet in a second, and jumped forward as Carl sat up. Edmond hit Carl in the center of his face with his right knee, followed by a fist to the right side of his head. As he fell to his left, Carl's right foot came up between Edmond's legs, bending him forward. Then he grabbed him by the neck and forced his head down as his knee came up. Edmond bounced back, stumbled, and came down hard on a rooftop stand pipe, falling forward into a sitting position. Carl looked over at the knife sticking out of the front of his shoulder and felt a burning sensation when he moved slightly. He looked over to Edmond, still sitting up against the standpipe, but now he was holding another silenced *.380* pistol. He fired off two rounds into Carl's chest, rocking him back to the right.

"Yes, just as I thought…the whole *outfit* is *Kevlar, right?*" said Edmond, watching Carl move back into an upright position.

"*Yeah! But still hurts like a son of a bitch…!*"

"And not impervious to sharp, pointed knives *either*," said Edmond. "*You broke my wrist…!*"

"Sorry…I didn't think it would matter once you were *dead!*" said Carl.

"*Aaahh*…means to an end… Understandable."

"*You stabbed me…!*" said Carl.

"*That*…I'm *not* sorry to say, was because I *was trying* to kill you!" said Edmond.

"How did you find me, Carl? I'm pretty sure I covered my tracks well…but *not well enough, huh?*"

"Yeah, you and that *damn pizza addiction*, Edmond. What's up with *that?*" asked Carl.

Edmond smiled, thinking back to his first kill.

"A habit…started a long time ago, Carl…*a looong time ago…*," said Edmond trailing off.

"Someone trying to take *you* out, huh?" said Carl.

"No, *nothing* like that… They had *started* a job they didn't get a chance to *finish*," said Edmond.

"*Oh well*, then I guess I'll have to finish the job *I* started…," said Carl.

"Oh? *Really?* Okay, Carl… I'll ask you, *how will you finish…?*"

"*Blood drop and stiletto…Edmond,*" said Carl.

"*Blood drop and stiletto…?*" said Edmond, truly puzzled.

The blood from the wound on his head had collected just above his right eye, becoming too heavy to stay on the ridge of his eyebrow, and rolled down into his open eye, making it close, blurring the vision in the left eye as well. He felt the hard impact to the front of his throat, a sharp burning sensation followed immediately by a metal *clink*. His right arm still pointing the gun at Carl began to tingle as if asleep, then no feeling at all. The numbness swiftly coursed through his body before it dawned on him: *his spinal cord had been severed.* His vision cleared for a brief moment, and he saw that the stiletto knife missing from Carl's shoulder was now in the middle of his neck.

Touché!

Edmond's eyes remained open, his right arm still ridged holding the gun, as Carl slowly stood then walked toward him.

CHAPTER 65

One More Fact Added

Stephanie, without telling Alex, had been tracking Patrick. If he wasn't going to contact her, she would have to contact him. What she found out gave her more questions than she had answers for. He seemed to have had an accident *"somewhere"* that required his business partners to operate on his face because he *fell* into a glass door *after* suffering a *mini stroke*. Then halfway through recovery, he *disappeared* into the night, and a few days later, he withdrew *$40,000* out of his savings. His car was left in the office building parking garage. No activity on his credit cards. No more sightings at his bank or apartment. Patrick had fallen off the face of the earth. Talking to a few people at his practice, she also found that his surgical assistant, Jennifer Dawson, was among the missing as well. First she thought, *Could they have run off together?* And if so, *why?* But after talking to Lisa Matthews, the night nurse supervisor and Jennifer's *"girlfriend,"* she was told a family emergency had come up, causing her to leave for home. Following that lead, Stephanie discovered that none of Jennifer's family members had heard from her in months. Coincidence or just bad timing? Or did both of these *"two missing persons"* have something to do with her crime lord cases?

Back at her desk in the station, Stephanie was going over the information she had about the crime lord cases and Patrick's disappearance, looking for anything she had missed or a possible connection between the two.

"So what do you think happened to them?" asked Alex.

Stephanie looked up with a questioning expression on her face.

"*Patrick and Jennifer...*," he said.

"How do you know about...*that?*" she said surprised.

"Uhh...*gold shield, detective, nosy*...to name a few things. But being your partner for *eight* years, I kinda know your mindset and investigative habits, Annie."

"Yeah...yeah. Guess to you I *am* an open book. Well, both those trails hit blank walls, and I just wonder if they have something to do with the crime lord cases, maybe loose ends being eliminated. Just don't know, Al."

"Yeah, my thoughts exactly, Annie. How long has it been since you've seen or heard from Patrick?"

"A few weeks after I got out of the hospital, he called a couple times, never came by though. He mentioned a research project he was working on but didn't go into any details. Only that it was a follow-up to that mother-daughter accident he worked on."

"What was *that* about? Did you get their names?" asked Alex.

"No, but it had something to do with '*skin graft*' from the daughter to the mother..." Stephanie stopped talking, her mouth slightly open as she stared at Alex. She picked up her desk phone and dialed a judge she knew...

Four hours later, after getting a warrant for Patrick's client list, they rang the doorbell of Norma Roberts's townhouse. When she opened the door, they were surprised at how young she looked. This couldn't be the almost sixty-something Patrick had operated on. Invited into the living room, Stephanie and Alex noticed several pictures of her on the mantel and end tables. Vanity maybe? Setting the tray with hot tea and fixings on the long table in front of them, Norma settled back onto the sofa.

"I hope nothing has happened to Patrick...*Dr. Procter*. After the amazing gift he gave me, I'll totally be in his debt for life!" she said.

"Yes, ma'am. It appears the plastic surgery he performed for you gave you a very youthful look, a very good job indeed," said Alex.

"It was *faaaar* more than just the average run-of-the-mill plastic surgery! It was a miracle! When we were hit, me and Lizzie, my daughter Elizabeth, the broken car glass cut my face and upper chest to pieces. I'd be scarred for the rest of my life if it wasn't for my Lizzie and Patrick."

"How so, ma'am?" asked Stephanie.

"She…*Lizzie*…told him, *made him promise*, to…*to fix me!* Told him she…*she knew*…she could be the donor…*knew*…*she wouldn't make it*…," said Norma, tears welling up in her eyes.

"We're sorry for your loss, ma'am…*Norma*," said Stephanie. "Did Patrick tell you anything about what he was going to do for you? Maybe go into some *details* about the procedure?" asked Alex.

"No…no, just that he'd try to keep his promise to Lizzie…and *he did*, in such a *fantastic way!*" said Norma.

"How so, Norma?" asked Stephanie.

Norma got up and left the room, returned a few moments later, and sat back on the sofa. She placed her driver's license on the table. The picture showed an older woman; the eyes definitely were hers, the nose very similar. Then she put one of the photos from an end table next to the driver's license. It looked like a younger version of her taken much earlier in her life.

"That is a picture of my daughter, Lizzie…*on the right*," said Norma.

Without a word spoken between them, Stephanie and Alex saw their original conclusion of *"vanity"* missed the actual facts completely. The fifty-eight-year-old Norma Roberts had the facial appearance, though slightly fuller, of her twenty-two-year-old *late daughter*…

CHAPTER 66

Stephanie Gets Another Message

Leaving Norma's townhouse, Stephanie didn't know what to think about this new twist in the case. They both walked over to her car in silence. A white folded sheet of paper was under one of the windshield wipers.

"That's par for the course...*a parking ticket*," said Alex.

Stephanie pulled it from under the wiper and read it. "Not a ticket, Al, an invitation to aid in a search warrant on a building in the loop, downtown Chicago."

"No, no...let me guess! *Carl*, right?" he said.

"Yep! What *now*...?" she asked.

As they pulled up in front of the four-story brick building, Stephanie realized it was next to Patrick's office. The unmarked cars parked in front with lights flashing must be *FBI* or some other higher-up law enforcement agency. At the entrance they were met by men in *FBI* field gear with automatic rifles.

"And you are...?" one of the men asked.

They both held up their shields.

"Detectives Caldwell and Smith," Said Stephanie.

"Take the first elevator on the right, it's unlocked. Ask for *Special Agent McDonald*," he said.

Walking down the corridor, they saw agents going in and out of the first-floor offices, making notes, talking to the employees inside. The elevator stood open, another agent standing by the control panel. Alex nudged Stephanie and nodded toward the control panel. She noticed that the fire emergency key was in and turned to the *On* position. The doors closed, and they descended.

The doors opened onto a brightly lit reception area, copper-colored brushed-metal desk with a dark-brown marblelike top, computer monitor, and telephone off to the right side. Six dark-brown leather armless chairs, same color metal legs as the desk, against the wall to the left, end tables at either end with table lamps. Turning to the right they saw more agents armed with rifles further down, several clustered around a taller agent, completely bald, speaking to them. Stephanie and Alex were pointed to him; he turned and walked toward them.

"Detectives Caldwell and Smith?" he asked.

"Yes. Special Agent McDonald?" asked Alex.

"Yeah...," he said looking them over. "Normally, you wouldn't *be* here, not anywhere even *close to here*, but the *director* told me *'personally'* to loop you two in," McDonald said.

"For starters, real estate management had no idea there were *two lower levels* to this building. This floor didn't *'appear'* on any floor plans or building records filed with the city or construction company. That *fire emergency mode* setting for the elevator you rode down on isn't *indicated* on the control panel, and that's not even a *regulation fireman's key!* No records were found for the *new work* that was *recently* done down here, and I *betcha'* all this new equipment *won't* have a paper trail *either! *Come on...," McDonald said.

He led them into a wide corridor, a glass-walled staff lounge area on the left, with one of the glass doors missing. Staff members were seated at the tables. At the end of the corridor were men and women bathrooms, a *"family bathroom"* between them. The right side of the corridor had private rooms, all the doors open, agents and patients inside of a few of them. Going into the last room, they saw an agent gently cutting the bandages covering the face of the sedated patient in the bed. Once the bandages were removed, Stephanie and Alex recognized the man, even with faint hairline scars.

"He look *familiar...?*" asked McDonald.

"Yeah, he runs a house of women on the Westside, not a major, major player but still somewhat of a heavyweight," said Alex. They left, walked into the next room. Another patient was getting their bandages removed.

"What about *this one?*" asked McDonald.

"Yep, him too. Drug distributor, far Southside and nearby Indiana. Another lightweight, but still important nonetheless," said Stephanie.

Four other rooms had the same type of occupants, all in the healing process from the plastic surgery procedure.

"Our *'intel'* (intelligence) says these joes are *expendable*, fake crime leaders a few steps away from a *morgue slab!* And they aren't the only ones, *I'm told...*," said McDonald. "Care to *'enlighten'* me, Detectives?"

"Well, we're on the tail end of it ourselves, putting what pieces we have together, trying to make sense of it all. There were six others before them, somehow *they* disappeared in the night. We think these poor bastards are copies as well, made to look like the originals, and then later on, *unceremoniously* disposed of," said Stephanie.

"So what's the point? Force the real crime leaders to toe the line? Put these guys in their places just as *figureheads?*" asked McDonald. "*Who's gonna come out the winner?*"

"All good questions, McDonald, we just don't know yet. Maybe take the heat off of them? Stop us from looking into their businesses? Who knows for sure," said Alex.

"Could be, the one that's pulling the strings might look at this as a way to control them undercover, maybe even tap into their cash flow. We just don't know enough...," said Stephanie.

"Well, *whatever* the reasons behind all this, somebody next-door is ass-deep in it. One of those doctors was doing the surgeries," said McDonald.

Stephanie froze, couldn't think of a word to say. She just couldn't believe, *refused to believe*, that Patrick was involved.

"Why do you say that?" asked Alex. "You know something we don't?"

"Yeah. Follow me."

He headed back to the main corridor, opened the women's bathroom door, and walked over to the handicapped stall, the stall door swinging closed behind him. Stephanie and Alex stopped, both wondering what the hell was going on.

"Come on, *come on through...!*" said McDonald, his voice echoing.

Alex pushed the stall door, holding it open as he looked inside. A portion of the wall, to the left of the toilet, was open, revealing a tunnel. Following the sound of his voice, Stephanie behind him, they walked through the tunnel into the basement of Patrick's practice. There were more agents with rifles standing in the corridor.

"Things that make you go *'hmmmmm'? Ya think?*" said McDonald with an accusatory stare. "And to add even more *'insult to the injury,'* we've got someone back there that works in *both places!*"

Back in the alternate facility, they went into the last office behind the elevator well, another set of bathrooms at the end of the corridor. Inside, seated behind the desk, was Lisa Matthews. Stephanie's anger made her ball up her fists; she stayed behind Alex, not trusting herself to stay away from her.

"And you really don't know ANYTHING about ANY of this? *Right*, Ms. Matthews?" asked McDonald.

"That's right," she said with a slight smile.

"Nothing about the whereabouts of Dr. Procter or Jennifer Dawson *either*, I suppose?" asked Alex.

"Correct. As I told the detective behind you earlier, Dr. Procter hasn't been seen for several days, and Jennifer had a family emergency she had to go back home for."

"So how did you end up working here? *Coincidence*, Ms. Matthews?" asked Alex.

"No, Detective. I actually answered an ad online. I was totally surprised when they told me the address..."

"And I also *suppose* you don't know anything about the secret passageway between the buildings *either*? Right?" asked McDonald.

"*Secret passageway...?* First I've heard of it, Agent McDonald. Sorry," she said, the slight smile still on her face.

It was all Stephanie could do not to push past Alex and begin slapping the answers out of her. She looked up with closed eyes and took a deep breath. Opening her eyes, still looking at the ceiling, she noticed, off to the left, a black *X* in the upper corner.

"Alex, does this room look…*shallow*…to you?" she asked, looking from the back of the room to the front.

"*Shallow…?*"

"Yeah, not as deep as the other rooms along the corridor. You see any doors along the back wall?" Stephanie asked, looking from one side of the room to the other.

"No… You're right, this room isn't as deep as the others…," he said, now curious.

"Hey, Lisa. What's that *X* up there in the corner for?" Stephanie asked pointing.

Lisa turned around, looked up. McDonald and Alex looked up as well. When she turned back, the slight smile was gone from her face.

"Nothing…*nothing*, I'm sure. Construction mark, *probably*…," she said.

"Hmmm. Let me take a closer look…" Stephanie said, walking from behind Alex.

Lisa stood suddenly, about to block her way when McDonald took her by the arm, pulling her to the right. Stephanie walked behind the desk. Close to the back wall she heard a faint *pinging*, obviously coming from behind it. Where the *X* was marked, she noticed thin straight spaces around it. A patch for a mistake or something else to fit into the pattern of the wall.

"Things that make you say *hmmmm*…?" she said looking at Lisa.

Reaching up, she pressed the *X*, felt it give a bit, and pressed harder. They heard a soft *clink*; a section of the wall moved back a few inches and stopped. McDonald snapped his fingers, pointed at Stephanie. The agent in the room quickly moved to the other side, his shoulder flat on the wall behind her. Drawing her gun, she nodded at the agent, slowly pushed the wall inward, swinging it to the left against the inside wall. A woman was in the bed directly ahead of her, and another patient was in the bed on the right, face bandaged like the others. Both were connected to medical monitors and *IV* drips, both heavily sedated. Stephanie holstered her gun and walked into the room.

"This, *I assume*, is Jennifer Dawson," she said.

Alex walked in the room behind her. McDonald, still holding Lisa by the arm, stood in the room opening.

"And *who is this mystery man* going to die for, I wonder...?" asked Stephanie.

Opening the top drawer of the bedside nightstand she found a pair of surgical scissors and began cutting the bottom of the bandages on his right, up to the eye opening. Pulling the gauze across to the left of his face, she literally jumped back, bumping into Jennifer's bed.

"*Shit! SHIT!*" she said, anger solid on her face.

"*What the hell? Who is it?*" McDonald asked, leaning forward.

Alex pulled the bandages back, already knowing what and whom he'd see.

"A copy of her boyfriend, *Dr. Patrick Lawrence Procter*," said Alex.

CHAPTER 67

You Can Run, But…

Patrick, once he had taken the money out of his savings account, found a *"no-tell hotel"* just off of the downtown *Chicago* loop to gather his thoughts. The manager didn't ask twice about what his name was after Patrick gave him *$500* in cash; but just in case, he had the alternate identification at the ready if necessary. He thought back to his college days with Larry, both of them knowing they wanted to be plastic surgeons, not just to help people but the big money that came with being good at it. They had laughed about maybe changing someone's face that was put into a witness protection program, forced to be somebody else for the rest of their lives. Or until whoever they were hiding from caught up with them and finished what they needed to finish. That stuck in their minds, struck a chord deep down inside them. It wasn't funny at all…*now*. Would they have to one day hide because of a botched surgery? An angry client that felt they charged too much? Who knew…?

Being in college made it easier for Larry to start a new identity. A library card, credit cards, all in a name other than his own were easy. The toughest thing was getting a new Social Security number; how he did it, he never asked, but thanked him very much when he got one for him as well. Once they got their new driver's licenses, they both relaxed. Now it would be simple to manage and maintain the dual identities. They never mentioned the second IDs anymore, but they each made sure they kept both current.

The next day he went to a nearby Target store and bought new clothes, a medium-sized travel bag to pack it all in, and two wallets to keep his IDs separate. He knew that one day his Dr. Procter identity would cease to exist. But right now, the big question was, why had they harvested his face? What did Marc Aurell have in mind for him down the road? And now that he was gone, what would they do with the poor guy that was wearing his face? He needed to put as much distance between him and Marc Aurell as he could, keep moving around, not staying in one place too long. *And what about Stephanie?* he thought. How could he tell her what he had done? What he was forced to do because they were holding Jennifer over his head, Marc's *"assurance"* to keep him in line until…*who knows when!* Lisa was the only one who really knew what he was doing. Maybe she was the only one that would be safe. But how long would that last? When it was all over, would they get rid of her? Tie up all the loose ends? *Shit!* He was going in circles! Number 1 was his major concern, his only concern: *himself!*

It was time for him to leave, get out of town, and go to another state. He'd buy another car then stick to the open road once he got out of here. Maybe head up to Wisconsin, work his way back down South, and hopefully get into California. Maybe he could get a passport, leave the country altogether. He would use the money in the numbered account that he created from the money Marc had paid him. Man! They made running away look *"soooo"* easy on television and in the movies, but he had no clue as to what to do next. *Food!* *Food* would be next. He didn't remember the last time he had eaten. Way too scared to even think about food until now. Once it got dark, he'd go out to a fast-food restaurant, get food to go, bring it back, and eat it here. But for right now, he was suddenly tired; he lay back on the pillow and went fast asleep.

CHAPTER 68

He Never Saw It Coming...

Stewart was surprised that the two detectives had put everything together so fast. Just over twenty-five months and things had fallen apart. He had expected that this would go on at least a few more years before he cashed in and moved on, this time out of the country altogether. What had gone wrong? Who had talked? Even though he hadn't been able to contact Edmond in a few days, he was quite sure that the sociopath was either on a pizza binge of doing some other freelance work for Marc Aurell, *not* telling the authorities about the plan to take over the city. Either way, it was time for him to leave.

This time the money had grown to almost *$7,000,000* in just the last few months, with *$1,750,000* already sent overseas to secure his new home and identity. With this amount of money, he could live very well for the rest of his life. To be on the safe side, Stewart had changed hotels several times, finally renting a three-story townhome in Darien, Illinois. In the back of his mind, something was telling him to cut and run, get out now while no one knew where he was, but he decided to stay, *needed to stay!* All because of a woman...

At first, it was just an exercise in control, free sex from Ruthie to show her he held all the cards, truly life and death over her and her family, while he was also being satisfied sexually. But seeing the way her brother had reacted to killing his double, it was only a matter of time before he broke and put a big glitch into the works. Even though no one would believe what he could tell them, it definitely would lead to more questions being asked. Killing him was a no-brainer and calling Ruthie to his place just four days later showed her that he really didn't care if she suspected he had her brother killed; he was still in control. But it had changed for him. Seeing her go through all the usual steps he wanted her to do, *commanded her to do*, had no effect on him; the silent tears dropping on his thighs as she knelt between his legs made him feel something he had never felt before... *empathy!*

And now, this one last time, he had to see her; even if he couldn't tell her how he felt, he *had* to be with her. Stewart had packed *$1,500,000* cash in a separate briefcase just for her, not nearly enough to make up for her brother's death but something he would leave for her without a word, maybe to ease his conscience, letting the letter inside do his talking, explaining for him.

Stewart watched as Ruthie walked out of the dressing room, the thin, red silk dress as if spray-painted onto her body. She was holding a white hand towel in each hand. As she walked toward the bed, he saw the tops of her stockings through the side slits. Looking down, the red patent leather stiletto-heeled ankle straps reflected the room lights. As she got closer, Stewart traveled up her body with his eyes stopping at the swell of her breast showing through the deep v-cut, each nipple clearly erect beneath the material. Finally looking at her face, he was overwhelmed by how beautiful she was, makeup flawless as ever. Stopping almost two feet in front of him, she slowly began to turn until he could see the u-cutout back, garter belt, and the slight hint of her cheeks separation. Stewart leaned forward, placing his hands on her waist, pulled her to him, and then softly kissed the valley of her back. Stepping forward away from him, she continued her turn, facing him again, then slowly sank to her knees, sliding the white hand towels under the front edge of the bed.

Stewart watched as the long, red fingernails reached over, unzipped his pants, freeing his excitement. As she began, he couldn't believe the incredible warmth steadily spreading over his entire body. His breathing came in shallow gasps as he quickly succumbed to her expertise, his head falling back as he moved his arms behind him for support. His thoughts turned to the *"what if"* questions: *What if he showed her the money before he left? What if he asked her to come with him? What if she said yes? What if he told her he loved her? What if he told her he had her brother killed...?*

The sharp stabbing pains in both of his sides were almost simultaneous. Stewart felt the blades sinking deep into his body, stopping at the handles, then quickly moving upward toward his armpits. Trying to push forward, he was pushed back with the knives traveling slightly around to his back. His head snapped upright, looking down on her face, deeply into her eyes, as he began to have trouble breathing. He was able to reach out with his right hand, grabbing her left shoulder, only to have her effortlessly knock it away as she stared coldly into his eyes. Stewart's energy was draining out of him as fast as his blood, his mind working overtime to grasp what was happening to him. Falling to his right, he stared at her as she calmly sat on her legs watching him. The bedroom door opened, and a woman walked in wearing sneakers, blue jeans, and a gray sweatshirt. As the blood began to flow out of his mouth, he saw the impossible: *Ruthie!* Looking back down to the *"Ruthie"* siting on the floor, Stewart watched as she took one of the hand towels and rubbed it across her forehead, bringing it back down to her lap. The three dark lines across her forehead hit him like a physical blow in the face: *Alan!*

"I told you, *you son of a bitch!* I told you *I'd kill you!*" said Alan in a controlled, low voice. Stewart tried to talk, but only more blood came out.

"I didn't want any blood on Ruthie's hands, *you asshole!*" said Alan as he stood up. "That's why *I killed you, you bastard!*"

Ruthie slowly walked into the room to the other side of the bed, unable to take her eyes off the knife in Stewart's left side, the bloodstain spreading across the bed.

"I'll...I'll call Mason... Yeah. Yeah. I'll call Mason, Alan. He'll... he'll know what to do...*what to do...*," was the last thing Stewart heard as his world faded to black.

CHAPTER 69

Ruthie Gets a New Sister

Mason hadn't asked what she needed him for and told her not to say anything else over the telephone. He called Michael, not knowing what to expect, being more reassured that he said he'd bring Melissa along.

As soon as Ruthie opened the front door, she fell into his arms, crying uncontrollably, Michael and Melissa easing past her and heading into the townhouse. They heard water running in one of the upstairs bedrooms; both pulled out the silenced *.380* automatics, their backs hugging the wall away from the banister. The water stopped, and movement was coming from the end bedroom on their right. Michael peeked around the doorframe into the room and saw the woman standing a few feet away from the bed, looking at the dead man lying on his back. A black-handled knife was clearly visible under each armpit. It was Stewart. He signaled Melissa behind him to lower her gun and walked into the room. It was evident that he was killed while having sex, probably had no idea what was going to happen to him. No need to check if he was still alive, too much blood on the bed for that. He walked past the woman, turned to look at her, and quickly stepped back, surprised. Melissa, captivated by the way the woman was dressed, as well as her shape, saw Michael's sudden move backward and in a few steps turned to look at the woman in front of him. *Ruthie!* How in the *hell* had she passed them, let alone changed into this outfit she was wearing?

"Quite *a-mazin'*, sugar, seein' you dressed like this. Always a *pleasuh'!*" said Mason from the doorway.

Michael and Melissa were both at a loss for words.

"Boss! How the *hell* did Ruthie get up here before us? And why did she change clothes?" said Michael.

"Dear boy and gurl, please have the pleasuh' of meeting Ruthie's *dead brutha'*, Alan."

Both their mouths fell open as they looked Alan up and down, still not believing what they saw.

"No! *No way! That's a man? She's…she's too damn gorgeous, boss! No way!*" said Melissa.

Alan smiled and turned to look at them.

"Thank you, young lady, sorry to surprise you…," said Alan.

Mason walked over and hugged Alan from behind and kissed him on the neck.

"Thank you for coming, Mason. Sorry to trouble you."

"Never a 'tru'ble, darlin', '*special'ly* when y'all lookin' like *this*…," he said, turning Alan around.

They kissed on the lips and then gazed into each other's eyes for a moment.

"Michael, if ya please, give Danny ah' call. Tell him we'll need him and his people's *'ex-pert-tise'* to tidy up tuh place. Stewart's presence needs ta' be gone, don't need no questions 'bout him her'a," said Mason.

"Let's get back ta' Ruthie, we'll wait 'til Danny gets her'a," said Mason, holding Alan's hand as they walked toward the door of the bedroom.

Less than half an hour later, several charcoal-gray panel trucks pulled up in front of the townhouse. Danny stepped out of the first one as it stopped at the curb. Side and rear doors opened on the other trucks as men, women, got out carrying a large black case in each hand. Two men pulled a king-size mattress, wrapped in plastic, from one of the vans and headed for the front door, while two others followed them with the matching lower box spring, also plastic-wrapped. Danny, once inside, went straight to Mason, nodded his head, and extended his right arm toward the main entry. Mason, without saying a word, stood, walked over to Ruthie, and helped her to stand. Alan supported her from the other side, then all three went out the front door. Danny turned to Michael and Melissa.

"*Show me...*," he said, and they led him and his people upstairs.

The bloodied mattress and lower box spring, each placed in thick, black zippered plastic contractor bags went into one of the vans first. As they cleaned, smaller draw-stringed contractor bags were brought out, placed neatly alongside the mattress and box spring. Michael and Melissa carried out the body bag holding Stewart, the knives pulled from his sides were laid flat on his chest. He was placed in a refrigerated hidden compartment in the floor of another van *(big enough to hold six adult bodies)*, the floor panels electronically locked. A wall-to-wall carpet was then rolled out to cover the seams. Finally, just over ninety minutes' total time, the last of the men and women came out carrying their large black cases, packed them up, and drove away.

Danny came out with Stewart's black briefcase in a latex-gloved hand, a lint-free cloth lightly doused with chemicals in his other latex-gloved hand, wiping down the front door hardware, just as he had done with the briefcase. He closed the door, already set to lock automatically. He turned when he reached the sidewalk, made a mental note that all the lights were off, then headed to the last van.

The interior of the windowless van was set up like a high-class lounge. All the seating areas were upholstered in dark-burgundy suede including the driver's and front passenger. Directly behind the driver's seat was a compact galley with sink, refrigerator, microwave, and electric convection oven, storage cabinets above. A bench seat at the end of the sink counter ran to the rear of the van, stopping at the outside wall of the bathroom. Three swivel *"captain chairs,"* a small bar, with refrigerator between the last two were lined up on the passenger side wall. A ceiling console held wireless headphones and two fold-down fifteen-inch diagonal video screens. Soft aqua-blue valance lighting along the tops of either side walls gave the cabin a warm, muted glow.

Danny got in and sat down in the front passenger seat. Mason was sitting on the bench seat; Ruthie had her head on his right shoulder. Michael and Melissa both had on headphones, a video screen down turned toward them, but they were staring in Danny's direction. After a moment, their attention returned to the screen.

"Where's Alan?" he asked.

Mason pointed to the bathroom, and as if on cue, the motorized door slid open. Alan walked out, high heels and stockings off, makeup removed.

"Sorry, I was beginning to feel a bit...*overdressed*...but still *comfortable*," he said.

"That's a good thing, darlin'. One less thang for y'all to get *u'sta*," said Mason.

"Ay, lad. Wid 'ya being dead twice 'ovar, '*Alan,*' best stay ta rest! I'll give'ya a neuw' name, start ya off a'gin," said Danny.

Ruthie sat up, looked at Danny, and shook her head *no*, then looked at Alan.

"For the longest time I have, and I know our sisters have, thought of you as one of us: *another girl, another sister!* So have you, honey. And you've had a girl's name, *a secret name*, all this time, we just stopped using it...," said Ruthie. *"Look at you...look at you, honey...!"*

They all looked at Alan still wearing Ruthie's red dress.

"*Christina. Christina Alexia!*" said Alan.

"*Christina Alexia!*" said Ruthie.

They all smiled.

"Aye, lass, *aye!* Ah'll get the paper trail a'goin', hav' tha' IDs by weeks'end," said Danny.

Alan sat down next to Mason and reached across his lap to hold Ruthie's hand.

"Ruthie. Stewart was *a'tonin'* for his sins, seems he done lef' ya a bit o'green, wid'a note...," said Danny, standing and walking over to Ruthie. He handed them to her then returned to his seat. She opened the trifolded single sheet of paper.

"This started out as just another assignment from a crime lord, another opportunity to make a large sum of money, then leave. Nothing I hadn't done before," she read.

"But as I began to use you, I began to have feelings for you. Unfortunately, those feelings came after Marc Aurell asked me to eliminate your brother. This won't make up for his loss, sadly, but it's all I can do before leaving you. Stewart."

She refolded the note and looked down at it in her hand. She spoke softly without looking up.

"I'm glad, Mason, that you insisted on Alan wearing that bulletproof vest. He really would have died twice if not for you," said Ruthie.

Looking up now, she spoke to Danny. "So how...*how much* was Alan's life worth to this *Marc Aurell?*" she asked, eyes tearing and wide open.

"Ah mill ana' half, all cash," Danny said.

"How much do I owe you for the...*cleanup*...Mr. Danny?"

"Ya moneys na' good wid' me, darlin', Ah got ya covered, lass," he said. "Ya be famli' now! Where cana' take ya?"

"Home. Home would be nice now," she said and laid her head back on Mason's shoulder.

Danny leaned over, whispered to the driver, and he started the engine.

"Michael, Melissa. Would y'all be so kind as ta' drive tha' car back home and folla' me to Ruthie's with hers? Pick me up in 'bout ah' h'our...or two?" Mason said.

Alan laid his head down on Mason's other shoulder. Looking down at him, he turned, looked at Ruthie, then back to Michael and Melissa.

"Betta' I call ya in the mornin', dear boy, Ah'm gonna have some *con-solin'* ta do *tonight*...," he said.

Michael and Melissa stepped out the power sliding passenger side door, it closing as the van pulled away from the curb. Danny stared out the windshield, the information he read on the other sheets of paper from the briefcase, which he had kept, going through his mind. This was far bigger than anyone had thought, deeper embedded into the city's operating system as well. A lot of higher-ups in city government were going to take a fall, probably disappear quietly, when he handed these papers over to Carl...

CHAPTER 70

Can't Deny It Now

Stephanie and Alex spent four and a half hours at the federal building talking to Special Agent McDonald, going over all the details that they had pertaining to the dead crime lord cases. With the discovery of the *"Patrick"* double and how it connected to her, he pressed even harder to get answers. Finally, a call came through and caused him to scream into the phone, then slam it back down onto the cradle. He suggested, not very politely, they leave his office.

On the way back to the Southside, neither one spoke, both angry at what they had suspected was made into a painful reality. Alex, stopping in front of Stephanie's building, parked, engine still running. Her anger, changed into a melancholy acceptance, left her feeling saddened, somehow knowing that she would never see Patrick again. How did he get into the middle of all this, and more to the point, why didn't he tell her? After that firefight she had, were *"they"* holding the fact that *"they"* tried to kill her once and *"they"* could do it again and maybe next time succeed? Patrick should have trusted her enough to tell her...*something!* Maybe she could have helped him, gotten to the bottom of these cases quicker. Now she possibly would never know.

Alex, his head slightly down, was deep in his own thoughts. With Patrick being neck-deep in this investigation, how would that affect Stephanie? Would the higher-ups think she knew more than she did, maybe even blame her for stalling the progress of the cases because her boyfriend was now known to be involved? Or would they assume she was in *"their"* pocket as well, from the very beginning, paid off to look the other way? Either way, she'd be looked at sideways from now on out. He just wondered what he could do to help her, possibly even save her...

He felt the back of her fingers on his right cheek. He turned and looked at her and saw the sadness in her eyes. Stephanie leaned forward, gently kissed him on the lips, and pulled back. For a few seconds, they stared at each other before leaning together again. This time the kiss was more passionate yet somehow limited to very close friends sharing a tender moment together, no expectations of anything else afterward.

"Thank you for being there for me, Al," she said touching his right cheek with her fingers.

"I'll be there, Annie, no worries about that. *Ever,*" he said.

She unbuckled her seat belt, stepped out of the car, and watched as he pulled away.

Stephanie walked into a dark apartment, street lights and muffled sounds coming from below. She pulled open the small dresser drawer on the right of the door, placed her holstered gun and keys inside, then closed it and the front door. Head hanging down, she stretched out both arms, leaning on the top surface of the credenza.

"Why didn't you tell me? Why did you let me walk into...*that?*" she asked into the dark.

"Would you have believed me?" said the deep *DJ* voice from the living room.

Stephanie paused, shaking her head.

"No...probably not. When did you know...?"

"Only two days ago. I wanted to make sure before the *FBI* started their investigation, something I had no control over. If it helps you any, I don't think he was in on the double of himself," said Carl.

"What were they going to do? The doubles usually wind up dead, taking the heat off the originals, *right...?* Then what were they going to do with Patrick? Keep him in that hole? Work him until they didn't need him anymore? Kill him later, no one being the wiser...," she said.

"Something like that. Could have even trained someone else in the surgery procedure *to* take his place, keeping him around as a living reference source...*for a while*...," said Carl.

Stephanie walked over to the sofa and sat down next to him, laid her head on his left shoulder. He raised his arm slowly and put it around her.

"Are you looking for him?"

"Yes."

"And when you find him...?" she asked.

"A few people would like to speak with him...," he said.

"Will...will I ever...*see him again...?*"

Carl looked down at the top of her head, knowing the real answer. "I don't know, Stephanie. I guess it will depend on what he has to say...to the people who want to speak with him," said Carl, the half-truth having to do for now.

"If they tell you to...*kill him...?*"

"No, Stephanie, no. I promise you, I won't let him die," he said pulling her closer.

"*Promise...?*" she asked.

"*Promise!*" he said.

Stephanie put her left arm across his stomach and her feet up on the sofa. Soon Carl felt her rhythmically breathing, fast asleep. There was still a slight tenderness to his left shoulder from Edmond's knife wound, not painful enough for him to wake her though. Patrick showed a level of disappearing he hadn't expected form an amateur, but after some of Eduardo's *"FBI people"* spoke with his friend Larry, they were able to track him down. At the right moment he'd be brought in...but not back to *Chicago*.

Carl looked down and kissed the top of her head. He took a deep breath as he laid his head back against the sofa. Saddened, he knew she would only see Patrick once again.

CHAPTER 71

One Step Ahead of You...

Patrick awoke, sunlight streaming onto his face, his stomach growling from not being fed the night before. The urge to get out, leave, suddenly became too strong to ignore, so he opted to get food once he got to the train station. Not calling a cab, he walked the seven blocks to *Union Station*. It was early morning, and the rush-hour commuters were still streaming in, stopping for coffee, a bite to eat, newspapers, the list unending. One of the electronic travel boards showed the next train to *Milwaukee* would be leaving in just over two hours, plenty of time for a meal.

Sitting at the back of the restaurant, Patrick kept an eye on the door as he ate the breakfast combo of eggs, sausage, pancakes and toast, sweetened coffee with hazelnut creamer. A group of people walked in wearing surgical scrubs, making him jump, but he quickly relaxed, remembering the full growth of beard and mustache on his face. Would he ever get used to being on the run? Maybe it *would* get easier the longer he had to stay out of sight; he wasn't sure, only hopeful. How many people were doing this on an *everyday* basis? How long would it be before he cracked or stopped looking over his shoulder? He shook his head slightly, took another sip of coffee. So be it!

I'm out and alive. That's all that matters, he thought. *One step at a time...*

Someone was following him; he heard the footsteps behind him and quickened his own pace. The footsteps began to fade; whoever it was, they were falling further behind. As he passed the alley, he saw another shadowy figure out the corner of his eye walking rapidly toward him. Patrick broke into a light jog, made it to the corner, turned right, then ran down to the next alleyway, ducking into it. Swallowed by the darkness, he pressed flat against the wall, holding his breath. He saw two figures run past the opening, their footfalls fading fast. He pushed off the wall and stopped abruptly when he saw the shape of a man in the middle of the opening. The man looked forward, put his hand to his ear, then turned right and walked into the alley, scanning from side to side as he moved. Patrick was frozen in place, heart beating so fast he didn't know which he'd have first: *a stroke or a heart attack*. Finally, the man stopped directly in front of him, quickly reached out, and grabbed him by the shoulder...

"*Heeeeey!* Sorry, buddy, didn't mean to scare you," said the man.

Patrick sat up startled as he looked at the man. He took a few deep breaths to calm himself down.

"We're in the station, *Milwaukee Intermodal.* That must have been *some dream* you were having there. You okay?" he asked. Patrick nodded his head *yes*.

"Didn't eat dinner last night...maybe some food would do me some good...," he said.

"Yeah, *thatadoit* all right! Well, plenty of food places inside, I'm sure you'll like one of 'em. *Have a great day!*" said the man as he walked down the aisle.

Patrick sat for a moment, clearing his head a bit more before he got up and followed.

The sun was shining as he checked into the BnB townhouse, the keys and instructions in a lockbox at the train station. *William Robert Harper*, his alternate identity, was going on a trip to *Milwaukee* for a family reunion; that's what he had told the travel agent back in *Chicago*. He had a week here to decide on which way he would head: up North to Canada or back down South, get lost in the lower states. *Stephanie. Dammit!* he thought. He closed the front door, turned to the left, and dropped the keys on the credenza. Patrick knew that he would have to contact her before he completely disappeared. But what was he going to say to her? That he was so blinded by his research that he couldn't turn down an offer from a criminal, a criminal he *hadn't even met?* Yeah, *yeah*, that would go over well. He could see the look on her face now… How mad *would* she be? Those guys he operated on, they were all *dead!* He truly didn't know that's what was going to happen to them, but just the same, he was an *accessory after the fact.* What kind of time was he looking at for that? Five years? Ten years? *For each? What the hell! What was he really going to do?*

The doorbell rang twice. Who knew he was here? Then it dawned on him: *one of the agents from the BnB checking on him.* Patrick walked over to the door, opened it. The fist hit him hard in the nose, closed his eyes, and sent him falling backward into the entry foyer. Turning slightly, Patrick bumped into the wall on his right shoulder. Before he could figure out what had just happened, another punch hit him in the left side, bending his body forward, followed by a third to his left jaw, literally knocking him to the floor. He managed to get one knee under him, slowly rising, when he felt a kick to his stomach from underneath, flipping him over onto his back.

"*YOU SONAVABITCH!*" was screamed at him. *Stephanie!*

He turned in her direction and saw the *Wisconsin* state trooper holding her back, another state trooper coming around them to help him up.

"*Why didn't you tell me? Why didn't you say SOMETHING TO ME?*" she screamed.

"*Detective! DETECTIVE!* Calm down or I'll have to *cuff you!*" said the state trooper.

Stephanie turned away from Patrick, walked over to the door, and put her forehead on the frame.

"*Okay! All right! All right!*" she said, her forehead still on the doorframe. "Those men…*died!* They all DIED, *Patrick! What the HELL were you thinking?*"

The second trooper helped Patrick into a sitting position on the floor and spoke into the mic on his shoulder requesting an ambulance.

"I didn't know, *Steph!* I SWEAR I didn't know they were going to *die!*" said Patrick, wiping the blood from his mouth. "I didn't know they were *dead* until I saw the pictures on your table. I *swear, Steph!*"

"*Regardless, Patrick, regardless! You're STILL an accessory! And that's for the six that we KNOW ABOUT...!*" said Stephanie.

The sound of the ambulance siren grew louder. Stephanie turned around and looked down at Patrick. "I'll do what I can to help, Patrick... I'll make some calls..."

The first state trooper stepped in front of Stephanie as the *EMTs* came in, quickly attending to Patrick. After a few moments, they had his face wiped off, and he was on the stretcher, then out the door.

"Did you need a ride back to the airport, Detective?" asked the first state trooper.

"No, no, I'll wait...check on Patrick after he's processed," Stephanie said.

"It could be a while, Detective, especially since he's wanted in *Chicago...*," said the second trooper.

"Yeah...yeah, I know... Maybe I'll catch a ride with whoever takes him back... Thanks, trooper."

"Yes, ma'am. Good day."

The two troopers left, closing the door behind them. She leaned against the wall, exhaling deeply as she lowered her head, tears suddenly falling from her eyes.

Inside the ambulance, Patrick wondered how Stephanie could possibly help him or if he even *wanted* her involved. He was beginning to feel relaxed, a bit tired; but with all the things that had just happened in the last few minutes, he was surprised to still be conscious.

"Stephanie was worried about you, she needed to see you," said the deep voice from the front of the ambulance. "This was one thing I could do for her."

"Yeah. Yeah, I'm sorry I put her through all this," said Patrick. "I don't want her to ruin her career trying to help me."

"No, Patrick, she'll be just fine. I promise."

"Hey…? *HEY! How do you know?* I *gotta* have a trial. *Jail time even…?*" said Patrick, feeling more tired now than just a few moments before.

"No, Patrick. No trial. No jail time," said the deep-voiced man.

Patrick could barely keep his eyes open. *Did they just turn the siren off…?*

"Wha'…? *What's hap…pe…ning…?*" he said.

"You're going to *sleep*, Patrick, just sleep. And when you wake up, a few people will have some questions for you…" Patrick's head drifted to the left, and he was fast asleep.

Carl tapped the side of the headset in his right ear.

"We'll be there in about twenty-five minutes. You cleared for *Chicago* and *New York*?" asked Carl.

"Yes, sir. The second plane will be touching down in forty-eight minutes to take Detective Caldwell back to *Chicago*, sir," said the man.

"Very good. Thank you." Carl ended the call.

A New Day for the Gangs

The average person had no idea that the majority of street gangs were originally started to patrol their local neighborhoods as the residents' protection against police brutality. The ongoing violence, dating far back in history, of those few overzealous police officers that were not above physically harming people in the neighborhoods, sometimes just for being in the area. A series of beatings with whatever was at hand, not limited to fists, police batons, pistols, rifle butts, etc., to show their *control* over as well as what they thought of them. But the younger ones began to organize, group together on their own, making *their* presence known in the face of those officers: *regardless of what you do to us, we're not backing down.*

A well-known so-called "*street gang*" that started in *California* went one step further by organizing free-breakfast programs and food drives in the communities, proving they could be proactive for social agendas while still monitoring the "*above-the-law*" police officers. Unfortunately, these organizations, as they advanced forward, became radicalized by several new members; they were more militantly inclined than social reformers. So over the years, they turned from *neighborhood protectors* into *neighborhood predators*, oftentimes far *worse* than the rogue law enforcement officers. The day of the "*new gangster*" had begun.

Terry jerked up into a sitting position, covers thrown to the left on the bed. Sweat was standing out on his forehead, his heart racing as he rapidly took in several deep breaths. His dream had him back in the abandoned building watching everyone dying all over again. But this time Stewart was shooting *them*, yelling in their faces while he pulled the trigger, then throwing them over the railing. He was falling; he felt the blood flying from his body as the ground rushed up to meet him. Just at impact...*he woke!* Terry slowly looked down to the left. Robin, his girlfriend, was still sleeping soundly. Easing his legs out of the bed, he quickly stood and unsteadily made his way to the bathroom. After he gently closed the door, he sat on the toilet, head in his hands. It was over a month since he heard from Stewart or had seen Edmond slowly driving by. His second-in-command, Nate, said the few other new gang leaders he got word from hadn't heard anything either. *What the hell?* He killed all these people then *bounced?* Who could *do* shit like that? And was he *really* gone? Terry had to find out one way or the other; he couldn't keep living like this! He needed to talk with the other gang leaders, find out what they knew. This shit *had to stop...!*

The next day, sitting in the park, *everyone's* neutral territory, Terry waited for his meeting to begin. A Hispanic male—Angel, he remembered—sat down to his left on the end of the bench. Nate nodded okay.

"That's my son, Manny. Six years old and his momma says he's a handful. Probably grow up to be a musician or DJ," he said, pointing at a little boy by the *Jungle Gym*.

Terry looked in that direction.

"That little boy he's *talkin'* to, that's *my* boy, Ricky. He's gonna be a *leader* someday, but not in *this shit*...somethin' a lot *betta'!*" said Terry.

"Yeah, man, *I hear that!*" said Angel. "You hear anything from those...*pendajos* (dumbasses)?

"Naw, man, *nothing!* Been a while too," said Terry.

A White male walked past them and sat down on the bench to Terry's right.

Tyler. He was another one of the secondary gang leaders at the abandoned building that night.

"Hey…what's going on with you two?" he asked. "*All still quiet?*"

Terry and Angel both nodded *yes*.

"Cain't take this not knowin' somethin', man. Creepin' me *the fuck out!*" said Tyler.

"Me too, man…," said Terry.

"Likewise…," said Angel.

They all sat quiet for a moment, watching the children play, laughing and talking to each other.

"It should be like this *all the time*…," said Terry, waving his hand across the park.

"My dad would bring me here a lot. He said this was a *'special place.'* Holds a lot of memories, good memories," said Tyler.

"*Buen fantasma…good ghost…spirits*," said Angel.

"How did we get away from *bein'* like *them?*" said Terry, nodding at the children in the park. "*What happened…to us?*"

"You all got caught up in somebody else's hype. Somebody else's idea of leadership that *degenerated* into all this… *'street gang violence,'* Terry," said the man sitting on the next bench.

They turned toward him, an older Black man, bald with black, wire-framed glasses and a salt-and-pepper goatee. His legs were crossed at the ankles under the seat, arms outstretched on the bench back, slightly looking up into the sky. None of them had noticed him before; they weren't aware that he was sitting there.

"The so-called criminals back in my day had a code, *'code of honor'* they called it, that they *all* lived by. Sure, they still broke the law, but it didn't involve *'children.'* Even with the drug sales, if it got out that they sold drugs to a kid, their *own* people would *whup they ass!* They all took *care* of their neighborhoods, looked after the people in them," said the man.

"*Familia*…," said Angel.

"That's right, Angel, *'family.'* Family is *everything*…," said the man.

They all thought of their own families, looked again at the children playing.

"My brother *Robert* and me would go down to the field houses in the neighborhoods back in the '60s, a lot of the *Motown* singing groups would give free shows, giving back to the people...Terry. Helping them out, some kind of way, with their music," said a light-skinned Black man, a reddish brown afro standing out on top of his thin frame.

When did he walk up? they wondered. *How long had he been standing there?*

"We knew the *'gangbangers'* went to school with most of them, but they very rarely did shit like *y'all* do, didn't even *'try'* to enforce recruitment, Tyler. Yeah, they went up against other gangs but only if that gang did something *stupid* to *them!* They didn't go *looking* for a fight," said the thin man.

"We all could appreciate the music at the field houses, not having to worry about if some *'dumb shit'* would start shooting!"

"Yeah...," said Terry. "That's my generation..."

"People don't talk to each other anymore, a lot of signals get crossed," said the older man on the bench. "What you were told somebody had said probably didn't even come up in the conversation, Angel."

"True *'dat!'*" said Tyler. "People always talking *shit...just to start stupid shit up!*"

"Look at them...," said the thin man standing, nodding at the children. "They don't know about *'territories.'* They don't know about *'hating somebody'* because they are a different color, if they got money or not, or if they belong to a *'rival gang.'* That's your future, all of you, right over there! Take care of it...and them!"

The thin man walked over to the older man sitting on the bench.

"Show them *something different* than what *you're all* doing right now...," said the older man, looking back over his shoulder. *"Familia...is everything!"*

"Hey, *'Rufus,'* let's go. Mom and Dad are waiting...," said the thin man.

The older man looked up at him, smiled, and stood.

"All right, *'quiet man,'* lead on...*lead on*," he said as they walked slowly off together.

The three of them looked down, lost in their own thoughts. Those two guys made a lot of sense; it *was* about family, the kids. They really *were* the future. Tyler looked toward the two men and didn't see them…*anywhere! What the hell?* They couldn't have gotten away that fast, not at the speed *they* were walking. He turned and saw the questioning looks on Terry and Angel's faces too.

"*Who were they?*" asked angel. "Did *you* know them, Terry? Your *familia?*"

"*No!* No, but it felt like…*they were!* It felt like they were…*kin-folk*…," said Terry.

"*Family!*" said Tyler. He stood and walked in front of Terry and extended his hand. Terry looked up at him, didn't hesitate.

He stood as well, shaking Tyler's hand. They both looked at Angel; he was already on his feet. He, in turn, shook their hands too.

"What just happened here? *What da we see? What da we* say to our *people?*" said Terry.

"*Nothin'!*" said Tyler. "Do what the old guy said, '*Show 'em!*'"

Tyler walked away as Terry and Angel went to introduce their children to each other.

Nate leaned against the tree and watched as Terry and Angel walked into the park toward their kids. Somehow he knew things were going to be different; he felt the three of them were going to change the way gangs operated, dealt with each other. Maybe there *was* hope. Maybe he *wasn't* going to die, shot down because of some *stupid shit* somebody else did. He'd wait and see, talk with Terry about what to do next.

Maybe even get up the nerve to ask why they kept looking right and left, talking into thin air…

CHAPTER 73

Carl's Thoughts Interrupted

Carl awoke with complete clarity. Every detail of the room was in sharp focus as the ache in his hip and thigh told him the day would definitely be off to a slow start. That last shot *"Charlie"* gave him as the chopper lifted off was partly cause for his pain. It went through the back of his thigh, exiting out the front, lodging in the roof padding of the chopper cab. He had just felt a mild sting, still hyped from the adrenaline rush of the firefight maybe. As the chopper banked to the left, he had the guy lined up with his *Mac 10* and dropped five rounds into the man's neck and head, literally knocking him back into the tree line. Nerve damage was what the doctor onboard the carrier had said was in store for him. Nothing they could do about it except the usual pain killers, then just cringe and bear it. Over all these years, it had gradually taken longer for him to function normally, but once in the field, it was totally unnoticed.

He began the painful routine of trying to walk by first sitting up in bed. The arthritis was the second cause of his morning pain: a product of all the humidity, rain, and heat that they all had suffered through, the gunshots just adding insult to the injury. Now it was just another reminder of all the things he had left there but somehow still always carried with him. He lost track of all the *VC (Viet Cong)* he and his crew had killed in the name of *"service to their country."* But the flashbacks…*the flashbacks*…every once in a while recalled *all* their faces, *vividly*, in his mind. Carl looked at the clock—*5:20 AM*, right on time, as usual. No matter how tired he was, he could not sleep more than three or four hours a night.

He eased into a standing position, feeling the sharp knifelike pain start at the bottom of his right foot and travel up his leg to the hip. The first try always knocked the breath out of him, making his heart skip a beat with the intensity until his mind could take control again. Slowly he walked forward, forcing the agony to stay in his leg and diminish with each step, finally being able to walk with a normal stride. There were loose ends to tie up and a few of them to be eliminated altogether before he disappeared again. Carl had gotten very good at leaving places and was getting even better at leaving the people he had *met* in those places as well. Sometimes, very rarely now, would he miss someone, and he knew, this was going to be one of those rarities.

As he walked into the bathroom, he thought of her: *Stephanie.* How could he ever forget Stephanie? She had qualities he didn't expect to find in a woman, especially a young woman. She was someone that he could feel at ease with, someone he knew he could trust, and that was something that hadn't happened since being with his crew over in *Nam.* His darkness, his deep darkness, the government had seen that in him somehow, saw it way below the surface, drew it out of him, then perfected and let it loose on all those unsuspecting people. And his crew were caught up in that darkness as well, following right along with him, *anywhere it led!* Stephanie had seen that darkness, and she didn't run from it but stuck side by side with it. She stood her ground and looked at *it*, and *him*, squarely in the eye, letting them both love her as she loved them, the best she could *(or would)* allow herself.

Opening the shower door, he turned both handles, his arms getting hit with the sudden forceful water spray. He stepped into the stream, closing the door behind him. The small enclosure changed to hot and steamy quickly as Carl's thoughts settled on wishing he *could* stay with her, but he knew it wouldn't work. The women, earlier in his life, all left because he treated them like queens, being *too* good to them, so they all said. He felt that whatever they wanted or needed, if he could do that or get that for them, he'd be more than happy to accommodate. And Stephanie was no different. He knew he had not only touched her body but something else, something deep inside her, that neither one of them could come up with the words to explain. But Carl also knew that she would never be able to stay with him, because no matter what they did together, he just wasn't that important to her. She wouldn't let him, or *anyone* else, be that close... He saw that distance between them in her eyes, felt it when she pulled him close, ready at any moment to push him away, escaping once again from the contact of another person that truly cared for her. He wanted to know what had happened to make her turn her back on people close to her but opened herself so fully to those who couldn't care any less. Lifting his face into the warm spray, the summation of Stephanie was undeniable: She needed to know that people would *be* there *for* her, but she didn't need to *have* any of those people *around* her. She waited to be *shown* they weren't going to leave but did *nothing* to tell them *to stay*. Someone had to have left her in the past, someone extremely close as well as important, and she was making sure she wouldn't be hurt that deeply again.

He hadn't planned on letting her see Patrick again, but he somehow knew that it would just add to the hurt, *mistrust* she carried inside if she didn't see him. Knowing Patrick wouldn't return to *Chicago*, Carl had already resigned himself to the hatred she must be feeling toward him now, knowing he, too, would be out of her life as well. No matter what, he'd always keep tabs on her, be there when she really needed him.

Carl stood for a bit longer under the steamy spray, and as he reached for the soap, he heard the bathroom door softly open. *Shit!* Thinking *too hard* again about his problems had made him lose focus! He opened his eyes, moving his back to the wall opposite the showerhead, fist clenched as the frosted shower door slid open. Quickly stepping forward, Carl relaxed, looking down into the warm blue eyes of...*Meagan Aymsworth*. He held her gaze as she stepped into the shower, naked, her right hand on his chest for support as she slid the shower door closed.

"I know...*I know*...we've worked together before, me being your information link inside, you being in the field...," she said looking down at the shower floor. "But this time...*this time*...it was different...*for me*."

"What changed for you, Meagan?" asked Carl, holding her waist lightly.

"When you went into that warehouse...*helped to move all those drugs!* You could have been *killed* if they found out *who you were*," she said looking up into his eyes.

Carl couldn't tell, but he sensed she was crying.

"Not something I would have let happen, *willingly anyway*, and you know Eduardo and his men were on hand for my backup...," he said.

"I know...*I know*, but I was still...*worried!*"

"Then I'm sorry to have *worried* you, Meagan. I'll try not to do that *too often* in the future," he said with a smile.

"*And cut down on the rooftop knife fights too...?*" she said with a slight smile herself.

"I'll *try*...," he said, still looking into her eyes.

"I know I'm not Stephanie...*won't even* try to pretend, but I wanted...*I needed*...to be here, because...*because* I thought you were so...*alone*. And I didn't *want you* to be alone... *I didn't want to be alone...either...is all...*," said Meagan, both hands on his chest now, a standing fetal position, her forehead resting softly against his chest.

"Meagan, you can't be *anyone* else except...*Meagan*. And you're doing *a fantastic job at doing that!*" He felt her body relax a bit. "I truly appreciate that you worry about me, *want* to be with me, but have you *read* my file? Do you know what I'm *capable* of doing, what I have done...*in the field?*"

She nodded yes, still looking down, eyes closed.

"Yes, I do, and it scares me...*scares me a lot*... But it *doesn't matter* to me..." She reached up, putting her arms around his neck, stretching up on her toes to rub her cheek against his.

Meagan's eyes were still closed as Carl's arms slowly embraced her. Looking up, she lightly kissed his lips, pulled back slightly, and opened her eyes. This time Carl *knew* she was crying and leaned down, kissed her lips. Their intimacy slowly increased, their embrace tightened. The thoughts of other loose ends, final instructions to the cleanup crew he'd leave behind...*and Stephanie*...began to fade from his mind.

CHAPTER 74

The One That Got Away

Evan had always wanted to take a cruise but held off because he didn't think he should go alone. What would people onboard say, or did they have groups of single people that they put together for the duration of the trip? Either way, his buddies had finally talked him into it saying that he needed to get away from his computer screens and program code writing, live a little, maybe even meet someone while he was gone.

So here he was: in a deck chair watching the sky and ocean meeting, a cool breeze blowing across his body. The ship suddenly dropped then rose back just as quickly. He grabbed his drink as it slid slightly toward the edge of the low table next to the chair. He raised it to his lips, and as he sipped, the ship dropped again, rose back, sloshing some of the liquid into his nose. A bit embarrassed, Evan picked up the napkin and wiped his nose, shifting his eyes from side to side to see if anyone was looking. This time when the ship dropped, he sat up, startled. Something was wrong; *he felt it!* But the sun was still shining! What the *hell* was going on? He looked left at the deck chair next to him; it was empty. Quickly looking to the right, another empty deck chair! Then he noticed he was the only one as far as he could see to either side! Drop! Rise! *Drop! Rise!* He was thrown from his chair toward the rail, hitting hard against the palms of his hands and center of his chest. *Drop!* Evan fell back into the chair, hitting his head against the wall. *Rise!* Thrown forward again, he caught himself against the seat in from of him! He was on an over-the-road bus, sitting close to the middle, next to a window on the passenger side! The roadway was flying past, obviously on an interstate. The sun was beginning to set off to the right.

"Even though the bump may be a small one, it can wake you from a sound sleep at times…," said the man sitting next to him.

For a second, Evan was panicked, disoriented, and gripped the arms of the chair firmly.

"*What's…what's going on? How the hell did I get here? Why the hell am I here?*" he said in a controlled whisper.

"One, you were going to be the fall guy for a doctor working for a major *crime lord*. Two, I brought you here from a hidden plastic surgery recovery room. And three, I'm helping you start a new life out of harm's way," said the man.

An image flashed into Evan's mind: *working on a computer system in a new facility.* A man in a lab coat staring at him from an open doorway.

"I was…*installing*…a new computer system…*somewhere!* I was being stared at…*too hard!* A man…*a man in a white lab coat…*," said Evan.

"That was probably the plastic surgeon. They figured you were a good match, size-wise, to double him. You would be left, along with a suicide note, for the police to find. End of their search for him while he disappeared *scot-free*," said the man next to him.

"That's crazy! How could…how could *anyone* think I was him? We…*we looked that much alike?*" asked Evan.

"He was a *plastic surgeon*, Evan. And you look *exactly* like him now…," said the man.

Evan turned to the window, dark enough outside for it to reflect his face. He did not recognize it; it wasn't him!

"*What did he do to me?*" he said to the window, feeling his face with both hands.

"What he learned to do best: *make an expendable double.*"

They rode along in silence for a while, Evan looking down at the floor.

"Now what do I do? I can't go back to my job. What would I say? Who would believe me?" said Evan.

"It's been taken care of, Evan. The organization I work for has given you a new identity, as well as a new position with one of our *IT* companies down in Missouri. Bank accounts, credit cards, health insurance, apartment, even a new car, all supplied for you. You'll be a transfer from the home office in Iowa to the assistant manager position. And if anyone decides to check, your back story is solid," he said.

"But...*why? Why me?*" Evan asked.

"*Simply because*...you were at the wrong place at *their right time*...," said the man. "All your new information is in your wallet with a nice sum of cash to get you by until you get to the bank. The other information you'll need will be given to you by your new secretary, she's the only one that will know about you, so feel free to ask her anything," said the man.

"And you...why are *you* doing this *for me?*"

The man looked down at the floor for a moment then turned back, looking Evan in the eyes.

"Because someone did it for *me* when I didn't know what had really happened... I'm just paying the favor forward," said the man.

Evan stared at him for a moment, then nodded his head in agreement.

The bus had slowed down and pulled over into a rest stop area so the passengers could stretch their legs and, perhaps, purchase snacks, food, and/or souvenirs.

"This is where I leave you, halfway point to your new home and job. Your new name is *Gregory Williams*, and your secretary's name is *Patrice Nelson*. It'll be another few hours before you arrive, but if you want to give Patrice a call, begin to get to know her, I'm sure she won't mind," the man said.

"Will I talk with you again?" he asked.

"Only if you get into trouble that I have to *personally* get you out of...," he said extending his right hand.

They shook, and the man stood, walked down the aisle to the front door of the bus. Evan sat back, looking up at the ceiling, a thousand and one thoughts going through his mind. He didn't even know that guy's name…

Carl walked over to the rest stop parking area and opened the driver's side door of the *1973 Buick Riviera*. The black pearlized finish with the charcoal-gray half-vinyl roof reflected the last rays of the setting sun. Meagan was sitting in the charcoal-gray suede passenger seat, wireless keyboard on her lap. A map of the local area was displayed in colors on the windshield in front of her, several open dialog boxes showing information from the seven tracking devices planted on and in Evan.

"Are you receiving everything, Brenda?" asked Meagan.

"Everything is good here, Meagan," said Brenda over the car speaker system.

"Everything is good here too, Meagan and Brenda," said Patrice.

"Carl? Nikki said, *'Don't forget your final report.'* She needs the wrap-up," said Brenda.

"No worries," said Carl. "I'll have it to her in a few days, once we get back."

"Okay. You both be safe on the road. Bye, everyone," said Brenda.

Meagan switched off the windshield display and slid the keyboard under the dash, locking automatically back in place. She leaned over and kissed Carl on the cheek. He turned and kissed her on the lips, watched as she buckled up, and settled into the seat for the long drive back to *Chicago*.

Evan, now Gregory, settled into his new position and new life with the help of Patrice. He grew closer to her until a relationship naturally began, never being made aware of her reports to the home office. The two tracking devices placed inside his body were sending information about his heart, respiratory, temperature, noting any changes that might be pertinent to the face-lift procedure. And with his six-month mandatory company physicals, up-close facial scans were taken by hidden cameras, all added to the growing research follow-up started by Dr. Patrick L. Procter.

CHAPTER 75

A "Blind" Watchful Eye

New players continued to stream in, all seeming to bring along guests who, the following week, brought in more guests. Jerry was told by Robert that the profits had gone up a steady *32 percent* since Stewart came into the game. The staff, with a generous increase in pay, had stopped asking questions about Warren and began to take a more active role in pleasing the customers professionally, as well as, in some cases, *personally*. But Jerry was still waiting for the other shoe to drop, not having seen Stewart or his hired gun in quite a while.

The upper level of the gaming house was full to its capacity: people laughing, enjoying the food, and gambling with total abandonment. He looked around at his security, knowing each one not only by sight but by their names. Jerry heard a glass break, jumped slightly, then relaxed when he saw the waitress stand up, bending over to say something to the customer who laughed as she walked away, obviously going for replacement drinks. After all this time *(almost ten months)*, the image of Warren, dead on the elevator floor, was still fresh in his mind. Shaking his head a bit, another sip of his drink eased the memory back into a dark corner. *Time to check on the lower VIP level*, he thought and headed toward the stairs to go down.

The lower level wasn't as crowded, but more people than normal were partying down here. Walking past the seating vignettes, Jerry greeted the new and old patrons as longtime old friends, asking if they were enjoying themselves and if there was anything else they needed. Passing by a few more seating areas, three familiar faces came into his view.

"You three are here *almost* as much as *I am!*" said Jerry smiling.

"Ah' quite *con'curr*, Jer'ry. Ya mak' it *soooo* hom'y he'er, we real'ly don't want ta' leave!" said Mason, both arms on the back of the sofa.

"It feels…*safe here*…really *protected* here," said Ruthie, looking up smiling at him.

"Almost like we're…*all connected*…you know, lost family members that you didn't know about are suddenly found," said Christina.

Jerry nodded, understanding what she meant. He still wondered how Mason had gotten involved with Ruthie, of *all* people—*a real woman*—knowing that he preferred men. What was *really* surprising to him was her sister, obviously her twin, *very possibly* the three darker caramel lines on her forehead the only difference between them. Was this a *ménage à trois*? If so…*lucky dog, Mason!*

"I'm glad we could make you all feel that way. The doors are always open to you all, *of course!*" said Jerry smiling.

"Biz'nuss has picked up a'mite, Jer'ry, Ah'll hav'ta tell somma my *'cli'ents'* 'bout yo'ur place here. Good food. Good peo'ple. *Ev'en betta' gam'blin'!*" said Mason.

"I'll appreciate that, *friend*. Coming from you, that means *a lot to me!*" said Jerry.

Under the table, Christina squeezed Mason's left leg, then he turned to look at her. He saw the look in her eyes, the slight nod of her head; he nodded back.

"Jer'ry…tha't *in'da'vid'u'al'* tha't we both was…*quite*…up'set by…" Mason said, looking into Jerry's eyes, "will no *lon'ga'* be ah' bu'den to ya…"

Christina held her head down for a moment, turned toward Jerry, and smiled, tears welling up in her eyes. It took him a minute to figure out what they had just told him; then it was very clear: *Stewart was dead!* He let out a sigh and lowered his head.

"Thank you. *Thank you…all!*" he said.

Looking back up at them, they were all smiling at him, and he smiled back.

"Okay. *Okay!* Your money's no good here...*ever! Period! Enjoy yourselves! Enjoy!*" said Jerry as he walked away, happy, knowing Warren had been avenged.

His cell phone vibrated; he took it from his pocket and read the text message then headed up to the entry lobby.

In the lobby entry's new security office, his guards were watching the monitors showing the hidden interior loading area behind the outside grain silos. Four black windowless vans, side doors open, were loading heavy plastic boxes taken from the base of the nearest silo.

"You got the plates? Faces?" asked Jerry, looking over the man's shoulder at the monitor.

"Yeah, boss. Those low-light, hi-def cameras work like a charm," the man said.

"Audio?"

"Hear a rat *pissin'* on cotton down there...*everything's* recorded too."

"Good. *Good!* I hope we don't ever have to use any of this, but I *wanna* be safe *now* than sorry *later*..." Jerry said.

They both continued to watch in silence until the last truck was finished loading and gone.

Jerry had been hesitant to let *The Monster's* drugs be stored in his empty silos, especially after *The Monster's* death was leaked to the news. But that day when he walked into the club and was told by Billy, his security head, somebody was waiting for him in his office, he automatically thought it was the cops. Opening his office door, he felt his heart skip several beats when he saw *The Monster* sitting at his desk. He was offered *$250,000* a month as a storage fee, shook hands on the deal, and *The Monster* was gone. Literally falling down onto the sofa in his office, he breathed a few heavy sighs of relief, knowing he would have agreed to ANYTHING *The Monster* would have asked for...*payment or not!*

"Get a copy of that over to the safe house. No uploadin', downloadin', or *somethin' loadin'!* I don't want that *shit* going through the air...*period!*" Jerry said.

"You got it, boss!" said the man.

Jerry turned and headed back downstairs.

Eduardo switched off his monitor after the last black van drove away and picked up his desk telephone.

"*Annabella*, if you need to allocate any additional storage space, order what you need. Send a copy of the requisition to my inbox please," he said.

"Of course, Eduardo. Anything else tonight?" she asked.

"No, *bella* (beauty), *buona notte* (good night)," he said.

"*Buona notte*," she said.

CHAPTER 76

Who Was He...Really?

Carl had popped into her mind again, or maybe this time she was just more aware of it. He not only had saved her several times but helped to close a case that only a few people had even tried to connect the dots. Where did he come from, and how did he know to get involved with the case in the first place? Stephanie rolled onto her back, stared at the ceiling as the outside lights played across it. Cars moving back and forth on the street somewhere below; the muffled voices of several conversations being carried on in other apartments and low *smooth jazz* was floating about, seemingly from everywhere. What was it that made Carl protect her? And how did he get under her skin the way no other man had? Carl had touched her, no doubt, and to her surprise, she *really* missed him.

Just over a month had passed since she last spoke with him, and he had told her about Patrick. Still trying to wrap her mind around all that information, she was forced to finally accept the fact that he was deeply involved with the crime lord cases. Did his plastic surgery research mean that much to him that he looked the other way when they approached him? And how much pressure was brought to bear on him once he found out they were holding Jennifer? He told her the man behind it all, *Marc Aurell*, someone he *never* met face-to-face, convinced him to come onboard. Stephanie guessed that with the promise of all that new equipment, plus alternate surgical theaters and recovery rooms not only impressed him but eventually *showed* him what this man *could do.* Shaking her head slightly from side to side, she still refused to believe that Patrick could have known they were going to *kill* the doubles; he just *couldn't* be that cold-blooded. That twist must have come down the road, when he was already knee-deep in Marc's agenda.

And why did they have a double of Patrick? Obviously, they wanted a fall guy, someone to pin most, *if not all,* of this crazy shit on. If Patrick was really hurt, like Lisa said, were they trying to take him out then but found out they *still* needed him? And if he *was* incapacitated, who did the work on his *double?* Someone *else* that knew his new procedure? One of his *business partners?* And if Patrick was *expendable,* what was the *need* for a double in the *first place?* None of this made any sense to her. Too many unanswered questions, ones she *thought* would be resolved when Carl called her and said they had tracked Patrick to *Milwaukee.* She was *really* stupid to think she would be able to travel back to *Chicago* with him hoping, finally, to find out what was *really* going on. After talking to the state troopers, who told her Patrick was being processed for transport, how long would she have waited there if Carl hadn't called? And even during the flight back to *Chicago,* she was still under the impression that both of them, Patrick and Carl, would be back soon.

Now, going into the fifth week, Stephanie hadn't heard a word from either of them. She turned, this time rolling onto her right side, looking out the window. The snow, falling like an old romantic movie, gave her a warm feeling inside, the thought of Carl holding her, loving her, all unknown feelings she had not felt before. What was he thinking of at this moment? Was it about a new case he was working on? Was it as dangerous as the last one? And what would the body count be? My GOD, the body count! Would his new case be just as deadly? How did he, how *could* he, function with all those souls connected to him? Would it involve another female in distress? *Was he touching her like he touched me? Was he even thinking of...me?*

A guilty feeling suddenly filled her mind, her eyes opening wide. What the *hell* was going on with her that she was thinking about *this man* she barely knew? Not to mention poor Meagan! She had been on the periphery of the case, helping her catalog all the facts, actually pointing out a few details that didn't make sense to her but turned on a bright light bulb after Meagan had explained them to her. She had even seen how Meagan looked at Carl when he suddenly popped up in the office as a patrolman, not knowing who he was yet frozen in her tracks like a deer caught by a cars high beams. Now with her missing, she wondered if Meagan was collateral damage? Did she find out something that she wasn't meant to? Or worse yet, did Carl have anything to do with *her* disappearance? That last thought made her shiver and just as quickly gave her a pang of jealousy that she *might be* with him! A crazy thought, no doubt, but the tears rolling down her cheeks were as much a surprise to her as these thoughts about Carl.

She started to sit up, making it halfway, then fell heavily back to the bed, sinking into her pillow. Stephanie turned, her face buried in the pillow now, knowing she couldn't stop the flood of tears she had tried so hard to hold back. Opening her eyes, she let them flow freely. As she turned her head, again toward the window, she saw that the snow had gotten brighter outside, almost glowing, sparkling, and she smiled, continuing to cry silently…

CHAPTER 77

Gone. . .but Not Forgotten

Meagan's arm lay across his chest as Carl gently rubbed from her wrist, up to her elbow then back again. He knew he would have to train her, give her an edge just to stay alive, if she was going to be in the field with him. Looking into Meagan's face, he wondered what she was dreaming, what she had thought during the case with Stephanie. How had all those bodies piling up affected her? And how had it affected her thoughts of him? It was an even bigger mystery why she was drawn to go away with him in the first place? She had always been his *technical/information* backup, accessing the computer data from the inside of the local law enforcement facility or some remote location, not really needing to meet him but running into each other occasionally. She was his connection to the *Consortium*, to *Nicole*; she knew almost his every move. Looking back down into her face, he was suddenly saddened by what he might be getting her involved with. Sliding to his left, Carl lifted Meagan's arm, lightly holding it up until he was clear of the bed, easing it down to the sheet. Her face rolled to the pillow as she let out a small sigh, not waking.

Out in the living room area of the apartment, Carl turned on the satellite radio; the soft *smooth jazz* music flowed into the room, wrapping him up like a warm blanket. He lowered himself into the plush, extra-wide club chair, legs outstretched, crossed at the ankles. The snow was falling outside, sparkling in the moonlight on its way down, giving him an even warmer feeling than before. He hadn't said goodbye to Stephanie, just left, because he really didn't think she would care that much. Or was that what he was *telling* himself, his justification for leaving without a word? Regardless of what they had shared together, he thought it just wasn't enough to have changed her mind about him in the least. Carl wondered what she *actually* felt working the case with him and if it *had* affected her in some way. A strong thought popped into his mind that she was thinking of him now, probably wondering the same things he was. It was crazy, *absolutely*, no doubt about it.

That last-minute decision to bring her to *Milwaukee*, confront Patrick, was something he thought he owed her. He had felt guilty knowing that Patrick's next stop would be *The Consortium* facility in *New York* and that, in all probability, they both would not see Stephanie ever again. He had hoped that Patrick would have told her *something* to explain his actions, not only how he managed to get in so deep but more importantly, *why*. But he was a scientist that came across an amazing thing, through deduction or luck; whatever the reasons, it *consumed* him. And as a scientist, he was duty-bound to expand and understand it further, going to those unknown limits.

Nicole made the arrangements with the *Wisconsin state troopers*, pulling the strings to get uniforms, an actual squad car and ambulance, so Eduardo's people could step in for the troopers and *EMT* techs. The lie he told Stephanie to get her on the plane back to *Chicago* still sat...*unsettling*...in his mind. He had been with women before, many of them, so why was Stephanie making him...*think?* Could she have touched him more than *he* was willing to admit? And if it were true, what the *hell* was he doing here with Meagan? During the drive back to *Chicago*, he wondered how Meagan's life would change now that she was going to be with *him*. How much danger would she *really* walk into because of *her choice?* It suddenly dawned on Carl that now there were three women he would *go to hell and back* for, and his heart told him that *Nicole* would *always* be *number 1!*

He heard movement behind him. Meagan softly padded across the floor from the bedroom, then he felt her standing to his right, slightly behind his line of sight. He held out his right arm, fully extended, waiting. Naked, she walked around the right arm of the club chair and sat down on his lap. Snuggling down on him, he folded both his arms around her, pulling her even closer.

"I dreamed of Stephanie in her bed, she was crying…," said Meagan.

"I thought of her as well…"

"Do you want to…*go back to her?*" asked Meagan.

"No…no. When she needs me…*needs us*…we'll go back then," said Carl.

"I'd understand if you went back…*alone*, I really would. I know you and I are only *together* for…*a short while*…"

Carl wondered how she could be so confident in her computer expertise yet so insecure in her personal relationships. That comparison made him want to protect as well as love her even more. He bent down and kissed her on the top of her head. When Meagan looked up, he lightly kissed her on the lips, holding it for a moment longer than she thought he would. She laid her head back on his chest.

"You're a very strong, intelligent woman, somewhat of a *rarity* in this day and age. You being *beautiful* is just a *bonus* that adds even more to who you *are!* Stephanie is the same way but will *never* allow herself to *be with* anyone, she'll always be *over there…just out of reach*. I'm here *with you*, Meagan, because I *want to* be here with you. A short while together…? No, I don't think so, darlin', *no, I really don't think so*…"

Meagan seemed to melt into him as he felt her first tears hit his chest. Hugging her tighter, he looked back out the window and saw that the snow had gotten brighter, almost glowing, sparkling, and he smiled.

EPILOGUE

Carl had gotten in my way again! I know that my planning left nothing out, nothing to the imagination was missed, but he was still able to stop it! What went wrong?

The chair leaned back with the shifting of weight, adding to deeper thoughts.

I need to get closer to him somehow. Find out what his thoughts are, how he really operates. With that, I may even be able to find a way to stop him...or eliminate him altogether...and take his controllers down with him. They have their hands in affairs all over the world, but I have people watching them as well. I don't know how to begin to bring them down or take them over, but I will continue to gather my information and create a foolproof plan that neither they nor their puppet Carl can alter.

The sudden banging of a fist on the tabletop reverberated in the darkened empty room. Lighting from the street below cast the window's shadow on the opposite walls, changing shape with the traffic headlights moving along the roadway.

No, anger will not help me. I need to have a clear head to think this through. Those so-called crime lords did their parts, no question of that, and the ones I disposed of gave me that much more control with my own people in their places. They will stay in place, and the originals still left alive will know not to go against me! The loss of the duplicate crime lord bodies was unfortunate, an error I will not repeat...

A prolonged car horn broke the deep concentration, a soft lingering tune of *"smooth jazz"* fading away as it passed by, and moved the focus of thoughts up to the star-filled night sky.

I must assume that Stewart, along with his associate Edmond, are no longer viable or among the living: there has been no activity on either bank account or answers to my recorded voice mails. My secondary eyes and ears continue to function regardless, and the information flow will remain current for the moment. I will bide my time for now...

Fingers began to drum lightly on the desktop, the rhythm advancing the train of thought.

Dr. Procter was ignorant, weak. A scientist with the usual myopic focus on his personal work. He really was not thinking ahead far enough, unaware of pertinent details. His double would have taken the attention from him, negate suspicion altogether, yet he chose to escape, having no idea how to successfully achieve that goal. Once the facts started to fall into place, it was only a matter of time before Carl would come to the correct conclusion! The good doctor was the cause of his own liability. He will not be missed...wherever he and his double have settled.

The chair made no sound as it was pushed back from the desk, and within a few moments the room was just as still and just as quiet, showing no sign *whatsoever* that anyone had even been there...

ABOUT THE AUTHOR

Charles Anthony Hunter was born on the Southside of Chicago, Illinois, in *1955*. His family was one of the first to move into the Stateway Garden Projects, a group of ten- and seventeen-floor elevator buildings, designed to give low-income families a step-up to eventually owning their own homes. His mother and father (Julia and Alfred Sr.) always stressed education. As a matter of fact, his first books were a set of encyclopedias.

He went to Raymond Elementary School and Dunbar Vocational High School, where, in the latter, he was introduced into the world of writing with several English classes. Going to the University of Illinois, in Champaign, Illinois, at the age of sixteen, he was given additional English writing classes *(helping some of his classmates with their essays for his extra credit!)* geared toward short stories *(even though his major was architectural layout and design, his admitted first love!)*. He credits his late brother, Michael Hunter, with the inspiration for a lot of what he wrote while in school. Michael was acknowledged by family and friends as a master storyteller, keeping cousins, aunts, and uncles on the edge of their seats with stories he would make up on the fly, especially the stories of *Mammy Josephine, the Conjure Woman of the Bayou*. Charles says, "He might be gone, but he was still here with me, critiquing my work."

Charles's wife, Debra, and their son, Victor, read the book as it was being written, giving him valuable input that helped along the way to the end, keeping him from going a bit *too far* with the details!

Charles still keeps up with his architectural designs on the side *(a hobby in addition to designing a six-story townhouse as a back-to-school class assignment for him)* while listening to his streaming smooth jazz. Even though Charles plans to continue his architectural drafting parttime, he feels sure that his next full-time vocation will be writing. He has several sci-fi stories as well as two sequels to this book, waiting to be written.